BROKEN ENGLISH

THE POLITICS OF LANGUAGE
Series editors: Tony Crowley, *University of Manchester,*
Talbot J. Taylor, *College of William and Mary,*
Williamsburg, Virginia

"In the lives of individuals and societies, language is a factor of greater importance than any other. For the study of language to remain solely the business of a handful of specialists would be a quite unacceptable state of affairs."

Saussure

The Politics of Language Series covers the field of language and cultural theory and will publish radical and innovative texts in this area. In recent years the developments and advances in the study of language and cultural criticism have brought to the fore a new set of questions. The shift from purely formal, analytical approaches has created an interest in the role of language in the social, political, and ideological realms and the series will seek to address these problems with a clear and informed approach. The intention is to gain recognition for the central role of language in individual and public life.

BROKEN ENGLISH

Dialects and the Politics of Language in Renaissance Writings

Paula Blank

London and New York

First published 1996
by Routledge
11 New Fetter Lane, London EC4P 4EE

Simultaneously published in the USA and Canada
by Routledge
29 West 35th Street, New York, NY 10001

Typeset in Garamond by Keystroke, Jacaranda Lodge, Wolverhampton
Printed and bound in Great Britain by Biddles Ltd, Guildford and King's Lynn

British Library Cataloguing in Publication Data
A catalogue record for this book is available from the British Library

Library of Congress Cataloguing in Publication Data
Blank, Paula, 1959–
Broken English : dialects and the politics of language in Renaissance
writings / Paula Blank.
p.   cm. — (The Politics of language)
Includes bibliographical references and index.
1. English language—Early modern, 1500–1700—History.
2. English literature—Early modern, 1500–1700—History and criticism.
3. Language and languages—Political aspects—England—History—
16th century. 4. Language and languages—Political aspects—England
—History—17th century. 5. English language—Variation—England—
History—16th century. 6. English language—Variation—England
—History—17th century. 7. Dialect literature, English—History and
criticism. 8. Language and culture—England—History—16th
century. 9. Language and culture—England—History—17th century.
10. Renaissance—England. I. Title. II. Series.
PE1081.B57   1996
820.9'003—dc20   95–52389
CIP

ISBN 0–415–13779–9 (hbk)

CONTENTS

FIGURES

ACKNOWLEDGMENTS

I would like to thank the American Council of Learned Societies, and the College of William and Mary, for grants that supported the writing of this book.

Parts of Chapters 1 and 4 of the book appear, respectively, in the following: "niu ureiting: Language Reform in Renaissance England," in *The Project of Prose in the Early Modern West*, eds Roland Greene and Elizabeth Fowler, Cambridge, Cambridge University Press (forthcoming); and "The Dialect of the *Shepheardes Calender,*" *Spenser Studies* X, 1989, pp. 71–86. I thank the editors and publishers of these volumes for permission to adapt those essays here. I would also like to thank the copyright holders for granting permission to reproduce the following material: Figure 1.1 – STC 541, Henry Cockeram, *The English Dictionarie* (1623), by permission of the Folger Shakespeare Library; Figure 1.2 – RB 61311, John Hart, *An Orthography* (1569), by permission of The Huntington Library, San Marino, California; Figures 1.4 and 1.5 – William Bullokar, *Booke at Large* (1580), by permission of the British Library Board. While I have made every effort to communicate with copyright holders of material used here, I would be grateful to hear from any I have been unable to contact.

I have been very fortunate in my colleagues and in others who have shared their expertise in helping me to develop this book. Elizabeth Fowler, Roland Greene, Lynn Kiesling, Adam Potkay, and Monica Potkay provided helpful comments on portions of the manuscript. I thank Julia Hall and Alison Foyle for supporting and supervising the project, and Claire Chandler, Carol Chitni, and Diane Stafford for their help with all the details. I am now as always grateful to Derek Attridge and to Barbara K. Lewalski for their generosity, and for advice that has been invaluable to me. It is also a pleasure to thank Talbot Taylor, especially for many energizing talks about talking about language; and Tony Crowley, for support and direction through a long and rewarding correspondence.

Finally, I thank Paul Aron, my best reader and everything else.

A NOTE ON THE TEXTS

I have attempted to retain original spellings wherever possible, with a few exceptions: I have modernized Renaissance printing conventions regarding the use of *vv* for *w*, *f* for *sh*, and the distribution of *i/j* and *u/v*. I have also replaced diacritics used in place of *n* and *m* with these letters, respectively, and have modernized certain conventions regarding punctuation, such as the use of slash marks to indicate the end of a clause or sentence.

INTRODUCTION

This book is about Renaissance literary dialects, the representation of linguistic differences in English literature of the sixteenth and early seventeenth centuries. It is also about the rhetorical description of those differences, the ways that Renaissance writers define and interpret the English language in all its contemporary diversity. As early as 1414, language was closely associated with national identity; English representatives at the European Council of Constance cited the "difference of language" as one "which by divine and human law is the greatest and most authentic mark of a nation and the essence of it."[1] *Broken English* examines some of the early modern discourses that contribute to the "nationalization" of English. But rather than exploring how English was understood in relation to other languages (the international "difference of language"), my subject is the Renaissance discovery, and elucidation, of differences within the national vernacular. By focusing on how writers represented dialects, I suggest the ways in which "English" itself was a construct of the period, produced, in large part, by discriminations made among competing "Englishes" then current. *Broken English* shows how Renaissance authors contribute to the construction of early modern English by distinguishing its dialects, and making a "difference of language."

In its emphasis on the history of ideas about the English language, my book falls within a traditional field of inquiry sometimes referred to as "attitudes towards language." I am especially indebted to R.F. Jones's seminal study of attitudes towards language in the Renaissance, *The Triumph of the English Language* (1953).[2] The "triumph" of Jones's title refers to the success of Renaissance efforts to promote the status – social, political, religious, literary – of English as against Latin (so recently the lingua franca of European culture) and other foreign language competitors. But Jones's work, though far more comprehensive than my own study, obscures the fact that English itself was divided by internal contests of the same kind, that the very meaning of "English" was subject to contemporary debate. The first vernacular grammars and dictionaries, products of this period, rose partly in response to a new consciousness of linguistic differences within national borders. Robert Cawdrey, the first English lexicographer, thus prefaces his dictionary of "hard words" by asking his readers:

1

> Do we not speak, because we would have other[s] to understand us? . . .
> Therefore, either wee must make a difference of English & say, some
> is learned English, and othersome rude English; or the one is Court talke,
> the other is Country-speech, or else we must . . . use altogether one
> manner of language.[3]

Cawdrey was not alone in invoking the problem of the "difference of English," or the stratification of the vernacular along the lines of class or social community, as the inspiration for his work. Many of the early English grammarians and lexicographers devoted themselves, implicitly, to the identification of the "best" the vernacular had or could achieve, to advancing a national language associated, often enough, with the elite dialect already known as the "King's English." In the Renaissance, it is the discovery of dialect that turns linguistic inquiry into a question of cultural authority, for the triumph of the King's English would depend, in part, on the defeat of alternative versions of the language.

By "dialect," I am referring throughout this study to alternative Englishes, to versions of the language that were defined by their value or status relative to other English dialects, including the King's English. By "dialect" I am also invoking languages ascribed not to individuals but rather to communities, whether or not that ascription is historically accurate. In the sixteenth and seventeenth centuries, the "real" dialects of English, including regional and class dialects, were rarely described in any systematic way. Renaissance study of the vernacular generally encompassed only two aspects of the language – English diction, and English spelling and pronunciation (these latter two were rarely considered independently). The dialects I explore here, in turn, are characterized by distinctive words or distinctive phonologies (represented orthographically). But my concern, I must emphasize again, is not with "real" dialects; I do not attempt here to recover, or to reconstruct, the variety of ways English was spoken in the period. Indeed, judged as a chapter in the story of English – if that story is confined to a chronicle of forms – this book may seem flawed or limited to many readers. But if the book says little about the progress of language *change*, I hope it says more about language *reform* – the ways that early modern writers deliberately reproduce English in their works. The "broken English" of my title refers only to the written language, to literary dialects (even when these are presented, notably, in dramatic literature, as scripts of speech). The story of English I tell reveals how the study of the "difference of language" began – and arguably, continues – as an imaginative enterprise rather than a strictly scientific one.[4]

Having confessed the parenthetical relationship of this study to a philological history of English, I should add that it would also occupy a doubtful place in any traditional history of English dialect literature. The study of dialect literature has generally been the province of medieval studies on the one hand, and eighteenth-, nineteenth-, and twentieth- century studies on the other. There are very good reasons, moreover, why the Renaissance is often left out of the story. The use of dialect in literature, especially regional language, is traditionally understood as a kind of grass-roots movement originating with native writers or, at least, with writers in close sympathy with the people for whom they speak. Most medieval authors, lacking a clear notion of a standard or prestige dialect, simply wrote in the language of their birthplace. Modern dialect authors, from Robert Burns to Hugh Macdiarmid, are typically bilingual; they may choose to write in their native dialects if it suits their interests, which may be aesthetic, or ideological, or both. In the late sixteenth and early seventeenth centuries in England, there was no such thing as dialect literature so understood. Shakespeare made use of southern English but not the dialect of his native Warwickshire; Jonson was of border descent but northern English is only one of numerous dialects he brought onto the literary scene. Put simply, dialects, for Renaissance authors, have nothing to do with "home."

On the contrary, the social and regional dialects that appear in Renaissance English literature are always recreated by authors who are culturally identified with more elite forms of the language. The Renaissance saw the rise of dialect comedy, and juxtaposing a peasant dialect with the King's English was, often enough, played for laughs. One of the first genres to incorporate dialect was the early sixteenth-century popular jest book; many jests hinge on provincials and foreigners being unable to speak the language properly. But the new linguistic relativism of the age also produced more serious experiments: Shakespeare's brief foray into southern English in *King Lear*; Spenser's incorporation of northern English words in *The Shepheardes Calender*; and Jonson's use of thieves' cant in *The Gypsies Metamorphosed*, among many others. The re-emergence of dialect in the literature of the Renaissance is not always a laughing matter: Renaissance authors who give voice to southern and northern English (dialects that had all but disappeared in formal writing since the fifteenth century), or to underworld language, or archaic words, were not always in collusion with those contemporary language theorists who prescribed their silencing.

Indeed, the idea of "dialect" itself – the word first comes into use in the middle of the sixteenth century[5] – is implicated in Renaissance ideas about literary language generally. In later chapters I will suggest that words usually characterized as examples of Renaissance "poetic diction" – notably, archaic words and neologisms – are better understood as dialects of early modern English; that the "deformations" of poetic language, no less than southern or northern English, were produced and interpreted within a culture of competing forms. Thus, one of the earliest English grammarians, Alexander Gill, divided the nation into its several linguistic regions: "There are six major dialects: the general, the Northern, the Southern, the Eastern, the Western, and the Poetic."[6] Along with regional languages implicitly defined, geographically and socially, by their relation to the "general" language (i.e., an elite variety of London English), Gill defines "Poetic" language as a province of the vernacular. *Broken English* is concerned, above all, with the "Poetic" dialect of early modern English, and the *imaginative* borders that mark, for the first time in the history of the language, the "difference of English."

3

Chapter 1, "The Renaissance Discovery of Dialect," initiates my study by showing how the idea of dialect conditioned the production of the first vernacular grammars, dictionaries, and proposals for spelling reform. Although early English linguists did not labor under the auspices of an academy, although there was no centralized forum for the debate, these works show that the English were deeply preoccupied with what the Italians called the *questione della lingua* – the discrimination of the "best" forms of the vernacular. The chapter suggests that the early history of linguistic prescriptivism in England, the idea of "authority" in language, arose as a corollary of Renaissance ideas about linguistic diversity. While the notion of linguistic authority was already current in the sixteenth and early seventeenth centuries, writers were not yet constrained by any established system of rules, and this proved a great convenience for the many reformers who sought, independently, to change the language. I seek here to demonstrate the extent to which Renaissance linguists, no less than Renaissance poets, invented the difference of language. The opening chapter reveals the era as one of diverse, unsystematic, yet prodigious efforts to "authorize" the vernacular.

Subsequent chapters examine several of the dialects of Renaissance English literature, along with the rhetoric of difference associated with each. In Chapter 2, "The Thieves of Language," I explore the early modern rhetoric of value as associated with English words, especially neologisms or invented words. I focus on a variety of linguistic practices that are figured by Renaissance writers, again and again, as economic "crimes" – the "theft" of words, the "begging" of words, the unregulated "coining" of words, the "counterfeiting" of words, the contraband "trade" in words. The chapter examines the continuities between literary uses of invented words and thieves' cant, the underworld language allegedly devised by its own speakers. The real "thieves of language," I suggest, were authors such as Ben Jonson, who perpetrated the "crime" of neologism as a means of literary enrichment. Jonson and other literary authors were the main producers of linguistic value in the first era in which the "difference of English" was accounted.

Chapters 3 and 4 concern the representation of regional English in Renaissance literature, and the cultural nexus of place, language, and social identity in the early modern period. I introduce these chapters with a discussion of the rise of literary regionalism, the earliest English works that were bounded, geographically and ideologically, by the provinces. Chapter 3, "Regions of Renaissance English I: South of the Border," focuses on representations of southern English, widely recreated by authors as a literary *vox populi*. Shakespeare exploits this dialect in *King Lear*. Edgar, heir to Lear's throne, appropriates southern English when he murders the foppish courtier sent to apprehend his father. In these works and others, aristocrats (and poets) briefly usurp the site of the marginal, the poor, or the dispossessed to speak resistance to those who are better positioned socially.

Chapter 4, "Regions of Renaissance English II: The North Country," explores the relationship between northern English and archaisms as articulated in linguistic and literary works of the period. I focus on the Renaissance search for an authentic or "original" English and Spenser's claims to have reproduced such a language in the synthetic diction of *The Shepheardes Calender* (1579). E.K., Spenser's own editor, predicted that readers of *The Shepheardes Calender* would find Spenser's diction the "strangest" part of the work.[7] Modern readers have worked hard to demystify Spenser's idiom, but such efforts beg the question of why E.K. insisted so strongly on its strangeness, and why Spenser's earliest critics concurred with E.K.'s view. I argue that the language of *The Shepheardes Calender* is an experiment in linguistic "originality," a diction that is both deliberately old and deliberately new. The chapter shows how Renaissance writers culled and even created old words (and, occasionally, northern words) not only as an act of cultural restoration, but because such words were "foreign" to London audiences.

In Chapter 5, finally, I look at the Renaissance rhetoric of language, laws, and blood – a triad of terms often invoked by early modern writers to identify the essence of a nation or race. The chapter examines efforts to Anglicize the British Isles, and the dialects or "broken English" of Anglicized Welsh, Irish, and Scottish characters in Renaissance drama. The "Englishing" of the empire, I suggest, was not only understood as a matter of translating forms; in its most radical construction, Anglicization was conceived as a means of racial translation, the recreation of one people as another. The chapter concludes by examining the Anglicization of King James's published works. I suggest that James's efforts to "English" his writing were part of a larger plan for a political union in which Scots was to be "naturalized" as English. Towards that end, James supervised the Anglicization of his own political tracts. But he never submitted his poetic language to the same degree of alteration – and his treatise on Scots poetics retained its native form. While some Renaissance poets and playwrights invoke the claims of English rule, both linguistic and political, over other nations, many dramatize and even champion the persistence of linguistic difference – again, understood as a difference in nature – even where political differences have been levelled through union.

As may already be evident from my synopsis of forthcoming chapters, the politics of Renaissance representations of dialect cannot be neatly or summarily identified. Dialect may be invoked as an object of ridicule or of admiration; it may be projected as another's language or assumed as part of an authorial voice. To a certain extent, it depends on the dialect being represented: Southern English generally fares worse than northern English; new words are more often censured than old ones. The fact is that it is difficult to fix the status of Renaissance literary dialects, or to place them definitively on a cultural map of the period. Yet it would be a mistake to conclude that Renaissance authors were not concerned with distributing those values, or with identifying loci of cultural authority within the national language.

Indeed, this book aims to challenge the idea of the Renaissance as a linguistic free-for-all, a view that still dominates the study of Renaissance diction and linguistic form. Many have concurred, with N.F. Blake, that "the spirit of the age encouraged innovation in vocabulary for its own sake."[8] Others have read the innovations of Renaissance literary language against a backdrop of an English indeterminately and randomly in flux: "Language was in a plastic state, so that it had an unparalleled freedom in both vocabulary and form."[9] The so-called "linguistic exuberance" or "linguistic enthusiasm"[10] of authors such as Shakespeare, Spenser, and Jonson needs to be re-examined as an expression of an age engaged in a struggle for possession of the vernacular, a struggle in which linguistic authority was just as much at issue as linguistic freedom. If there is any single "politics of language" that can be identified with Renaissance poetic practice, as well as the practice of early English linguists, it surely lies in the effort of each individual writer to discriminate among versions of the language and to authorize preferred forms, to draw (and then, at times, deliberately to transgress) the borders that separate one dialect of English from another. *Broken English* tells the story of how and why Renaissance writers portray a language that is fragmented, divided into difference, in an age before official measures were taken to render the language one.

1

THE RENAISSANCE DISCOVERY
OF DIALECT

Thus today we are, for the most part, Englishmen not speaking English and not understood by English ears.

Alexander Gill, *Logonomia Anglica*[1]

The earliest recorded use of the word "dialect," referring to a manner of speaking, dates from 1577, according to the *Oxford English Dictionary*.[2] John Bullokar's *An English Expositor* (1616), an early precursor of the *OED*, was the first vernacular dictionary to include the term:

> Dialect. a difference of some words, or pronunciation in any language: as in England the *Dialect* or manner of speech in the North, is different from that in the South, and the Western dialect differing from them both. . . . So every country hath commonly in divers parts thereof some difference of language, which is called the Dialect of that place.[3]

The term "dialect" was also current among literary authors from the latter half of the sixteenth century. In 1579, E.K., in his defense of the language of *The Shepheardes Calender*, warned his readers that, despite the example of Edmund Spenser's own poetic idiom, they ought not to corrupt "the commen dialecte and maner of speaking" by using too many archaisms in verse.[4] E.K., in contrasting archaisms with the "commen dialecte and maner of speaking," implicitly suggests that old words represent an "uncommon" dialect of English. Ben Jonson, in his *Poetaster* (1602), invokes the word in reference to another contemporary experiment in English diction – coining new words, often by borrowing or adapting Latin forms. The "Poetaster" of his title, also known as Crispinus, is forced to purge the Latinate neologisms in his own verse by means of an emetic administered by Horace. After Crispinus vomits up the offending words, Virgil advises him:

> You must not hunt for wild, out-landish terms,
> To stuff out a peculiar *dialect*;
> But let your matter run before your *words*:
> And if, at any time, you chaunce to meet
> Some *Gallo-belgic* phrase, you shall not straight

7

Racke your poore verse to give it entertainement;
But let it passe: and doe not thinke your selfe
Much damnified, if you do leave it out;
When, nor your understanding, nor the sense
Could well receive it. This fair abstinence,
In time, will render you more sound, and cleere;
And this have I prescrib'd to you, in place
Of a strict sentence.[5]

For these writers, the "difference of language" referred to as dialect was not always defined in regional terms; in the Renaissance, dialect refers to any manner of speaking or writing that is judged as either a "common" or "peculiar" variety of the language.

The English spoken in the sixteenth and seventeenth centuries was not a standard language, if by "standard" we mean fixed or uniform.[6] There were as yet no official, codified rules for vernacular usage. Yet Renaissance writers refer, again and again, to a variety of English they describe as the "commen dialecte" or common language. As early as 1490, William Caxton discriminates "comyn termes that be dayli used" from "rude," "curyous," and "auncyent" ones. Thomas Wilson urges his countrymen to avoid "straunge" or "outlandishe" English and rather to "so speake as is commonly received." Alexander Gill locates the *communis dialectus* in relation to northern, southern, eastern and western varieties of the language. The word "common" in these statements refers, it seems, not so much to a ruled language as to a shared one, to a "commonality" of usage and of understanding. George Puttenham, in his *Arte of English Poesie* (1589), defines language itself in such terms, as "a speach . . . fully fashioned to the common understanding, & accepted by consent of a whole countrey."[7] By a "common language," in other words, Renaissance authors intend a national language – an English pertaining, by consensus, to the "whole countrey." This language, also described by contemporaries as "pure" English or "true" English, was rhetorically distinguished from "uncommon" dialects in terms that suggest they are not English at all, but rather "strange," "counterfeit," or "foreign." In speaking of common and uncommon words, Renaissance writers affirm which ones are "really" English.

In the present chapter, I aim to show how the idea of dialect, or early modern constructions of the "difference of English," conditioned the rise of vernacular language study in the Renaissance, and the production of the first English dictionaries, grammars, and works on vernacular orthography. These treatises represent some of the earliest English attempts – like Virgil's in *Poetaster* – at linguistic "prescription," efforts to identify, and disseminate, the best forms of the language. Prescriptivism as a motivating force in English language study, along with the project of "standardizing" the language, has long been viewed as the legacy of the eighteenth century, and there is no doubt that modern notions of "correctness" in language have their origins in the work of men like Bishop

Lowth and Samuel Johnson.[8] Yet one of the purposes of this chapter will be to marshal the overwhelming evidence that prescriptivism has its sources in the linguistic researches of the sixteenth century, although it did not manifest itself as any official system of prescriptions or rules. Rather, sixteenth- and early seventeenth-century prescriptivism was diagnostic in its methods and its aims; its implicit end was discrimination – the differentiation of English forms, and the valuation of those differences. In England, the idea of authority in language was a corollary of a process, initiated in the sixteenth century, by which the relative value of alternative native forms was distributed for the first time.

In continental studies, this is hardly news: The sixteenth-century linguistic scene in Italy has long been characterized by what contemporaries referred to as the *questione della lingua* – the debate over which of the numerous dialects of Italian then current was worthy of being advanced as a national language. This "question," however, had been posed as far back as the fourteenth century. Dante's *De Vulgari Eloquentia* (*c.* 1303) may be understood as the ultimate source of debates on the vernacular throughout early modern Europe. This treatise is well known for the aggressive challenge it posed to the cultural status of Latin and for its defense of the modern Italian vernacular as superior to its classical ancestor. At the start of his work, Dante celebrates the vulgar tongue as "that language, which we learn without any rules by imitating a nurse," pronouncing it nobler than Latin "because it is natural for us, whereas the other is instead artificial."[9] Yet beyond a few initial remarks to that effect, Dante expends little effort advancing the claims of Italian over Latin in this treatise.[10] The status of Italian with respect to Latin was not Dante's primary concern at all, if we accept as evidence the emphasis in his own text. Dante, who declares at the start that his subject is "the correct and elegant use of the vernacular," spends the better part of the first book attempting to establish which of the numerous regional dialects of Italian then current was worthy of advancing as "correct and elegant," as superior – not so much to Latin as to rival Italian dialects. In Book I of his treatise, he leads his readers through a guided tour of the provinces and, one by one, discommends fourteen alternative varieties of Italian as he searches for what he calls an "illustrious" Latin vernacular. Dante's sixteenth-century heirs – not only in Italy but in France and England as well – would make analogous journeys in search of the national language.

The course of Dante's own journey is instructive: Promising "to help the language of the common people" (1.1), Dante claims that the *vulgare illustre* is a language that belongs, inclusively, to all Italians:

> For just as is the finding a certain vernacular which is peculiar to Cremona, so is the finding a certain one which is peculiar to Lombardy; and just as is the finding one which is peculiar to the whole left side of Italy . . . so also [one may find] that one which is of all Italy.
>
> (19.1)

9

At the end of Book 1, Dante at last announces his "discovery" of a vernacular that transcends regional borders: "I proclaim an illustrious, cardinal, royal, and courtly vernacular in Italy, which is of every Latin city, and seems to be of none" (16.6). Yet the dialect that, in Dante's riddle, is at once of all places and of none turns out to be the one that had been used by certain exceptional poets, the "doctores illustres" among whom Dante counted himself.[11] And in a final repudiation of the altruism that seems to have inspired his efforts, he declares the "illustrious" vernacular a medium that only the best, most "illustrious" poets, are worthy to employ (19.1). Although Dante originally hails Italian as superior in its natural state to the artificial Latin, the entire second book of the treatise is taken up not with the "unruled" vernacular, but with the rules for writing a *canzone*, Dante's favored literary form. Dante's work is not broadly nationalistic in the way it is sometimes characterized, for he is not as concerned with the advancement of "Italian" as with a particular kind of Italian that he – along with a small coterie of elite poets – was privileged to wield. The early chapters of the *De Vulgari* had invoked an ideal language to which the modern vernaculars could only aspire: Not Latin, but the original lingua franca, the language given to Adam in Paradise. In a sense, this is where the treatise ends as well. *De Vulgari Eloquentia* begins with Adam and ends with a new Adam – the poet Dante – whose "universal" Italian is also, in a sense, a language of his own making.

Dante's views on language were rediscovered by sixteenth-century Italian writers, who explicitly invoked the *De Vulgari* in the debate on the *questione della lingua*.[12] Remarkably, Dante's vision of a literary conquest of the language was ultimately achieved, thanks to the work of Pietro Bembo and his followers, who promoted the fourteenth-century Florentine dialect of the poets Dante, Petrarch, and Boccaccio as a national language. Bembo's poetic standard for Italian was one explicitly set by an elite:

> It is not the masses who give repute and authority to the literature [and language] of any particular time, but in every age the people, who are unable to judge directly by themselves, trust to the judgement of a small number of men considered more learned than the rest.[13]

Bembo, indeed, made explicit what was only implicit in Dante's treatise: The idea that literary language was, or should become, the representative language of the nation as a whole. This language was to be determined by a "small number of men considered more learned than the rest" – namely, poets. Bembo's determination was made official by the Accademia della Crusca, founded in 1583 to foster the development of the vernacular as an expression of emergent Italian nationalism. In 1612, the Accademia published its official *Dizionario*, which established the vocabulary of Dante, Petrarch, and Boccacio as a national treasury of words.[14]

The Italian question of the language was not so easily settled, however. Many sixteenth-century writers argued strongly against adopting a literary idiom as a national standard. Among these, Baldassare Castiglione stressed the idea that language was essentially an instrument of communication and must be determined by current, spoken usage; like Dante at the start of his treatise, Castiglione privileged native, "natural" speech against the artifice of written language. In his Epistle prefacing *The Courtier* (1528), Castiglione writes that the "force or rule of speach doeth consist more in use, then in anye thinge els: and it is alwayes a vice to use wordes that are not in commune speache." He explains his own choice of diction accordingly: "Therefore it was not meete I should have used many that are in Boccaccio, which in his time were used, and now are out of use emonge the Tuscans them selves." His Count Lewis, in the dialogue that constitutes the text of *The Courtier*, adds

> it [would be] a straunge matter to use those words for good in wryting, that are to bee eschewed for naughtie in every manner of speach: and to have that which is never proper in speach, to bee the properest way a man can use in wryting.

Because spoken usage sets the standard, Castiglione argues that no dialect can claim to be more authoritative than any other. He denounces Bembo's advocacy of an archaic Tuscan precisely because it is a version of Italian known only to a very few; the language of Dante, Petrarch, and Boccaccio, he asserts, is a "hard and secret" tongue. Castiglione stresses the importance of perspicuity, in writing even more than in speech: "Because they that write are not alwaies present with them that reade as they that speake with them that speak."[15]

But there's a catch to Castiglione's cult of usage, as another participant in the dialogue, Sir Fredericke, points out, taking Count Lewis to task on his notion of custom:

> Custome, that you make so much a doe off, appeareth unto me very daungerous. . . . If any vice of speech be taken up of many ignorant persons, me thinke for all that it ought not to be received for a rule. . . . Besides this, customes be many and diverse, and yee have not a notable Citie in Italie, that hath not a diverse manner of speach for al the rest. Therefore if ye take not the paines to declare which is the best, a man may as well give him selfe to the Bergamaske tongue, as to the Florentine, and to follow your advice, it were no errour at all.[16]

Sir Fredericke underscores the necessity of establishing a single, educated guide, a man of taste and learning whose function it is to choose among competing forms of the vernacular. Castiglione himself ultimately makes such a choice, promoting a language largely based on contemporary, courtly Tuscan, as a "universal and noble" pan-Italian language.[17] Although he designates the courtier, rather than the poet, as the ideal arbiter of national linguistic differences, Castiglione, like Bembo, ultimately forsakes the mother tongue (at least, in most of her guises) in favor of an elite dialect of his own choosing. "Custom" or "currency" is repeatedly invoked by Renaissance authors on behalf of an ideal of linguistic "commonality" – but such terms generally refer, on closer inspection, to the custom or the usage of a minority of speakers or writers.

The work of Pietro Bembo and his followers had a direct impact on the terms of the debate on language in Renaissance France. Joachim Du Bellay and Pierre de Ronsard, the principal poets of the circle known collectively as the Pléiade, contributed two of the most important treatises on the French vernacular produced in the period. Du Bellay's *Deffence et illustration de la langue francoyse* (1549) has been called "a great manifesto of patriotism."[18] He is certainly direct in expressing the political mandate of his work: "The same natural law which commands each to defend the place of his birth, obliges us to guard the dignity of our language."[19] According to Du Bellay, national language reform is dependent on the arts of language. Tracing the contemporary confusion of tongues to the Tower of Babel, he suggests that the diversity of languages is "born in the world of the desire and will of mortals," that "since men are of diverse wills, therefore do they speak and write diversely." The capacity to improve the language consequently lies in the "sole artifice and industry of men."[20] It is no surprise, then, that Du Bellay, just like Dante before him, devotes the entire second book of his defense of the vernacular to a poetics; that is, to the arts of language that will bring an end to the great confusion of languages and unify the national tongue. The *Deffence* has been aptly described as an "art of poetry in disguise."[21]

Du Bellay nominally censures those who favor the use of strange or "foreign" language that might be difficult for some of his countrymen to understand. He thus endorses the enterprise of translating Latin and Greek works into the vernacular on the grounds of accessibility. Like Castiglione, he characterizes his detractors as elitists harboring a privileged language:

> I well understand that the professors of languages will not be of my opinion: who through . . . ambitious desire . . . fear nothing so much as that the secret of their mysteries, which must be learned from them . . . be laid bare to the vulgar.

He derides the notion that "obscurity" in language should be valued for its own sake: "I do not see . . . that one should esteem one language more excellent than other, simply because it is more difficult." Yet Du Bellay's linguistic nationalism, once again, is not exactly a celebration of any and all native forms of speech, as he ultimately makes clear: "All that I have said for the defence and renowning of our language concerns principally those whose profession it is to speak well, as poets and orators."[22] Although Du Bellay at first invites "universal" participation in the defense of the French vernacular, invoking "the same *natural* law" commanding everyone to defend the place of his birth in the defense of the native tongue, Du Bellay concludes, as did his predecessors, by leaving the "dignity of the language" in the hands of those who make the laws of art, namely, contemporary French poets – himself among them.

A full account of the *questione della lingua* in Italy and in France goes beyond the scope of the present study. But it is essential to note that the "question," on the continent, always involved a discrimination among competing forms of the vernacular, and the designation of a superior form – the language favored by the individual reformer – that would provide a model for the national language. Moreover, many continental language reformers advanced elite dialects as that model, even as they claimed to champion the "common" or "natural" tongue. And many were poets or apologists for poetry prescribing a future for literary language.

While early modern England produced no full-scale treatises devoted to a defense of the vernacular, the question of the language was implicitly debated, and in similar terms, by English poets, poetic theorists, and language theorists alike. Yet there has been very little sustained historical inquiry into the "question of the language" as it was posed by these writers. Instead, English literary studies has been dominated by applications of M.M. Bakhtin's view of the linguistic culture of the Renaissance. For Bakhtin, the Renaissance saw the birth of a new linguistic order:

> We live, write and speak today in a world of free and democratized language; the . . . hierarchy of discourses, forms, images, styles that used to permeate the entire system of official language and linguistic consciousness was swept away by the linguistic revolutions of the Renaissance.[23]

The Renaissance, Bakhtin suggests, made the world safe for the democratization of language. According to the history of literary discourse that he rehearses over several of his works, we are the heirs of a sweeping revolution in linguistic consciousness fought and won in the age of Shakespeare, for sixteenth-century Europe saw the the triumph of heteroglossia over monologism and the rule of an "official" tongue. This revolution was enabled by the rapid decline of Latin as a literary lingua franca (the same decline presaged by Dante). While classical Latin had been reduced to a "dead" language by the beginning of the century, the national vernaculars survived as "the language of life, of material work and mores, and the 'lowly', mostly humorous genres" (*Rabelais*, p. 466). The revolution of the vulgar tongues, in Bakhtin's account, was a grass-roots movement, a kind of peasant's revolt staged against an aging linguistic tyrant. Together, he tells us, the vernaculars rose up and "invaded all the spheres of ideology and expelled Latin," thereby securing for posterity "the victory over linguistic dogmatism" (*Rabelais*, pp. 465 and 473).

In response, Renaissance authors, in fellowship with the popular voices that had been liberated by the revolution, spoke up for the dialects within the national vernaculars. Bakhtin observes the way that dialects suddenly make their way into numerous texts of the sixteenth and seventeenth centuries. According to Bakhtin, the "free play" of dialects was yet unhindered by the centralization of language, the eventual establishment of new linguistic norms:

> A single national language did not exist yet; it was being slowly formed. The process of transferring the whole of philosophy to the vernacular and of creating a new system of literary media led to an intense interorientation of dialects within this vernacular (*but without concentration at a center*).
>
> (*Rabelais*, p. 468; emphasis added)

In the wake of linguistic decentralization, new literary forms such as the novel would flourish:

> The novel begins by presuming a verbal and semantic decentering of the ideological world, a certain linguistic homelessness of literary consciousness, which no longer possesses a sacrosanct and unitary linguistic medium for containing ideological thought.
>
> (*Dialogic Imagination*, p. 367)

Bakhtin's literary history has a tendency towards Utopian idealization, but nowhere so clearly as in his chronicle of the Revolution. The rise of the European vernaculars, in fact, did not entirely dismantle the old linguistic hierarchies, for the standardization – or, more precisely, the centralization – of these languages,[24] well underway before the sixteenth century, quickly advanced new, prestige forms. In Renaissance England, grammarians, lexicographers, and spelling reformers were already concerned with advancing the King's English – the elite dialect that had already repossessed some of the domains of literature, religion, and politics once held by Latin – as a "unitary" national language. Bakhtin acknowledges that Renaissance writers were beginning to evaluate the dialects of English in terms of an emergent standard.[25] What he slights, however, is the idea that this "centralizing norm" was already engendering a new, modern myth of monoglossia, and one that was already becoming as powerful and totalizing as the last. Latin was dead – but long live the King's English.

Language historians have traced the rise of a standard, written English, derived from the East Midlands dialect of Middle English, to the late fourteenth and early fifteenth centuries.[26] But the more pressing question, for the purposes of this study, is not when the centralization of English got underway, but when individuals began to articulate the idea that one dialect of English represented a prestige form. By the middle of the sixteenth century, it is clear that the link between dialect and social class had already been forged. Thomas Elyot, in *The Book Named the Governor* (1531), advises nurses who attended noblemen's sons that they should:

> speke none englisshe but that which is cleane, polite, perfectly and articulately pronounced, omittinge no lettre or sillable, as folisshe women oftentimes do as a wantonnesse, whereby divers nobel men and gentilmennes chyldren . . . have atttained corrupte and foule pronunciation.[27]

Even educated men whose speech betrayed traces of their provincial origins were subject to linguistic censure. John Palsgrave, in 1540, notes that some university students:

> because of the rude language used in their native countries [counties] where they were born and first learned their grammar rules, and partly because that, coming straight from thence unto one of your grace's universities, since they have not had occasions to be conversant in such places of your realm where the purest English is spoken, they be not able to express their conceit in their vulgar tongue.[28]

After a visit to the recently inaugurated Merchant Taylors' School, which Spenser attended under the headmastership of Richard Mulcaster, it was reported that the teachers "being northern men born . . . had not taught the children to speak distinctly or to pronounce their words as well as they ought."[29]

A complete social history of the development of early modern English has yet to be written.[30] Although he does not attempt that level of historical specificity, Pierre Bourdieu, in his *Language and Symbolic Power* (1991), has offered a compelling paradigm for understanding the relationship between competing versions of the vernacular in the early modern period. Bourdieu concurs with many historical sociolinguists in linking early efforts to promote a standard language to the emergence of nationalism:

> Only when the making of the 'nation', an entirely abstract group based on law, creates new usages and functions does it become indispensible to forge a *standard* language. . . . Political unification and the accompanying imposition of an official language establish relations between *the different uses of the same language* which differ fundamentally from the theoretical relations . . . between different languages, spoken by politically and economically independent groups. All linguistic practices are measured against the legitimate practices, i.e., the practices of those who are dominant.

According to Bourdieu, the idea of a "common" national language invariably places alternative dialects in a new light: "Measured *de facto* against the single standard of the 'common' language, they are found wanting and cast into the outer darkness of *regionalisms.*"[31] The result of this process, Bourdieu explains, is the creation of a "linguistic market" in which individuals compete for social profit based on their ability to exploit the new system of linguistic differences. Where Bakhtin imagined a "free play" of dialects engaged in democratic debate, Bourdieu more accurately represents the struggle for dominance that characterizes the period in which the King's English inaugurated its reign.[32]

It is easy to overlook, or underestimate, this struggle in sixteenth-century England. The incursion of thousands of new words into the language, the variability of spelling, the profusion of literary styles seem to speak to Bakhtin's formulation, or that of numerous modern scholars who have emphasized license rather than rule, expansion rather than consolidation: "It might be fanciful, yet not altogether wrong, to view it [the introduction of new words during the Renaissance] as another aspect of their willingness to experiment, the spirit that sent them exploring across half the world."[33] There were no linguistic academies established in early modern England, no state institutions working, like the French Academy, "with all possible care and diligence to give definite rules to our language, and to render it pure, eloquent, and capable of treating the arts and science."[34] The English, it seems, had no use for such academies. Shakespeare apparently ridicules the aims of the King's "little academe," including the spelling reform schemes of the pretentious pedant Holofernes, in *Love's Labor's Lost.* The fact that the English, two centuries after the production of Shakespeare's play, still rejected proposals to form an academy, to "fix" the vernacular as the Italians and French had sought to do, further suggests that England was not disposed to participate in the movement, that, as Samuel Johnson later put it, language academies were somehow "un-English."[35] There is no doubt that the language was remarkably plastic in the early modern period, and that the precise nature of the King's English had yet to be articulated. But the idea that writers enjoyed "unparalleled freedom"[36] with the vernacular needs to be reconsidered in the context of a period in which – in England no less than in Italy and France – the idea of a "common" language worked as much to limit as to expand the freedoms of writers. The idea of an elite language did not pass away with the decline of Latin in favor of the European vernaculars but persisted – even in the absence of officially authorized vernacular forms. Although they labored individually, without the support of the state, English language reformers, the first English lexicographers, grammarians and spelling reformers, were busy defining the new terrain of a dominant language. And that definition depended, as Dante had articulated centuries before, on the social discrimination of competing "Englishes" – from the old spoken dialects of the provinces to the new literary dialects of a cultural elite. I turn now to the rise of English lexicography, and the "difference of English" set forward in these works.

* * *

> I grant that lexicographers collect artificial words, and even invent them, and truly disregard English ones, or even misunderstand them – You will hear ours among artisans and country people rather than among writers. In the meantime, until they become reasonable again, make use of existing benefits and hope for better things.
>
> Alexander Gill, *Logonomia Anglica*[37]

Like Dante's treatise, which sets up an adversarial relationship between alternative national "languages," the original English dictionaries, dating from the early seventeenth century, rose in response to a new, or at least, a heightened, awareness of linguistic diversity within the nation. Commentary on the dialects of English dates back to the twelfth century,[38] but concern about such differences gained increasing urgency from the late fifteenth century on. William Caxton, the first English printer, described the difficulty he faced in negotiating among the several varieties of the language:

> Comyn englysshe that is spoken in one shyre varyeth from a nother. In so moche that in my dayes happened that certayn marchauntes . . . taryed atte Forlond. . . . And one of theym . . . cam in-to an hows and axed for mete, and specyally he axyd after eggys. And the goode wyf answerde, that she coude not speke no frenshe. . . . Loo what sholde a man in thyse dayes now wryte, egges or eyren? certaynly it is harde to playse every man by cause of dyversite and chaunge of langage.[39]

Caxton does not speculate on which of the variant forms, *egges* or *eyren*, ought to prevail; he seems more eager to "playse everyman" than to promote the language of any particular social or regional group. But by the end of the next century, writers are not so even-handed about the dialects of English. George Puttenham is able to delineate the borders of the "best" English within sixty miles. In the well-known passage, Puttenham decrees that poets:

> neither shall . . . take the termes of Northern-men, such as they use in dayly talke, whether they be noble men or gentlemen, or of their best clarkes all is a matter: nor in effect any speach used beyond the river of Trent, though no man can deny but that theirs is the purer English Saxon at this day, yet it is not so Courtly nor so currant as our Southerne English is; no more is the far Westerne mans speach. Ye shall therfore take the usuall speach of the Court, and that of London and the shires lying about London within lx. myles, and not much above. . . . But herein we are already ruled by th' English Dictionaries and other bookes written by learned men, and therefore it needeth none other direction in that behalfe.[40]

Drawing strict boundaries around the small sociolinguistic region he calls "the usuall speach of the Court," Puttenham excludes the "terms" of the vast majority of sixteenth-century speakers from the domain of the "best" English. Clearly, something had changed in the hundred years since Caxton compared the variant dialect forms of the word "egg."

According to Puttenham, that change was wrought by the production of English dictionaries and "other bookes" that had put an end to debates like Caxton's once and for all. "We are already ruled" by the dictates of these books, Puttenham tells us, as if to say that the whole question of dialect and linguistic difference had long since been dismissed. Yet more than a hundred years after Caxton's "good wyf" mistook a native dialect word for French, writers continue to complain about linguistic diversity – and in similar terms. According to Gill, seventeenth-century England was a nation of "Englishmen not speaking English and not understood by English ears"; as late as 1656, English lexicographers are still writing of the need to have "English Englished."[41] The first English dictionaries, moreover, did not concern themselves with usual speech – or even the "usuall speach" of London and the court, as Puttenham would have it; they listed and defined "hard words," the new and unusual diction fashionable in some contemporary writing. The first English dictionaries were in fact a direct descendant of the foreign language dictionaries that preceded them: Both provided translations of words, largely foreign to native speakers, into an English that all could understand. These works are best understood as "dialect" diction-aries, providing readers with compilations of the new, specialized language of a social elite. Although the first actual dialect dictionary, John Ray's *A Collection of English Words not Generally Used*, did not appear until 1674, the first English dictionaries are predicated on the idea that, linguistically, the country was, as one seventeenth-century lexicographer put it, a "self-stranger Nation."[42]

The idea that English was a "foreign" language – even to native speakers – was felt to be a uniquely contemporary phenomenon, and with good reason. The period 1500–1650 saw the introduction of over 10,000 new words,[43] some of them borrowed outright from other languages, but many of them newly coined, invented by writers. The sixteenth-century debate over "inkhorn" terms is too familiar to rehearse here.[44] What is rarely acknowledged, however, is the implicit connection that is drawn between social or regional dialects, and "foreign" or strange-looking language, in that debate. Caxton had very nearly articulated that connection: Immediately after he compares the dialect forms of *egges* and *eyren*, he continues:

> Certaynly it is harde to playse everyman by cause of dyversite and chaunge of langage. For in these dayes every man that is in ony reputacyon in his countre wyll utter his commynycacyon and maters in suche maners and termes that fewe men shall understonde theym. And some honest and grete clerkes have ben wyth me, and desired me to wryte the moste curyous termes that I coude fynde. And thus bytwene playn, rude, and curyous I stande abasshed.[45]

For Caxton, the "dyversite" of language includes dialect along with "curyous termes" – no doubt he is referring to inkhorn words and borrowings, already controversial as early as 1490. For Caxton, too, both represent varieties of English that "fewe men shall understonde." Puttenham, almost a hundred years later, continues to fault neologisms, the "many darke wordes and not usuall nor well sounding" as too unusual for use.[46]

The idea that the first English dictionaries concerned themselves with a particular class dialect of the period becomes more obvious when we compare them with another, contemporary development in vernacular lexicography. The original English–English dictionaries, long preceding those produced in the seventeenth century, were glossaries of "cant," a language allegedly devised by a criminal underworld of outlaws and thieves. Contemporary observers describe the canting language as a dialect partly invented by its own speakers, a secret code based on neologism. One sixteenth-century historian, William Harrison, reports that beggars and thieves:

> have devised a language among themselves which they name "canting" but other, "pedlers' French", a speech compact thirty years since of English and a great number of odd words of their own devising, without all order or reason; and yet such is it as none but themselves are able to understand. The first deviser thereof was hanged by the neck, a just reward no doubt for his deserts.[47]

Harrison was not alone in his effort to tie the goals of social legislation – especially the punishment of transgression – with linguistic rule. For Gill, the use of cant was a criminal offence no less abhorrent than that of vagrancy, and one that should be subject to the harshest measures. In his discussion of the English dialects, he brutally denounces cant and its speakers:

Regarding that venemous and disgusting ulcer of our nation I am embarrassed to say anything at all. For that detestable scum of wandering vagabonds speak no proper dialect but a cant jargon which no punishment by law will ever repress, until its proponents are crucified by the magistrates, acting under a public edict.[48]

There was, in fact, at least one official measure taken to suppress the unruly language of the underworld. In formal indictments, it was illegal to designate certain criminals such as dicers, carders, or vagrants by terms that identified their true means of gaining a living, since these terms, many of them cant words, referred to "occupations" forbidden by the state.[49] Despite such censure, the criminal language of the underworld finds its way into a series of glossaries and, later, full-scale dictionaries as well.[50]

The most influential of these was a brief glossary appended to Thomas Harman's popular pamphlet *A Caveat or Warening for Commen Cursetors* (1567). Harman presents his work as an exposé of rogue life, a warning to potential victims who might be prey to tricksters and thieves plotting against them. His glossary, in turn, promotes a kind of linguistic vigilantism. Harman describes the underworld language as "the leud, lousey language of these lewtering Luskes and lasy Lorrels . . . a unknowen toung onely, but to these bold, beastly, bawdy Beggers, and vaine Vacabondes."[51] He proposes that the publication of his work, by exposing the "unknowen toung," will ultimately render the language obsolete. He then translates the "leud, lousey" language into "common" English:

Nab, a head.	A pratling chete, a tounge.	quaromes, a body.
Nabchet, a hat or cap.	Crashing chetes, teeth.	prat, a buttocke.[52]

and so on through a list that includes 120 terms.

Harman presents his *Caveat* as an eyewitness account, claiming to have gained his knowledge of cant through contact with real rogues. William Harrison, the historian, corroborates Harman's account of the underworld society, but he cannot provide any independent evidence of an underworld language. Although Harrison includes examples of cant in his *Description of England*, he lifted them directly from the *Caveat*, and later authors followed suit. Even Harman illustrates the dialect by means of fictional dialogues between fictional rogues:

Roge.
I couched a hogshead in a Skypper this darkemans.
I layd me done to sleepe in a barne this night.
Upright Man.
I towre the strummel trine vpon thy nabchet and Togman.
I see the strawe hang vpon thy cap and coate.

> Roge.
> I saye by the Salomon I will lage it of with a gage of benebouse; then
> cut to my nose watch.
> *I sweare by the masse, I wull washe it of with a quart of good drynke;*
> *then saye to me what thou wylt.*[53]

The canting language no doubt existed, in some form, but its authentication
ultimately depends on literary and semi-literary sources like Harman's pamphlet.
From the beginning, the elaboration and transmission of canting words was
the special province of early modern fiction. As later chapters will show, the
representation of English dialects, in general, was largely a literary enterprise in
this period.

For its sixteenth-century detractors, inkhorn terms are nothing more than
upper-class cant, and the attacks on educated neologizers bear a certain
resemblance to Harman's attacks on the canting crew:

> And I can not but wonder at the strange presumption of some men that
> dare so audaciously adventure to introduce any whatsoever forraine wordes,
> be they never so strange; and of themselves as it were, without a Parliament,
> without any consent, or allowance, establish them as Free-denizens in our
> language.[54]

According to such critiques, some neologizers, like the sturdy beggars of
Harman's report, are not licensed to invent words or to allow "alien" terms to
infiltrate the national borders of the language.

The lexicographers who compiled these terms tended to agree. The English
dictionary that is generally recognized as the first of its kind, Robert Cawdrey's
A Table Alphabeticall (1604), is presented as:

> conteyning and teaching the true writing and understanding of hard
> usuall English wordes, borrowed from the Hebrew, Greeke, Latine, or
> French etc., with the interpretation thereof by plaine English words,
> gathered for the benefit and helpe of Ladies, Gentlewomen, or any other
> unskillful persons.[55]

Cawdrey directs his work to women and to other "unskillful" people, promising
to make "hard words" available to all readers. But, like Harman, Cawdrey does
not entirely favor the practice of neologism. He entreats his educated readers to
refrain from using "any strange inckhorne termes, but [rather] labour to speake
so as is commonly received, and so as the most ignorant may well understand
them." In the interests of communication, "unusually" hard words are best
avoided. For convenience, I cite his caveat again:

> Do we not speak, because we would have other[s] to understand us? . . .
> Therefore, either wee must make a difference of English, and say, some is
> learned English, and othersome rude English; or the one is Court talke,
> the other is Country-speech, or els we must of necessitie banish all affected
> Rhetorique, and use altogether one manner of language.[56]

Cawdrey's reforms, it seems, are meant to be retroactive, obliterating the "difference of English" that had arisen in the age of new words. But Cawdrey's plan, like Harman's, had a serious flaw; despite his stated goals, Cawdrey gives neologism a certain cachet; those who understand "hard words," his work implies, enjoy a social advantage over those who do not. Both men, by publishing and circulating their works, help advance the new English dictionaries as "official" works that codified the language they set out, in part, to critique.

Cawdrey's successors similarly argue for the dissolution of the language barrier as a means of social reform. Henry Cockeram thus offers the contents of his *English Dictionarie* (1623) for "the generall use."[57] Yet Cockeram remains ambivalent about the unrestricted practice of inventing words; some measure, he believed, must be introduced to curb the potential for excessive neologizing. Cockeram's dictionary, no less than Cawdrey's, is thus designed to set the limits of innovation. To that end, he explains: "I have also inserted . . . even the *mocke-words* which are ridiculously used in our language . . . by too many who study rather to be heard speake, than to understande themselves."[58] A page of his dictionary reads as follows:[59]

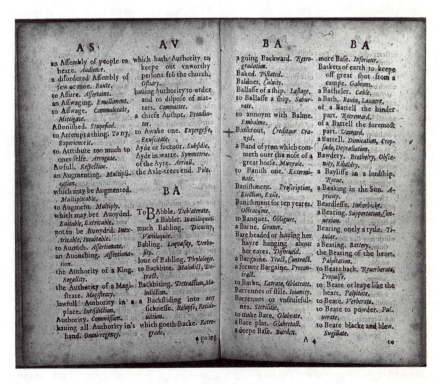

Figure 1.1 A plate from Cockeram's dictionary (1623)

21

Unfortunately, there is no way of knowing which of the terms that Cockeram includes here are the "mocke words" he is referring to; apparently, he thought his examples spoke for themselves. His intention – that his readers would promptly laugh such words out of use – is based on an assumption, common enough in such works, that his own linguistic preferences were somehow self-evident.

His contemporary, John Bullokar, also speaks out for linguistic and social equity in his dictionary, *An English Expositor* (1616). Yet Bullokar expresses some concern about the reaction of the educated classes to such a project. In his own defense, he addresses a separate prefatory letter "To the Courteous Reader," saying:

> I hope such learned will deeme no wrong offered to themselves or dishonor to Learning, in that I open the signification of such words, to the capacitie of the ignorant. . . . For considering it is familiar among best writers to usurp strange words . . . I suppose withall their desire is that they should also be understood.[60]

The ironic tone of Bullokar's final remark hints at what he really supposed neologizers were doing: Like gypsies and beggars, the inventors of inkhorn terms intended to keep their language a secret from the public. Just as Castiglione had warned, Bullokar suspected that some reformers championed words precisely because of their obscurity, because they were foreign to ordinary speakers. The idea of linguistic privilege, indeed, is key to the program of early English dictionary-writing.

John Ford, in a dedicatory poem affixed to Cockeram's dictionary, addresses the lexicographer:

> Born in the West? live there? so far from Court?
> From Oxford, Cambridge, London? Yet report
> (Now in these daies of Eloquence) such change
> Of words? unknown? untaught? 'tis new and strange.

What, finally, is "new and strange" in Ford's account? The "change/Of words?" Or the fact that an outsider – from the court, from London, from the universities – took it upon himself to determine the bounds of eloquence? The earliest lexicographers were not, as far as we know, powerful men; their qualifications for ascertaining the "best" English, from a seventeenth-century standpoint, may have been questionable.[61] None of these men, moreover, is entirely innocent of the offense they prosecute in their works. Gill, for one, assumed that contemporary lexicographers were the ultimate source of many of the terms they included: "I grant that lexicographers collect artificial words, and even invent them."[62] It was not uncommon in this period, apparently, for writers who disapproved of others' neologizing to engage in the practice themselves. Puttenham, who openly complained of the "many darke wordes and not usuall nor well sounding" used by contemporary writers, filled his treatise on poetics with a host of new words – of his own coinage.[63] He admits a certain hypocrisy here:

Peradventure the writer hereof be in that behalfe no lesse faultie then any other, using many straunge and unaccustomed wordes and borrowed from other languages: and in that respect him selfe no meet Magistrate to reforme the same errours in any other person.[64]

Like the lexicographers, Puttenham is a self-appointed magistrate of English, who openly expresses his concerns about linguistic innovation. Yet he apparently could not resist the temptation that neologizing held forth – no matter how "straunge" his new words might seem to others.

All of the earliest English lexicographers speak of eliminating linguistic differences, either by obliterating certain neologisms – including the invented dialects of the rich and the poor – or neutralizing them by publishing them more broadly. The first lexicographers, however, do not much concern themselves with the nature and the forms of a common language, but with the mysterious, recondite languages that most people could not understand. Despite their professed concerns for the public at large, the early English lexicographers make themselves the guardians of the privilege they had gained through knowledge, perhaps even "inventing" the linguistic secrets they promise to divulge. Like Dante, they, too, advanced uncommon (that is, rare or elite) dialects in the name of the "usual" language. Despite the rhetoric of social unanimity that animates Renaissance language reform, Cawdrey and his followers promoted dialects which, in sociological terms, fulfilled much the same role as the Latin of an earlier age. Renaissance spelling reformers, as we will see, similarly privileged new and unusual ways of writing as "national" scripts.

* * *

Why not my ear best?
Richard Mulcaster, *The Elementarie*[65]

As a printer, William Caxton might have applied the new technology to the problem of language variability; he might, for example, have regularized the many divergent spellings he came across in the manuscripts he published. Yet Caxton, despite his concerns about linguistic diversity, did not attempt this.[66] But by the middle of the sixteenth century, language reformers are ready to take the problem of English orthography into their own hands. Robert Robinson in *The Art of Pronunciation* (1617) explains that spelling reform is an attempt to amend the fact that "speech is so darkly set downe, that our words in speaking seeme as a different kind of language to the same in writing."[67] Yet despite the desire to make English orthography as transparent (i.e., as phonetic) as possible, most of the early language reformers advance schemes that are, by their own admission, very difficult for readers to comprehend.[68] Just as the first English dictionaries are compilations of "hard words," the new spelling systems are replete with "hard letters," which, in Caxton's words, "few men could understonde." Like the early lexicographers, the first orthographers present themselves as translators of English writing, which they re-form themselves.

The earliest crusaders for a reformed spelling along phonetic lines are Sir John Cheke and Sir Thomas Smith, whose interest in the subject grew out of the sixteenth-century academic controversy over the proper pronunciation of classical Greek.[69] Smith's recommendations for reforming the way the older Greek was pronounced were apparently outlawed by the Chancellor of Cambridge; what is more, Smith reports that the supporters of reform incurred:

> ejection from the senate, loss of exemptions, a considerable loss of status, and a sort of proscription of a man of honest and harmless life and unspotted reputation. [The] decree has almost imposed the penalty of parricide on what are possibly the true sounds of Greek letters.[70]

But this rebuff did not stop Smith from attempting the same sort of reform of English pronunciation and spelling. Smith's *De Recta et Emendata Linguae Anglicae Scriptione* (1568) may be understood as a manifesto for the movement as a whole. Every letter, he states, has a "nature" established by general consent; when a letter is silent, or expresses a different sound than its "nature" permits, that letter is abused. In Smith's view, there is nothing revolutionary about spelling reform, which rather marks a return, and a confirmation, of what had already long since been established by "mutual covenant and consent among men."[71]

Orthographic reform is thus continually put forward as a program sanctioned by nature and universally endorsed. Gill introduces his grammar, which includes his own design for a reformed spelling system, by invoking a lost ideal of pre-lapsarian linguistic unity; like Dante centuries before, his treatise begins with a brief history of the language from its origins, before embarking on a scheme implicitly designed to bring the language "home." The chief beneficiaries of such schemes were to be the uneducated; like the early lexicographers, the orthographic reformers explicitly proffer their works for the betterment of the "multitude." John Hart, for example, presents his *Orthography* "for the profite of the multitude . . . or the rude countrie English man, which may desire to read English as the best sort use to speake it."[72] Edmund Coote's *The English Schoole-maister* (1596) is pitched at:

> any unskilfull person [who] may easily both understand any hard english words . . . and also be made able to use the same aptly themselves. . . . And therefore it is made not onely for children . . . but also for all other especially that are ignorant.[73]

Their social goals, indeed, often extend beyond national borders. Hart labors on behalf of the Welsh, Irish, and Scottish. Gill confesses that "concern for humanity persuades me to come to the help of foreigners, and the universal bond of human society, which is united firmly by nothing so much as by the use of reason and language." He even professes the hope that, once reformed, English might properly reclaim the place of the original universal language:

> Since in the beginning all men's lips were identical, and there existed but one language, it would indeed be desirable to unify the speech of all peoples

. . . and were human ingenuity to attempt this, certainly no more suitable language than English could be found.[74]

Implicitly, Gill envisions his treatise as a "master text" which will help English achieve what he believed to be its imperial destiny.

But such ambitions for the national language depended, once again, on the reformers' careful discrimination among the dialects of English then current – and among those who spoke them as well. Hart, who writes on behalf of the "rude countrie English man," also makes it clear that "countrie English" had no place in a reformed language: "He should have a wrong opinion of me, that should thinke . . . I ment any thing should be printed in London in the maner of Northerne or Westerne speeches."[75] His reforms, he asserts, will be based on words "as they are called in the Court, and London speaches, where the generall flower of all English countrie speaches, are chosen and used."[76] Gill similarly identifies the King's English as the flower of the language, insisting that "writing will have to conform not to the pronunciation of ploughmen, working-girls, or river-men, but to that used by learned and refined men in their speech and writing."[77] Edmund Coote blames the tendency to misspell words on the inferior speech of provincials: "I know not what can easily deceive you in writing [i.e., spelling], unlesse it bee by imitating the barbarous speech of your contrey people."[78] Above all, Hart writes, improper forms of writing must be eliminated for the sake of the polity, a project aimed, implicitly if not intentionally, at those who threatened the polity by their use:

Such an abused and vicious writing, bringeth confusion and uncertaintie in the reading, and therefore is justly to be refused, and the vicious parts therof cut away, as are the ydle or offensive members, in a politike common welth.[79]

The best-known of the sixteenth-century orthographers today, Richard Mulcaster, is also the one who marshalled the most powerful defense of the old spelling against the threat of the new. In contrast to the various kinds of "niu ureiting" set forward by his contemporaries, Mulcaster advocates what he calls "right writing" – the phrase itself is a defense of the non-phonetic character of English spelling. In *The Elementarie* (1582), Mulcaster explains his position by means of another political analogy. English writing, he relates, was originally ruled by a tyrant, sound, until "consent in use did transport the autoritie, from sound alone, to reason, custom and sound joyntlie." In the last, perfect era of linguistic history (Mulcaster's own day), Art joins reason and custom to ensure that sound (and its lackeys, the phonetic reformers) may never again seize the throne of language:

Reason and custom, do assure their own joynt government with sound, by the means of Art. For sound like a restrained not banished Tarquinus desiring to be restored to his first and sole monarchie, and finding som, but no more than sounding favorers, did seke to make a tumult in the scriveners province, ever after that, reason and custom were joyned with him.[80]

Although Mulcaster appears to object to the monarchy of sound in favor of a "parliamentary" linguistic system,[81] his real antipathy to the phonetic spelling movement has its source elsewhere. If spelling is left solely to the government of sound, Mulcaster reasons, everyone will follow his own pronunciation and spell words accordingly. The tyranny of sound, for Mulcaster, is really the tyranny of individuals who propose unusual spellings on private grounds; the rallying cry of the most radical spelling reformer, he claims, is "Why not my ear best?"[82]

Mulcaster was no doubt the most "reasonable" of contemporary spelling reformers (he understood the intransigency of custom in matters of language), but his position, it must be pointed out, was not shared by the majority of men working on the topic. He was certainly right, though, about the more radical proponents of spelling reform, for their strategy, in every case, was to treat their own "ear" as the model for a newly perfected language. Thomas Smith, the first to set out to establish a fixed set of correspondences between sound and letter, understood that he had to fix the proper sounds of English first. His procedure, and the one favored by everyone who followed him, was to set down his own pronunciation and ignore any others.[83] E.J. Dobson has characterized the situation this way:

> Men who had once formed the concept that there was a correct manner of speech, and so were resolved to teach and learn it, must constantly have been asking themselves which of the many alternative pronunciations that they heard around them were to be preferred; the elimination and avoidance of others must inevitably, and quite properly, have been a conscious and indeed often arbitrary process.[84]

John Hart rationalized the procedure:

> Tonges have often and much changed . . . then if occasion in the fancies of men have had power to chaunge tongues, much more Reason shuld correct the vicious writing of the speach.[85]

According to Hart, "reason" dictated to him his new system. As he explains, the way to achieve national linguistic uniformity, the "one certain" and "general" manner of speaking, was to submit to the rule of the learned – that is, to his own rule – a prescription even Hart finds "strange" (see Figure 1.2 opposite).[86] Gill concurred that his predecessor's scheme was far too peculiar, charging Hart with reinventing, rather than describing, the vernacular: "[Hart] did not intend to represent our speech but to fashion it."[87] He offers his own orthography, on the other hand, as a faithful representation of the "common" language. Gill "reformed" Spenser's *Faerie Queene*[88] (see Figure 1.3 opposite).

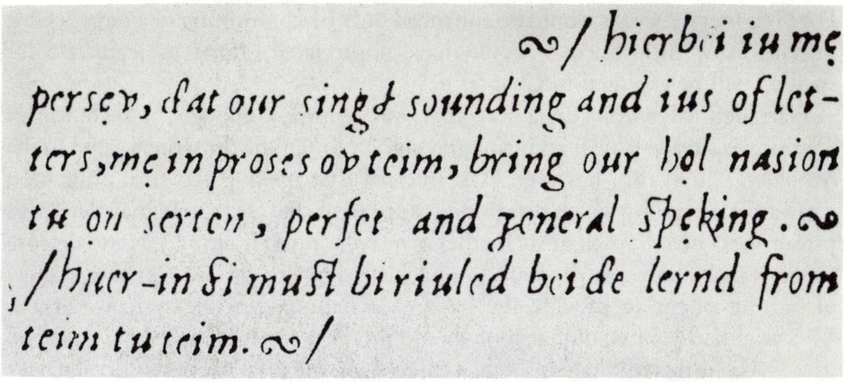

Figure 1.2 Hart on his new system of writing

Note: The text reads as follows: Hereby you may perceive, that our single sounding and use of letters, may in process of time, bring our whole nation to one certain, perfect and general speaking. Wherein we must be ruled by the learned from time to time.

Hart's text continues, "And I can not blame any man to think this manner of new writing strange, for I do confess it is strange to myself."

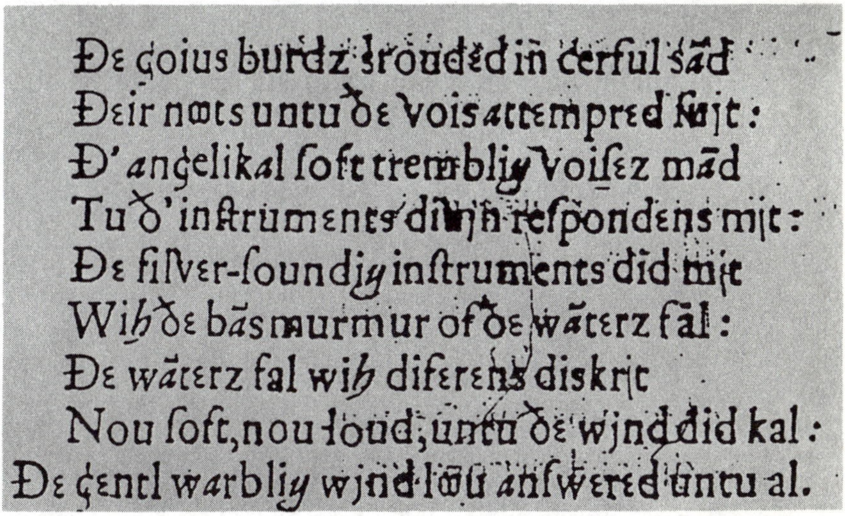

Figure 1.3 A sample of Gill's "reformed" *Faerie Queene*
Note: The original text reads as follows:

> The joyous birdes, shrouded in chearefull shade,
> Their notes unto the voice attempred sweet:
> Th'angelicall soft trembling voyces made
> To th'instruments divine respondence meet:
> With the base murmure of the waters fall:
> The waters fall with difference discreet,
> Now soft, now loud, unto the wind did call:
> The gentle warbling wind low answered to all.

27

For Gill, literary works would be enhanced only by conforming to a more legible system. How little Spenser would have appreciated efforts to regularize his spelling will be explored in Chapter 4.

Hart defined writing in a way that was common enough in such works: "Writing is a reasonable marking or graving . . . to signifie the writers mind to the beholder." From this, however, Hart inferred that spelling was also, ultimately, a private matter: "By which definition it appeareth that every man may devise his private maner for himself or such other as he will impart it unto."[89] Hart's defense of innovation, however, depended on his justifying why his own "private maner" of writing ought to provide the basis of a national writing system, why, as Mulcaster had pointed out, anyone should privilege "privat fantsie before general use."[90] The early spelling reformers seem to share the ideal of consensus; all chant the same litany of terms, promoting "usual," "customary," "general," and "universal" language. William Bullokar complained that Smith and Hart "brought in divers [letters] of new figure and fashion, having no part in figure or fashion of the old, for whose soundes they were changed in figure, or newly devised, strange to the eye,"[91] and cites Quintilian on limiting the role of private individuals in matters of national interest. But with unintended irony, he translates Quintilian into his own "privat" spelling:[92]

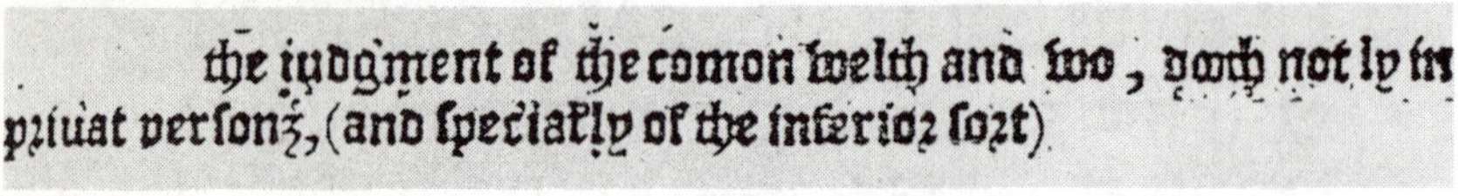
the iudgment of the comon welth and wo, doth not ly in priuat personz, (and specially of the inferior sort)

Figure 1.4 William Bullokar's translation of Quintilian

All of the reformers employ a similar strategy: They posit their own "fantsie" as "reason," "reason" as unanimity. Like Dante almost three hundred years before, they appeal to a community of thought, and a community of ideology, even as they make it their private business to determine the direction of national language reform.

It is instructive that the most radical of the new spelling schemes had something in common with systems of "swift writing" or shorthand that were developed in the same years, invented scripts that deliberately aim for obscurity. In 1588, Timothy Bright presented his brainchild in a treatise entitled *Characterie: An Arte of Shorte Swifte and Secret Writing by Character.*[93] John Bales suggests that the obscurity of his own version of "brachygraphie" would be of use to "men of state" who wish to "swiftlie and secreatlie decipher" their communications.[94] Although spelling reformers promise just the reverse – to eliminate the obscurities that "darkened" traditional writing – they, too, in a sense, created "secret" systems, codes that could only be cracked by their creators.[95] Bright, who puts his script at the service of statesmen, is eager to make it known that his shorthand is wholly "my invention . . . without precept, or imitation of any."[96] Edmund Willis, in *An Abbreviation of Writing by*

Character (1618) asserts that his system can be mastered "without any other Tutor."[97] These men are more explicit about their status as language "masters," inventors of new writing. At their most ambitious, the authors of the new short-hands aim beyond English; some saw their scripts as "universal characters" that might one day replace writing systems all over the world.[98] Yet Gill, after all, had exactly the same idea in mind for his reformed English.[99]

We have been told, repeatedly, that "[Renaissance writers] loved words" and that "the love of words shows itself in more than style of language: in the many books on the arts of language, in the proliferation of dictionaries, in the speculation of the history of English."[100] There is no reason to deny such a premise, but there is more to the story. In an era in which the meaning of "English" was still in flux, there was a widespread, intoxicating sense that the vernacular was up for grabs, its forms plastic enough to respond to the dictates and whims of individual proponents of change. Thomas Smith, in his treatise on English spelling, tellingly compared his new orthography to the "different and distinct language" of gypsies, "unknown to others and serving only them-selves,"[101] on the grounds that each could only be deciphered by a coterie of specialists. Like the gypsies of the Renaissance underworld, the first English language reformers practiced a kind of sleight of hand: Although they claimed to be the bearers of the royal seal, they were determined to put their private stamp on a still impressionable language. For all their talk of progressive social reform, the changes they envisioned were also implicitly designed to enhance their own claims to cultural authority. In their treatises, after all, their voice – no matter how strange or how new – becomes the voice of the nation at large.

* * *

The Renaissance "love of words" is most often associated with its literature, with Shakespeare generally cited as the chief exemplar of the characteristic "linguistic exuberance" of the age. Yet, for early modern literary authors as well as for linguists, there was more at stake in language reform than "innovation . . . for its own sake," as it has been suggested.[102] Throughout Renaissance Europe the "question of the language" was closely tied to questions, more specifically, about literary language. In Italy and France, as we have seen, linguistics – the study of language in general – was often incorporated into or even subsumed by poetics – the study of poetic language in particular. In England, it was just the reverse. Puttenham's treatise on poetics, for example, doubles as a contemporary theory of the vernacular; his prescriptions for poetic language are often intended as rules for usage generally.[103] For Puttenham, the "common" language and poetic language were to be coterminous, at least as far as pronunciation and diction were concerned. He cites many of the words I will investigate in later chapters as "vices in speaches and writing [which] are always intollerable" – and not only in poetry:

> Some maner of speaches are always intollerable and such as cannot be used with any decencie, but are ever undecent namely barbarousness,

incongruitie, ill disposition, fond affectation, rusticitie, and all extreme darknesse, such as it is not possible for a man to understand the matter without an interpretour, all which parts are generally to be banished out of every language.[104]

Poets who lapse into "barbarismus" or "forreign speech," which according to Puttenham includes any "strange" or "unnatural" pronunciation or spelling; "fond affectation," or neologism; "rusticitie;" or any language characterized by "extreme darkeness," only do so, he suggests, "for the nonce;" that is, on purpose "not to be understood."[105]

Gill, on the other hand, in his grammar of the "common" dialect, presents a more complex theory of the relationship between poetic language and the King's English. On the one hand, Gill makes a clear distinction between them: The "Poetic," he explains, is a dialect of English, formally distinct from the common language, no less than northern or southern English. Although the southern, northern, eastern, and western dialects represent the language of "ploughmen, working girls, and river-men," he claims that these people share, with poets, a propensity for "metaplasm":

> Metaplasm is when out of necessity, or for the sake of charm, a syllable or word is changed from its own proper form to another; and here belong all the previously mentioned dialects, except for the general one.[106]

Gill's examples of metaplasm (epenthesis, apocope, prothesis, etc.) are all derived from rhetorical theory; according to his scheme, all "uncommon" dialects represent language that has been altered, "out of necessity, or for the sake of charm," "from its own proper form."

Yet despite the "provincial" status of poetic English – its "distance" from the common language – Gill does not believe that the borders of the poetic dialect should overlap with those of other regional dialects. Some forms of metaplasm, it seems, are better than others. After providing a few examples of the idioms characteristic of southern, northern, eastern, and western varieties of English, he states that "of all writers, only poets are permitted to use dialects, yet they abstain from using them (except the general use)." According to Gill, poets may use regional dialects, yet they usually "abstain" from doing so; poetic diction corresponds with the "common" language, just as Puttenham suggested – but only because poets deliberately choose not to exploit the license they have been granted to transgress the borders of common speech. Gill reminds his readers of the undesirability of proliferating variant forms, and the common dialect emerges as the universal language of a cultural elite – including poets:

> What I say here regarding the dialects, you must realise, refers only to country people, since among persons of genteel character and cultured upbringing, there is but one universal speech, in pronunciation and meaning.[107]

What remains unclear, in Gill's treatise, is what distinguishes, from a social or an aesthetic standpoint, the "improper" forms of poets from those of plough-men. Perhaps the only answer he provides can be found in his remark that every poet tends to "[defend] the irregularity of his own dialect solely on the grounds of license."[108] Poets, it seems, are licensed to deviate from the King's English (ploughmen are not), but Gill seems uncertain as to how far that license ought to be extended. What is emergent in this debate is the question of whether it is possible or even desirable to identify, as a unique variety of English, literary language or "poetic diction."[109]

Like Puttenham and Gill, many Renaissance literary authors are concerned with the relationship between poetic language and "common" usage. According to the playwright Thomas Heywood, in his *Apology for Actors* (1607), Renaissance writers labored to mend a language that was "broken" by internal differences:

> Our English tongue, which hath ben the most harsh, uneven, and broken language of the world, part Dutch, part Irish, Saxon, Scotch, Welsh, and indeed a gallimaffry of many, but perfect in none, is now by this secondary means of playing, continually refined, every writer striving in himselfe to adde a new flourish unto it.[110]

Later chapters will confirm Heywood's sense that early modern literature was a laboratory of linguistic reform, with "every writer striving in himselfe" to add (but also, at times, to eliminate) forms. But rather than uniting English – transforming a "gallimaffry" of foreign forms into a unitary national language – the innovations of Renaissance authors often accentuate the "difference of English." In the chapters that follow, I will explore some of the "uncommon" dialects recreated by Renaissance authors, including southern and northern words, old words and new words, varieties of English that were controversial insofar as they were construed as strange or foreign – that is, as samples of a "broken" language.

It would be misleading, however, to suggest that Renaissance English literary writers advanced specific dialects of the vernacular as part of a larger linguistic movement, as some of their contemporaries on the continent did. Even the English lexicographers and grammarians described earlier in this chapter, perhaps, did not recognize that they were a part of a whole era preoccupied with the past, present, and future of the language.[111] Yet it cannot be a coincidence that, for the first time in the history of the vernacular, so many individuals took it upon themselves to modify or alter – sometimes dramatically – the way their countrymen spoke or wrote the language. In Renaissance England, no less than Italy or France, language reformers vied for the right to authorize a language that was, as yet, up for bids; throughout Europe, poets took the lead in authoring the mother tongue. Many English poets and playwrights shunned "peculiar" dialects, and worked to refine the "common" language. Yet many others opened the borders of literary language to words that placed their texts beyond the bounds of Puttenham's "usuall speech." Implicitly, literary language, for these writers, might itself be understood as a dialect of English – Gill's "Poetic" dialect – a semi-autonomous domain, self-authorized, a language designed to rival or even replace an emergent national tongue. These writers, consciously or not, sought, as Gill had feared, "to defend the irregularity of [their] own dialect solely on the grounds of license."[112] "Poetic license" is a phrase that we associate with a much later age, yet, along with the word "dialect," it comes into use in the middle of the sixteenth century.[113] The "broken English" of Renaissance litera-ture, from the provincial language of peasants in King Lear to the erudite archaisms of Spenser's *Faerie Queene*, was not always put forward in service of the King or his English, but rather in service of authors competing to prescribe the bounds of the native tongue. I will return directly, in Chapter 2, to the notion of "license," as applied to Renaissance English diction, and the rhetoric of law and transgression that pervades early modern accounts of new and unusual words.

2

THE THIEVES OF LANGUAGE[1]

It may be objected that such patching maketh . . . [a] hotch-pot of our tongue, and in effect brings the same rather to a Babelish confusion than any one entire language. It may again be answered, that this theft of words is not less warranted by the priviledge of a prescription, antient and universal, than was that of goods among the Lacedemonians by an enacted law; for so the Greeks robbed the Hebrews, the Latins the Greeks (which filching Cicero with a large discourse in his Book *de Oratore* defendeth) and (in a manner) all other Christian Nations the Latine.

Richard Carew, *The Excellency of the English Tongue* (c. 1595)[2]

Richard Carew's celebration of the national language was published in 1614 in a work devoted to celebrating things English, William Camden's *Remaines Concerning Britain*. While Camden hails the glories of the native land, its people, and its customs, Carew puts forward the superiority of English over rival vernaculars. For Carew, the "excellency" of English owes to what he calls its "copiousness," or wealth, with respect to other languages, the extent to which English appropriates foreign words for national "profit."[3] This "theft of words," according to Carew, is prescribed and legitimated by classical precedent, as well as by current European usage. Although Carew authorizes the "filching" of foreign words, many of his contemporaries sought to restrict such "thefts"[4] along with a variety of linguistic practices that are figured, again and again throughout the period, as language "crimes" – the "begging" of words, the unregulated "coining" of words, the "counterfeiting" of words, the contraband "trade" in words. Robert Greene, Thomas Dekker, Thomas Nashe, William Shakespeare, and Ben Jonson are among those authors who seek to expose and to indict illegal or illegitimate writing, but they are also, as we will see, chief among the perpetrators of such crimes.

Pierre Bourdieu's notion of a linguistic market is a useful one in understanding the predominance of economic and legal metaphors employed in sixteenth- and early seventeenth-century accounts of the language. For Bourdieu, language is not only constituted by signs to be deciphered, but by "*signs of wealth*, intended to be evaluated and appreciated, and *signs of authority*, intended to be believed and obeyed."[5] Bourdieu critiques a long tradition of Western linguistic theory which is based, he claims, on "the illusion of linguistic communism," the idea expressed, for example, by Auguste Comte, who wrote that "language forms a kind of wealth, which all can make use of at once without causing any diminution of the store, and which thus admits complete community of enjoyment; for all, freely participating in the general treasure."[6] Rather, Bourdieu suggests, the linguistic market operates according to "the unequal distribution of linguistic capital" and the competitive struggle for social "distinction" through language.[7]

Renaissance writers participate in the rhetorical tradition Bourdieu describes, continually speaking of the "treasure" of the language and of "enriching" the language, in a way that suggests that the "gain" accrued is a collective one.[8] In early modern England, "enrichment" generally refers to the introduction of foreign words, or new words of foreign derivation, into the native wordstock. It is often associated with the enterprising and profitable labor of contemporary poets; Francis Meres, for example, lists Shakespeare and Chapman among poets by whom "the English tongue is mightily enriched."[9] But the trope of "enrichment" is not always employed as part of a rhetoric of universal gain. The acquisition of new words is not, according to many Renaissance writers, a venture that is open to all; rather than a communal resource, the new English is often represented as a dialect that pertains to a particular group or social class. For Shakespeare, Jonson, and their contemporaries, the attainment of another language is not always a matter of borrowing freely from the national linguistic coffers, but of "filching" words for personal profit, and at another's expense.

In this chapter, I will explore the literary appropriation of social dialects in the early modern period. I begin with Shakespeare's Prince Hal, or rather return to his example: Stephen Greenblatt, notably, has made Hal the chief exemplar of a dominant Elizabethan culture predicated on the "mastery" of others' words. In Greenblatt's compelling reading of the second tetralogy, Hal's calculated transformation from thief to King is owed, in part, to his practice of "recording" alien voices.[10] During his Eastcheap days, spent among the taverns, Hal boasts of his facility with lower-class men and their dialects, telling Ned Poins that he "can drink with any tinker in his own language."[11] After demonstrating his proficiency with some impromptu translations ("They call drinking deep, dyeing scarlet" (2.4.15)), Hal turns his attention to the language of Francis the drawer, one, he asserts, "that never spake other English in his life" (2.4.24–5) than the few simple phrases necessary to his trade. To prove it, Hal devises a jest in which Francis, distracted by Poins' voice calling him offstage, is compelled to answer all of Hal's inquiries with the identical response, "anon." Every repetition of the word seems to strip it further of meaning, until "anon" becomes a nonce word signifying nothing more than Francis's dullness. The jest confirms for the Prince that Francis's language is barely a human one, comprising "fewer words than a parrot['s]" (2.4.98–9). But crucially, as Greenblatt observes, it is the Prince himself who, by the design of his jest, prescribes Francis's linguistic impoverishment.[12]

Hal's business in these plays, we might say, is to acquire power in a political economy where one man's gain is predicated on another's loss. His aim, as he details it in the famous soliloquy of Act 1, scene 2, is to "redeem" the time, to recover, in an economic as well as a moral sense, the time he has wasted in the taverns, as well as the crushing political debt incurred by his father's usurpation of the crown. But Hal can only redeem himself by means of contrast; his value is relational. By his own account, he glitters only as "bright metal on a sullen ground" (1.2.212). His culminating triumph in the play, the defeat of his "worthy" rival, Hotspur,[13] is thus figured as his final "transaction," for Hal schemes to profit from Hotspur's early gains:

> The time will come
> That I shall make this northren youth exchange
> His glorious deeds for my indignities.
> Percy is but my factor, good my lord,
> To engross up glorious deeds on my behalf;
> And I will call him to so strict account
> That he shall render every glory up.
>
> (3.2.144–50)

The play as a whole is preoccupied with Hal's value, figured, in part, as the value of coin. If Falstaff believes he sees the Prince's true worth: "Never call a true piece of gold a counterfeit. Thou art essentially made, without seeming so" (2.4.491–3), the play calls attention, again and again, to Hal's propensity for "counterfeiting."[14] Greenblatt suggests, convincingly, that Hal's value is not intrinsic but "dependent upon the circulation of counterfeit coin and the subtle manipulation of appearances."[15] Hal, I would add, is the "Robber-King" whose early life as a thief makes an appropriate apprenticeship for sovereignty, whose power is based on a series of transactions that are predicated on others' losses. Falstaff entreats the wayward Prince to "rob [him] the exchequer" as soon as he is King. But Hal has already stolen, or symbolically exchanged, his means to thrive.

In *Henry IV*, Part II, Hal's relationship to the Eastcheap crowd is explained to the King this way:

> The Prince but studies his companions
> Like a strange tongue, wherein, to gain the language,
> 'Tis needful that the most immodest word
> Be look'd upon and learnt, which once attain'd,
> Your Highness knows, comes to no further use
> But to be known and hated.
>
> (4.4.68–73)

Greenblatt describes Hal's attempt to master lower-class language as a mode of containment: Hal continually usurps subversive practices, including thieving and counterfeiting, as a means of reasserting the established social and political order which, as King, he will one day embody. But Hal's strategy, it seems, is not so much one of containment, of conserving or reconfirming a prior social order, but of attainment and acquisition; Greenblatt's model of subversion and containment cannot account for Hal's dynamic bid for advantage over others. Hal is not seeking to conserve his assets, but to break the bank, for he seeks to gain in value, to enrich himself and his country far beyond the holdings of his father. To "gain the language" of another is, as Hal's joke on Francis suggests, to take it away from him, to produce the poverty on which one's own wealth – linguistic, social, political – stands. Falstaff presents the riddle of Hal's moral and political status: "Shall the son of England prove a thief and take purses?" (*1 Henry IV*, 2.4.409–10). One thing is certain: If he also has the power to set the laws of the market, to determine values, to decide what is "current" coin, he will get away with it.

It may well be, in fact, that Hal is not playing fast and loose with the rules of the early modern market, but exercising (in advance) his sovereign right to produce and exchange values at will. Hal's practices in this play, in fact, reflect a traditional view of the relationship between the English crown and the valuation of coin, and one still current in the sixteenth century. According to this view, it is the king's prerogative to raise and debase the value of money; the king's effigy, and not some intrinsic quality of silver or gold, transforms bullion into coin.[16] Thus, in John Hale's sixteenth-century treatise on economics, *A Discourse of the Common Weal* (1581), a knight insists, to the assembled company (a doctor, a merchant, a husbandman, and a craftsman) that the value of coin is conventional, that "coine is but a token to goe from man to man."[17] In the same way, the King alone could establish laws to preserve and maintain the national treasury, for example, by setting embargos on the exportation of coin or bullion, or by prohibiting the importation of foreign coin, for, as another early modern economist put it, "the right of prerogative of exchange of bullion hath alwaie been a flower of the Crowne."[18]

Yet, as John Hale's "doctor" argues, there was no true monarchy of the marketplace in the sixteenth century. He explains that only "a man at first blushe would thinke that a king in this realme might doe this easily, and make what coin he would currant, and of what estimation it pleased him"; the great economic crises of the age – especially, an unparalleled rise of prices and a perennial shortage of coin – are enough to show that the king cannot dictate the laws of the market.[19] Whatever the historical reasons for these crises,[20] Hale's doctor, along with numerous sixteenth- and early seventeenth-century economic analysts, found three likely culprits. First and foremost, many believed that the "dearth" or rise of prices had been brought on by dishonest merchants seeking private gain, "for what oddes soever theare happen to be in exchange of things the merchants can espie it anone" and "save themselves in every alteration".[21] According to this view, merchants exported native wares at low prices and imported foreign goods at high prices, an illegal exchange that raised prices at home.[22] King James takes a similar stand against them, telling his son that merchants thinke the whole common-weale ordayned for making them up; and accounting it their lawfull gaine and trade, to enrich themselves upon the losse of all the rest of the people; they transporte from us things necessary, bringing back some-times unnecessary things, and at other times nothing at all. They buy for us the worst wares, and sell them at the dearest prices . . . being as constant in that their evill custome, as if it were settled lawe for them.[23]

Among these, the most dangerous and exploitative, according to many early modern writers, were the "exchangers," a new class of merchants who "traded" English and foreign currency to facilitate the importing and exporting of goods. In the years from about 1530 to 1630, the exchangers were increasingly held responsible for the devaluation of coin; indeed, according to one economic historian, "all economic evils were ascribed to the sinister operations of the exchangers."[24] The valuations of the exchangers, many complained, were arbitrary and dictated solely by a desire for profit. Thomas Milles, in his *Customers Replie* (1604), writes that

> Merchandizing exchange is the laborinth of errors and private practice, whereby (though Kings weare crownes and seem absolutely to raigne), particular banders, private societies of merchants and covetous persons (whose end is private gayne) are able to suspend their counsailes and controle their policies . . . lending money to Sovereigns and Emperers themselves, that onely can make coyne and should have to give largely and lende unto others. Thus, making Kings to be subjects, and vassalles to be Kings.[25]

Exchangers were in fact prohibited in the reigns of Edward VI and Mary, while Elizabeth attempted to deter them by taxing exchanges heavily. In 1576, in an attempt to centralize such transactions, Elizabeth revived the medieval office of Royal Exchanger, and issued a proclamation to all merchants, English and foreign, that "by the lawes and statutes of this Realm no man ought to make anie exchange or rechange of money, but such as Her Majesty shall authorize to keep, make, and answere for such exchanges and rechanges."[26] But all such prohibitions were in vain, and the fluctuations in the value of coin continued to be determined, in part, by private societies seeking to control the commonwealth, and by "vassalles" seeking to be "Kings."

The economic troubles of the sixteenth century were also ascribed, by some, to the circulation of "base money" (coin that was not gold or silver) that had been introduced in the reign of Henry VIII as a way of increasing the amount of currency in circulation. Numerous works, in prose and verse, express anxiety over the "alteracion of the coin":

> O most nobell Kinge,
> Consyder well this thinge!
> This coyne by alteracion

> Hath brought this desolacion
> Which is not yet all knowen
> What myschiff it hath sowen.[27]

John Hale's doctor is among those who believe that the alteration of the coin is the chief cause of the dearth, that the "common wealth" can only be measured by how much gold and silver the King commands. Moreover, "sence oure coine hath bene based and altered, strangers have conterfeted oure coine, and founde the meanes to have great masses transported hither."[28] William Camden concurred that the debasement of the coin led to crimes of the mint perpetrated, especially, by foreigners: "By reason of these said base monies, great quantity of forged and counterfeits were daily made and brought from beyond Seas."[29] Finally, many blamed the dearth on excessive importing which, they believed, could only lead to the depletion of the nation's treasure. Sir William Cecil, for example, warned that "this realm is over-burdened with foreign wares, and if the trade thereof should continue but a while, a great part of the treasure of the money of the realm would be carried thither to answer for such unnecessary trifles."[30] For many who still considered wealth to be constituted by the amount of money (coin or bullion) in the exchequer,[31] importing, left unregulated, might one day bring the nation to bankruptcy.

The controversy over new words in the sixteenth and early seventeenth centuries was conditioned by these contemporary anxieties over coin: The circulation of "base" coin, the introduction of "counterfeit" moneys into the system, the loss of native treasure to foreigners, and, above all, the sense that the monarch no longer had sole authority over the nation's currency, that private individuals, or private societies, were usurping the king's prerogative to determine the value of coin, became the rhetorical means by which the introduction of "new" words in the period was interpreted and debated. Above all, the question posed by the production of words in the period was one of social authority – who had the prerogative to "gain" words, to "mint" words, to discriminate among "base" words and the genuine article. And who, finally, stood to profit from the trade.[32]

Throughout sixteenth- and early seventeenth-century commentaries on the new "Englishes" in circulation, the value of a word often depends, crucially, on whose word it is alleged to be. I will be concerned, in the remainder of this chapter, with the Renaissance idea of social dialects – languages that are represented as pertaining, uniquely, to a given group or social class – and to the idea of sociolinguistic mobility – the acquisition of words as a means of social promotion or exchange. I will argue, here, that social dialects are not so much represented by early modern authors, as they are produced by them; that such languages are "counterfeited" by writers in pursuit of linguistic distinction. Indeed, the paradigmatic example of a social dialect in Renaissance literature may well be neologism – the "counterfeit" or "coined" words of the age. And as with coin itself, the Renaissance crisis over new words concerns contested authorities in the creation and distribution of linguistic value.

Renaissance writers often do not clearly distinguish between social dialects and regional dialects, because provincial language is generally defined in terms of social class. Puttenham, in his *Arte of English Poesie*, at first seems to locate the "best" English on regional grounds, when he advises poets to "take the usuall speach of the Court, and that of London and the shires lying about London within lx. myles."[33] But he also makes it clear that residing in or around London is not enough, for the poet must also abjure

> the speach of a craftes man or carter, or other of the inferiour sort, though he be inhabitant or bred in the best towne and Citie in this Realme, for such persons doe abuse good speaches by strange accents or ill shapen soundes, and false ortographie.[34]

It is not simply London English, but the London English spoken by the "superior sort," that Puttenham is recommending to his readers.[35] As I note in Chapter 1, Puttenham's claims that this dialect of English represented the "most usuall of all [the poet's] countrey"[36] was, in demographic terms, misleading to say the least.[37]

But the idea that the "best" English was also the most "usual" one pervades accounts of the vernacular in the period, and often leads to strained rationalizations for assigning linguistic authority to upper-class speakers. Instead of what was "usual," Ben Jonson, echoing Quintilian, invokes the idea of "custom" as the ultimate arbiter of English usage. In his *Discoveries*, Jonson hails custom as the guarantor of linguistic value: "the most certain Mistresse of Language, as the publicke stamp makes the current money." But Jonson acknowledges that the term "custom" is potentially misleading:

> When I name Custome, I understand not the vulgar custome; for that were a precept no lesse dangerous to Language, then life, if wee should speake or live after the manner of the vulgar: But that I call custome of speech, which is the consent of the Learned.[38]

Jonson, in fact, states explicitly what Puttenham only implied: There is not one but two kinds of "custom," and they are to be distinguished not by usage or frequency, but along the lines of class. Although he appears to champion common usage as the standard of eloquence, a standard available to any speaker of the language, Jonson reserves the determination of what is "customary" to a learned minority. Only the elite may certify the "currency" of language.

But we must recall that the identification of the "best" English with the upper classes, however pervasive throughout the period, did not guarantee "the consent of the Learned" on particulars. Alexander Gill, for example, rails against what he dubs the language of the "Mopsae"[39] – London women who affected certain pronunciations in order to appear better cultivated. Yet historians of the language have determined that the particular features that Gill associated with the Mopsae were fast becoming current in London English; Gill's linguistic sensibility is thus an inappropriately conservative one.[40] In the absence of a strictly demarcated upper-class dialect, good English was at least partly a question of personal taste.

The inability of the grammarians to arrive at a consensus concerning the forms of the King's English is not entirely a reflection of their biases, however, but also of the fact that the speech of upper-class Londoners was in flux throughout the period, largely because of a high rate of immigration from the provinces to the capital. While some provincialisms became fixed features of an emergent, lower-class urban speech, others made their way into the "common" language. Whatever class hierarchies may have characterized social and political life in the capital, the shifting nature of the population interfered with the progress of hierarchization in language. That is one reason, perhaps, why there are no full-scale portraits of lower-class urban dialects in the literature of the period.[41] In the absence of a clear, widely recognized "Cockney" or other lower-class London idiom, Renaissance authors tend to mark the social class of certain characters with a variety of broad linguistic cues, including proverbial language, vulgar oaths, and "low" salutations. These have all been carefully enumerated by scholars.[42]

Yet the representation of class dialects in Renaissance writing is not quite as haphazard, or as limited, as it may first appear. The most fully articulated, and the most pervasive, social dialect of Renaissance literature is represented by the linguistic practice we now call "neologism," that is, in the extraordinary wealth of new and unusual words introduced into English during the period.[43] Early modern neologism, I will suggest, is best understood not as a discontinuous, sporadic, idiosyncratic activity, but as the systematic production of sociolinguistic differences – a cultural project aimed at creating "new" vernaculars tied to social class. In the absence of "real" class languages – a universally recognized "Cockney," for example – Renaissance authors fill an existing social space with dialects of their own making.

As is well known, the period 1500–1659 saw the introduction of between 10,000 and 25,000 new words into the language, with the practice of neologizing culminating in the Elizabethan period.[44] Although the need for new words in English, especially in fields previously dominated by Latin, was real enough, linguistic innovation in the Renaissance generated a polemic that is known to historians of the language as the "inkhorn" controversy. While many contemporary observers commend the utility of the new words, many others object to them on the grounds of obscurity, the fact that understanding them depended on a knowledge of the foreign languages from which they were derived. Caxton had long since acknowledged the problem:

> [I] toke a penne and ynke and wrote a leef or tweyne, whyche I oversawe agayn to correcte it. And whan I sawe the fayr and straunge termes therin, I doubted that it sholde not please some gentylmen whiche late blamed me sayeng that in my translacyons I had over curyous termes which coude not be understande of comyn people.[45]

40

The contemporary critique of "inkhorn" language, again and again, revolves around the way they magnified social differences by recreating English as, in a sense, a "foreign" tongue "whiche common people, for lacke of latin, do not understand."[46] Some suggest, in fact, that the new interest in neologisms and foreign words was part of a deliberate scheme on the part of the educated to mystify the unlettered. Abraham Fraunce, in the prefatory epistle to "The Lawyers Logike" (1588), professes scorn for "that Hotchpot French stufft up with such variety of borrowed words, wherein our law is written," arguing that many lawyers exploit legal language to impress those who lack the education to understand it. Such men:

> having in seaven yeares space met with six French woordes, home they ryde lyke brave Magnificoes, and dashe their poore neighboures children quyte out of countenance, with Villen in gros, Villen regardant, and Tenant per le curtesie.[47]

Thomas Wilson also indicts "alien" words on behalf of a democracy of English speakers:

> Emong al other lessons, this should first be learned, that we never affect any straunge ynkehorne termes, but so speake as is commonly received. . . . Some seke so farre for outlandishe Englishe, that thei forget altogether their mothers language. And I dare swere this, if some of their mothers were alive, thei were not able to tell, what thei say, and yet these fine Englishe clerkes, wil saie thei speake in their mother tongue, if a man should charge them for counterfeityng the kynges English. Somme farre jorneid jentlemen at their returne home, like as thei love to go in forrein apparell, so thei will pouder their talke with oversea language. He that cometh lately out of France, wil talke Frenche English, and never blushe at the matter. Another choppes in with Englishe Italianated. . . . The lawyer wil store his stomack with the pratyng of Pedlers. The Auditour in makyng his accompt and rekenyng, cometh in with sise sould, and cater denere. . . . The fine Courtier wil talke nothyng but Chaucer. . . . Do we not speake, because we would have other to understand us, or is not the tongue geven for this ende, that one might know what another meaneth? And what unlearned man can tell, what [this language] . . . signifieth?[48]

The new English was, for many, a "counterfeit" English – that is, not really English at all – that erected barriers of communication among native speakers of the language and, moreover, accomplished this as a deliberate effort to achieve or confirm social preeminence. Whatever their usefulness, inkhorn words and borrowings effectively resurrected older, cultural distinctions between Latin and the vernacular. The new English, largely derived from Latinate forms, became, in the most literal sense, the new Latin of the age.

Yet for all the protests against the obscurity of neologisms, Renaissance writers did not recommend distributing the new "wealth" of words indiscriminately, as a way of levelling the "difference of English." For Wilson, for Shakespeare, and for Jonson, among many others, neologism is too often an affectation, too often abused by people seeking social promotion. To illustrate this, Wilson cites (or composes) a letter by a "Lincolnshireman" in search of patronage:

> You knowe my literature, you knowe the pastorall promocion, I obtestate your clemencie, to invigilate thus muche for me, accordying to my confidence, and as you know my condigne merites, for suche a compendious livyng.[49]

It is not coincidental that neologisms are put to use by a man seeking a "compendious livyying" from a patron; for the Lincolnshireman, new words seem to hold out the linguistic means of his financial gain. But it is crucial, too, that the very language of his suit advertises his failure, mocks his unworthiness to "gain" the living he seeks. Wilson and his contemporaries are primarily concerned, however, with those uneducated or "unLatined" English men and women who do not understand neologisms but who, nevertheless, endeavor to profit by them. John Hart describes the impact of neologism on his "countrie" men:

> Howbeit, I must confesse it [neologizing] beautifieth and Orators tale, which knoweth what he speaketh, and to whom: but it hindereth the unlerned from understanding of the matter, and causeth many of the Countrie men to speake chalke for cheese, and so nickname such straunge tearmes as it pleaseth many well to heare them: as to say for temperate, temporall: for surrender, sullender: for stature, statute: for abject, object . . .[50]

And Shakespeare's plays are full of comic characters – Dogberry, Bottom, Mistress Quickly, among them – who cannot command the "new" English, and who are ridiculed for trying.

What Hart is describing, of course, is what now goes by the name of "malapropism," an unintentional misuse of words. There is no reason to doubt Hart's word that malapropism was a historical phenomenon, a linguistic by-product of the new exchange in words. Wilson observed it as well, relating the following anecdote:

> [A poor man] standyng in muche nede of money, and desirous to have some helpe at a jentlemanns hand, made his complaint in this wise. I praie you sir be so good unto me, as forbeare this halfe yeres rent. For so helpe me God and halidome, we are so taken on with contrary Bishoppes, with revives, and with Southsides to the kyng, that al our money is cleane gone. These words he spake for contribucion, relief, and subsidie. And thus we see that poore simple men are muche troubled, and talke oftentymes, thei know not what, for lacke of wit and want of Latin and Frenche, whereof many of our straunge woordes full often are derived.[51]

In Wilson's account, the poor man's "want" is not only economic but linguistic; his malapropisms both announce and confirm his impoverishment. Malapropism is, in sociological terms, the "Cockney" of early modern writing. But the chief difference between malapropism and Cockney (for example) is that Cockney, at least in modern literary usage, is a "real" dialect imitated by writers; malapropism, whether a "real" phenomenon or not, consists of forms invented by authors ascribing a low social or educational status to certain characters. Ben Jonson notes that it had become fashionable among playwrights to create such characters: The Stage-Keeper, in *Bartholomew Fair* (1631), observes the stock figure of the "watch" (e.g. the Watch in *Much Ado About Nothing*) who "ha' stoln in upon 'hem, and taken 'hem away, with mistaking words, as the fashion is, in the Stage-practice."[52] In the early modern period, there is nothing random about these "mistaking words." Malapropism is a dialect that is produced by writers in a literary "fashion" of the period. Like Hal and his production of Francis's "singular" language, Renaissance authors, in effect, create social dialects to articulate the lines of social class. And like Francis's language, malapropisms do not represent an autonomous language, but are entirely dependent – formally and socially – on the educated dialect of neologism; they are "debasements" that serve to enhance the value of acquiring new and unusual words.

The debate over neologism – the so-called "inkhorn" controversy – was openly engaged by many early modern poets and playwrights as well. Samuel Daniel, at the end of his *Defense of Rhyme* (1603), reproaches other poets for "counterfeiting" words:

> We alwayes bewray our selves to be both unkinde and unnaturall to our owne native language, in disguising or forging strange or unusuall wordes, as if it were to make our verse seeme another kind of speach out of the course of our usuall practise, displacing our wordes, or inventing new, onely upon a singularitie. . . . And I cannot but wonder at the strange presumption of some men, that dare so audaciously adventure to introduce any whatsoever forraine wordes, be they never so strange, and of themselves, as it were, without a Parliament, without any consent or allowance, establish them as Free-denizens in our language.[53]

Daniel identifies literary neologism as an effort to distinguish poetry from "usuall" language, to make it "another kind of speach." He condemns writers who coin words as men who "audaciously adventure" to allow foreign words into the national language, who sponsor a kind of illegal immigration. Like the dishonest merchants described by contemporary economic theorists, such poets operate by a law that is only "of themselves."[54] Yet Thomas Nashe defended his own neologizing on the grounds that the practice had gained such currency among authors: "Come, my maisters, enure your mouthes to it. . . . My upbraided Italionate verbes are the least crime of a thousand, since they are growne in generall request with every good poet." Nashe, in fact, defends his "crime" by means of an analogy to the contemporary practice of "exchange." Native words are "base" coins that he converts to coins of higher value:

43

> Others object unto me the multitude of my boystrous compound wordes, and the often coyning of Italionate verbes. . . . Our English tongue, of all languages, most swarmeth with the single money of monasillables, which are the only scandal of it. Bookes written in them, and no other, seeme like shopkeepers boxes, that contain nothing else save halfe-pence, three-farthings, and two-pences. Therefore, what did me I, but having a huge heape of those worthlesse shreds of small English in my *pia mater's* purse, to make the royaller shew with them to men's eyes, had them to the compounders immediately, and exchanged them foure into one, and others into more, according to the Greeke, French, Spanish, and Italian.[55]

Another exchanger on the new linguistic market, Nashe unabashedly enriches his language by means of this "crime."

Nashe was, and remains, notorious for his verbal prolixity, and his fondness for conspicuously neologistic diction. Yet it is crucial to note that Nashe was ruthless, at times, in attacking the verbal innovations of others. In his famous literary quarrel with Gabriel Harvey, Nashe condemns the "inkhornism" of his rival:

> The floures of your Foure Letters . . . I have . . . assembled . . . together into patheticall posie, which I will here present . . . leaving them to his wordie discretion to be censured whether they be currant in inkehornisme or no: Conscious mind; canicular tales; egregious an argument (when as egregious is never used in English but in the extreame ill part); Ingenuitie; inckehorne pads; putative opinions; . . . energeticall persuasions; Rascal-litie; materiallitie; artificiallitie; . . . Nor are these all, for everie third hath some of this over-rackt absonisme.

Harvey responded in kind:

> He is of no reading in comparison, that doth not acknowledge every terme in those Letters to be autenticall English. . . . But the vayne fellow (for so he prooveth himself in word and deede) in a phantasticall emulation presumeth to forge a mishapen rablement of absurde and ridiculous wordes . . . such as Inkhornisme, Absonisme, the most copious Carminist, the Carminicall art, a Providitore of young Schollars, a Corrigidore of incongruitie . . . and a number of such Inkhornish phrases, as it were a pan of outlandish collops, the very bowels of his profoundest Schollerisme.[56]

Both authors, of course, were guilty of the some of the most outrageous neologizing of the age. Renaissance "inkhornism" is a game in which each player makes up his own rules and then legitimates those rules – most often, by proscribing those of others. For those authors, including William Shakespeare, who exploited the new trade in words, profits depended, crucially, on regulating the linguistic ventures of others.

The period from 1580 to 1619, the era of Nashe and Shakespeare, seems to have been the heyday of neologizing in England; according to one of the most recent estimates, more than 10,000 new words were introduced into English in these years alone. Shakespeare may have been personally responsible for more than 600 of these.[57] One recent historian of the language concludes that the playwright "embraced the generous [linguistic] liberalism of his time. . . . And by so felicitously using the words newly bequeathed to English, he, more than any other writer of the English Renaissance, validated the efforts of earlier and contemporary neologists."[58]

Yet "liberalism" is a misleading term to apply to linguistic practices of the period. Shakespeare is no more "generous" towards his contemporaries than Nashe or Jonson; if he proves himself a partisan of linguistic "enrichment" by the sheer number of words he added to the native treasury, he also calls attention to what he saw as a contemporary embarrassment of linguistic riches. In *Love's Labor's Lost*, notably, Shakespeare creates what has been described as "a comedy on the English *état de langue*,"[59] a work that draws, explicitly, on the early modern rhetoric of a traffic or trade in words, the idea that "as with Merchandize, with terms it [English] fares/Nations do traffic Words, as well as Wares."[60] Shakespeare must be distinguished from contemporaries such as Richard Carew, who saw such commerce as a certain means of national profit. According to Carew, borrowing from foreign coffers was no cause for shame, since English grows rich from the trade:

> Seeing that we borrow (and that not shamefully) from the Dutch, the Britain, the Roman, the Dane, the French, the Italian, and Spaniard; how can our stock be other than exceeding plentiful? . . . For our own parts we employ the borrowed ware so far to our advantage, that we raise a profit of new words from the same stock, which yet in their own Countrey are not merchantable.[61]

Others, pursuing the same analogy, noted that English imported far more words than it exported to others, and warned of a kind of linguistic trade deficit. John Cheke believed that "borrowing" led not to enrichment, but rather to the impoverishment of the language:

> I am of this opinion that our own tung shold be written cleane and pure, unmixt and unmangeled with borowing of other tunges, wherin if we take not heed by tijm, ever borowing and never payeing, she shall be fain to keep her house as bankrupt.[62]

Richard Verstegan, another advocate of a "pure" and "unmixt" native tongue, argued his case in similar terms:

> Wee are dayly faine to borrow woords for it (as though it lacked making) out of other languages to patch it up withall, and that yff wee were put to repay our borrowed speech back again to the languages that may lay claime unto it, wee should be left little better than dumb. . . . But doubtlesse yf our selves pleased to use the treasurie of our own tong, wee

should as litel need to borrow woords, from any language, extravagant from ours, as any such borroweth from us, our toung in itself beeing sufficient and copious enough, with out this dayly borrowing from so many as take scorne to borrow any from us.[63]

The fear that an unregulated foreign trade might ultimately devalue English wares was, as we have seen, common enough in economic treatises of the period. The idea that many foreign words and borrowings were merely "trifles," the sense that the new trade in words did not represent enrichment but a kind of cultural bankruptcy, circulated alongside celebrations of the "common-wealth" of the new English. Shakespeare, unlike Cheke or Verstegan, was no "purist" when it came to the native tongue.[64] But he did, it seems, share with them the sense that there was a serious danger of "loss" in excessive borrowing. In *Love's Labor's Lost*, especially, Shakespeare dramatizes the warning expressed, thirty years later, by Ben Jonson: "A man coins not a new word without some peril, and less fruit."[65] The rhetoric of crime, of illegality, of "peril," speaks, through-out the period, to the ongoing concern that the new trade in words ultimately endangered both the language and the speakers who exploited them.

For all of Shakespeare's celebrated "linguistic enthusiasm," *Love's Labor's Lost* reveals a playwright who did not advocate "liberty" but rather license – i.e., a regulated freedom – with new and alien words, who saw neologism as a privilege and not as a right. Many of the characters of *Love's Labor's Lost* surfeit on the "great feast of languages" served up in the play and, like Jonson's Crispinus, who is forced to vomit his words on the prescription of a better poet, must be purged of their unnatural diet. But the catharsis or emptying out that occurs in this play is generally figured in economic rather than medical terms, as "labor" that is "lost." Shakespeare's comedy is centrally concerned with the danger of linguistic inflation[66] and linguistic bankruptcy, a loss that is predicated, as Cheke and Verstegan warned, on an apparent "wealth" of words. Shakespeare's King of Navarre emerges as a comical Henry V who is at a clear linguistic disadvantage with the woman he courts, who fails to win her or, for that matter, to recover the debt that her nation owes.[67] While Katherine, and her nation, submit to King Henry and the British conquest, King Ferdinand's princess refuses to strike any "world-without-end bargain" (5.2.789) with him. From the King of Navarre to his constable, Dull, Shakespeare's play is replete with characters who, in the words of Costard, have "stol'n the scraps" (5.1.37) of others' languages. But they may stand to lose more than they gain: This kind of crime, it seems, ultimately doesn't pay.

Love's Labor's Lost is a play that seems little occupied with the "traffic" of the world; along with the King, Shakespeare seems to abandon politics and other social realities in his creation of a "little academe" devoted solely to intellectual, and amorous, pursuits. Yet Shakespeare's academy is continually figured in the play as a kind of market, where wit – commodified in words – may be bought and sold. Berowne condescends to Boyet as a mere tradesman of wit:

> This fellow pecks up wit as pigeons pease,
> And utters it again when God doth please.
> He is wit's pedlar, and retails his wares
> At wakes and wassails, meetings, markets, fairs:
> And we that sell by gross, the Lord doth know,
> Have not the grace to grace it with such show.
>
> (5.2.315–20)

The Princess confirms Berowne's characterization, and charges Boyet with "spending" his wit prodigally, with the hope of being "counted" wise:

> Good Boyet, my beauty, though but mean,
> Needs not the painted flourish of your praise:
> Beauty is bought by judgment of the eye,
> Not utt'red by base sale of chapmen's tongues.
> I am less proud to hear you tell my worth
> Than you much willing to be counted wise
> In spending your wit in the praise of mine.
>
> (2.1.13–19)

But Boyet is not the only verbal spendthrift in Navarre, nor the only courtier who stoops to participate in such a market. In the opening scene of the play, the King invites his fellows to "subscribe" (1.1.19) to the laws of the new academy, to set their names to their oaths. Their aim, as the King describes it, is to be counted wise by posterity; they make their vows with the hope that "the endeavor of this present breath may buy/[The] honor" of eternal fame (1.1.5–6). Among the statutes of the academy are the injunction that no woman might come within a mile of the court, "on pain of losing her tongue"; and that no man might speak with a woman, on pain of enduring "public shame" (1.1.124–5; 1.1.131). As Berowne predicts from the start, the men, at least, stand to forfeit: "These oaths and laws will prove an idle scorn" (1.1.309). With the arrival of the French princess and her coterie, their vows indeed prove a "base sale" of words.

But no sooner have the men perjured themselves and broken their oaths than they subscribe themselves anew – this time, to their loves. One by one, they declare their passions through poems; they also "mask" their courtship by disguising themselves as "Muscovites." The women deride these antics:

> *Ros.*: They were all in lamentable cases!
>   The King was weeping-ripe for a good word.
> *Prin.*: Berowne did swear himself out of all suit.
> *Mar.*: Dumaine was at my service, and his sword:
>   "No point," quoth I; my servant straight was mute.
>
> (5.2.273–7)

What they "buy," for all this expenditure, is nothing but the "public shame" they feared; as Rosaline says:

> They are worse fools to purchase mocking so.
> That same Berowne I'll torture ere I go.
> O, that I knew he were but in by th'week!
> How I would make him fawn, and beg, and seek,
> And wait the season, and observe the times,
> And spend his prodigal wits in bootless rhymes.
>
> (5.2.59–64)

Perjury is not the worst of the language crimes committed in this play. As Berowne foresaw, the courtiers' transgression lay, not in breaking their word, but in subscribing to such words in the first place. When the news of her father's death arrives by messenger, and the princess, with her French commission, makes a hasty departure, the "spending" of their "prodigal wits" has indeed proven "bootless," "the endeavor[s] of this present breath" vain.

In this sense, the King and his courtiers have a great deal in common with the comic trio long recognized as the target of Shakespeare's satire on the linguistic manners of his day – the pedant Holofernes, the curate Nathaniel, and the pretentious Spaniard, Armado. Armado is described by the court as a man who "hath a mint of phrases in his brain," "a man of fire-new [newly coined] words," and of "high-borne" words (1.1.165; 1.1.178; 1.1.172). He is a familiar contemporary figure: the braggart-linguist. His language is often obscure to his clown, Costard, for whom he translates his "hard words". Speaking of Costard's "enfranchisement," Armado explains, "I mean setting thee at liberty, enfreedoming thy person: thou wert immured, restrained, captivated, bound" (3.1.123–5). Although Holofernes and Nathaniel deride Armado's "verbosity," they are also characterized by their penchant for "high-borne" words, especially for Latin, and for Latinate neologisms. Their exchanges tend to multiply words, to inflate language by sheer addition: When the constable Dull mistakes the Latin *haud credo* for a kind of deer, Holofernes remarks:

> Most barbarous intimation! yet a kind of insinuation, as it were *in via*, in way, of explication; *facere*, as it were, replication, or rather *ostentare*, to show, as it were, his inclination, after his undressed, unpolished, uneducated, unpruned, untrained, or rather unlettered, or ratherest unconfirmed fashion, to insert again my *haud credo* for a deer.
>
> (4.2.13–19)

Like Armado, they invariably prefer several words where one will serve. Holofernes thus describes his introduction to Armado with a string of synonyms: "I did converse this quondam day with a companion of the King's who is intituled, nominated, or called Don Adriano de Armado" (5.1.6–8). He uses the Latin words *caelo* and *terra*, only to gloss them with a series of English alternatives: "The deer . . . now hangeth like a jewel in the ear of *caelo*, the sky, the welkin, the heaven, and anon falleth like a crab on the face of *terra*, the soil, the land, the earth" (4.2.3–7). Their exchanges thus offer a wealth of linguistic alternatives, yet the effect is all expenditure: They add words, inflate language, without accruing any additional meaning. They, too, believe themselves "counted wise" by their contemporaries, although they purchase, like the king, only mockery for their efforts; they, along with Costard, Mote, and Dull, assume the status of "clowns" for the entertainment of the court, who nominate them, collectively, as, "the pedant, the braggart, the hedge-priest, the fool, and the boy" (5.2.542–3).

If Armado, Holofernes, and Nathaniel profit at all from "stealing" the scraps from the feast of contemporary languages, they do so only at the expense of others who, they believe, are unworthy to partake of them. Armado frequently uses neologism to distinguish himself from Dull and others of his class: "Sir, it is the King's most sweet pleasure and affection to congratulate the Princess at her pavilion in the posteriors of this day, which the rude multitude call the afternoon" (5.1.87–90). He prefers to associate himself with Holofernes: "Arts-man, preambulate, we will be singuled from the barbarous" (5.1.81–2). Holofernes and Nathaniel, for their part, insist on distinguishing themselves from the Spaniard, whose pretentions they critique in their own "thrasonical" language:

> *Hol.*: His humor is lofty, his discourse peremptory, his tongue filed, his eye ambitious, his gait majestical, and his general behavior vain, ridiculous, and thrasonical. He is too picked, too spruce, too affected, too odd as it were, too peregrinate, as I may call it.
> *Nath.*: A most singular and choice epithet.
> *Hol.*: He draweth out the thread of his verbosity finer than the staple of his argument. I abhor such fanatical phantasimes, such insociable and point-devise companions, such rackers of ortography, as to speak "dout," fine, when he should say "doubt,"; "det" when he should pronounce "debt" – d,e,b,t, not d,e,t: he clepeth a calf, "cauf"; half, "hauf"; neighbor *vocatur* "nebor." . . . This is abhominable – which he would call "abbominable"; it insinuateth me of insanie: *ne intelligis, domine?* to make frantic, lunatic.

> (5.1.9–26)

In Holofernes, as has often been noted, Shakespeare mocks contemporary orthographic reformers, some of the most radical of the new linguistic authorities of the age. Holofernes, like Armado, uses linguistic authority as a measure of social advantage. When Dull offers up a riddle to his betters: "What was a month old at Cain's birth that's not five weeks old as yet?" he gets more than he bargained for in return:

> *Hol.*: Dictynna, goodman Dull, Dictynna, goodman Dull.
> *Dull.*: What is Dictynna?
> *Nath.*: A title to Phoebe, to Luna, to the moon.
> *Hol.*: The moon was a month old when Adam was no more,
> And raught not to five weeks when he came to fivescore.
> Th' allusion holds in the exchange.

Dull: "Tis true indeed. The collusion holds in the exchange.
Hol.: God comfort thy capacity! I say, th' allusion holds in the exchange.
Dull.: And I say the pollution holds in the exchange.

(4.2.36–47)

There is surely a kind of "collusion" against Dull in these exchanges; his mala-propisms confirm, above all, the social agenda of their neologizing. Although Nathaniel excuses Dull because he is illiterate, he also deems him uneducable: "As it would ill become me to be vain, indiscreet, or a fool,/so were there a patch on learning, to see him in a school" (4.2.29–32). Yet for all their condescension towards the constable, they are the beggars of language, dependent on language as a means to thrive, to achieve social ascendancy, as Costard knows: "O, they have liv'd long on the alms-basket of words" (5.1.38–9).

Living off words is, precisely, what defines the faltering economy of Navarre. And it is Costard, once again, who inadvertently discovers the nature of that market. After Armado offers him "remuneration" for serving as his envoy, Costard considers his reward:

> Now will I look to his remuneration. Remuneration! O, that's the Latin word for three farthings: three farthings – remuneration. 'What's the price of this inkle?' – 'One penny.' – 'No, I'll give you a remuneration': why, it carries it. Remuneration: why, it is a fairer name than French crown! I will never buy and sell out of this word.
>
> (3.1.136–42)

He later receives a "gardon" from Armado, which he adjudges to be "better than remuneration, aleven-pence-farthing better; most sweet gardon! . . . Gardon! Remuneration!" (170–2). Here, to be sure, is the metaphor of word-as-coin fully realized. For Costard, the Latinate "remuneration" and the French borrowing, "gardon," have a specific monetary value, an intrinsic worth: "Three farthings – remuneration. . . . I will never buy and sell out of this word." Yet neither word, of course, can be definitively priced; the words "remuneration" and "gardon" have no specific value – except, perhaps, a social one. Costard's confusion, however, speaks to the whole of Navarre, and to Shakespeare's England, where words are often confused with value itself, where they become the medium of all manner of personal and professional negotiations, and the proceeds of a labor that is, finally, lost.

By the end of the play, the courtiers reject a "bootless" expense of words, in favor of "plain," "honest," native language. Berowne seems to speak for them all:

> O, never will I trust to speeches penn'd
> Nor to the motion of a schoolboy's tongue,
> Nor never come in vizard to my friend,
> Nor woo in rhyme, like a blind harper's song!
> Taffata phrases, silken terms precise,

50

Three-pil'd hyperboles, spruce affection,
Figures pedantical – these summer flies
Have blown me full of maggot ostentation.
I do forswear them, and I here protest
By this white glove (how white the hand, God knows!),
Henceforth my wooing mind shall be express'd
In russet yeas and honest kersey noes.
And to begin, wench, so God help me law!
My love to thee is sound, sans crack or flaw.

(5.2.402–15)

Berowne subscribes himself here once again, this time to English wares – russet and kersey – instead of importations, like silk and taffata, and other foreign borrowings. Rosaline's response, however, exposes Berowne's continuing dependency on such terms, as she corrects him, "Sans 'sans,' I pray you" (5.2.416).

James Calderwood explains the new linguistic market envisioned at the end of the play:

> Language is a public medium in which everyone has a stake. Surely the social order needs a true language no less than a true currency. In the marketplace of love – where seller, buyer, and money take the form of lover, beloved, and language – a valid linguistic currency must effectively unite what is meant with what is understood.[68]

Love's Labor's Lost proceeds, no doubt, towards the idea that there must be accountability in language. But what is at stake in the play is not only the need for sincerity, but the risks of insincerity, the "costs" of stealing words, of borrowing words, of inflating words. In *Love's Labor's Lost*, Shakespeare satirizes the new "authors" of English, but, no less than Nashe or Harvey, he is also setting limits on linguistic innovation – limits that he, it must be said, transgressed with impunity. Although Shakespeare may have deemed some of Armado's "fire-new words" inauthentic or pretentious, he uses many of them elsewhere; while "preambulate," "peregrinate," and "verbosity" only occur in this play, "peremptory," "thrasonical," "audacious," "impudency," "excrement," and "eruption," for example, all occur in contexts where no satire is intended.[69] Similarly, although Shakespeare seems to be making fun of Holofernes' insistence on (false) etymological spellings such as "abhominable" (the pedant assumes it derives from Latin *ab homo*), the same form appears eighteen times in the first Folio, and *abominable* does not occur not at all.[70] Shakespeare's satire, it seems, is not directed at particular words, but at particular people – namely, those who practiced neologism, who set themselves up as linguistic authorities, solely to be "counted wise" by others. Yet it is difficult, in practice, to dissociate Shakespeare entirely from those characters who concern themselves with barring others from the new trade in words. For Shakespeare, too, the profit of distinction depends on revoking a verbal license in others.

51

It is difficult to know whether Shakespeare had contemporary continental language academies in mind when he created the "little academe" of Navarre. Yet it is clear that the idea of a centralized linguistic authority – whether administered by Parliament, or by pedants – was a crucial part of a cultural polemic in England as well as on the continent, throughout the early modern period. In 1665, three-quarters of a century after Shakespeare composed *Love's Labor's Lost*, John Evelyn asked that the newly instituted Royal Academy of London legislate the production of a dictionary, to include "all pure English words"; moreover, he declared, the nation would be served by the production of:

> a full catalogue of exotic words, such as are daily minted by our Logodaedali ... and that it were resolved on what should be sufficient to render them current, *ut civitate donentur*, since, without restraining that same, *indomitam novandi verba licentiam*, it will in time quite disguise the language ... since there ought to be a law as well as liberty in this particular.[71]

Shakespeare, it seems, had no desire for any royal administration of the "question of the language," nor to see the matter placed in the hands of professional academicians. Yet the central problem, for Nashe, for Shakespeare, for everyone interested in profiting from the new traffic in words, remained the same – determining what law, and whose, should regulate the production of language, who had the license to coin, to borrow, to trade words without "peril." In the sixteenth century, there was one group of neologizers who were charged – universally – with holding that license illegally, who had "stolen the scraps" of language as part of a larger, criminal conspiracy. To these "thieves of language" I now turn.

* * *

Samuel Rowlands, in *Martin Markall, Beadle of Bridewell* (1610), describes how, in 1501, Cock Lorell became the leader of all vagrants in England, and organized them into a new society:

> After a certaine time that these up-start Lossels had got unto a head, the two chiefe Commaunders of both these regiments met at Divels-arse-a-peake, there to parle and intreate of matters that might tend to the establishing of this their new found government; and first of all they think it fit to devise a certaine kind of language, to the end that their cousenings, knaveries, and villainies might not be easily perceived and knowne, in places where they come.[72]

The story of the rise of a Renaissance underworld of beggars and thieves, in its various renderings of the period, always includes the same basic elements: the creation, at the turn of the sixteenth century, of a "society" or "fraternity" of criminals, governed by independent "laws," who hatch and carry out their conspiracies by means, in part, of an invented language.

Thomas Harman's *A Caveat or Warening for Commen Cursetors* (1567), one of the earliest and certainly the most influential of sixteenth-century "cony-catching" pamphlets, established the terms of the new genre. Presenting his work as an eyewitness exposé of rogue life, Harman claims his purpose is a philanthropic one – not directed towards "commen cursetors" but towards their victims, the "conies" they seek to "catch." In his Epistle to the Reader, Harman defends his choice of the term "cursetors," in reference to vagabonds, in the title of his work:

> Although, good Reader, I wright in plain-termes – and not so playnely as truely . . . [yet many find] a greate faulte . . . callynge these Vagabonds Cursetors in the inteytelynge of my booke, as runneres or rangers aboute the countrey, derived of this Laten word (curro): neither do I wryght it Coorsetours, with a duble oo; or Cowresetors, with a w, which hath an other signification: is there no deversite betwen a gardein and a garden, mayneteynaunce and maintenance, streytes and stretes? those that have understanding knowe there is a great dyfference: Who is so ignorant these dayes as knoweth not the meaning of a vagabone? . . . yet this playne name of vagabone is deryved, as other be, of Laten wordes, and now use makes it commen to al men. . . . I have set forth this worke, simplye and truelye, with such usual words and termes as is among us wel known and frequented.[73]

Harman's discussion of his Latinate diction, not to mention his remarks on orthography, may seem out of place in a popular chapbook, especially one with such a sensational theme. Yet the Epistle advertises its author as an advocate of "plain" words against those that "nede to have an interpretar," a defender of "true" English against a "false" and "alien" one, a linguistic patriot who will translate the foreign into the familiar. Harman's Epistle, in fact, situates his later account of the "canting language" – the dialect of a criminal underworld – within larger debates on the vernacular of the period – especially, the polemic surrounding new and alien words, and the authorization of English.

One of Harman's imitators, Thomas Dekker, creates a character called the "Bellman," a national "alarmist" who, like Harman, warns his countrymen of an underworld plot. The Bellman's conspiracy theory originates in Babel: At the beginning of time, he reminds his readers, there was one, universal language, and in those happy days:

> two could not then stand gabling with strange tongues, and conspire together (to his owne face) how to cut a third mans throat, but he might understand them.[74]

The confusion of tongues at the Tower gave rise to nations and to foreign wars, but also to the internal "confusion" within English boundaries – both social and linguistic. For Dekker, and for his fellow pamphleteers, the canting language, itself, represented a kind of Babelish confusion. Harman declared cant to be "half-mingled withe Englyshe," but did not identify the derivation of the other half. According to Dekker, many cant words (including the word "cant" itself) were Latin in origin:

> As for example, they call a "cloak" in the canting language a *togeman,* and in Latin *toga* signifies a "gown" or an upper garment. *Pannam* is "bread," and *panis* in Latin is likewise "bread." *Cassan* is "cheese," and is a word barbarously coined out of the substantive *caseus,* which also signifies "cheese." And so of others.[75]

Rowlands, Dekker's contemporary, determined that cant was rather more cosmopolitan than that, and incorporated not only English and Latin, but also Dutch, Spanish, and French forms,[76] and William Harrison noted that this "mingled"[77] language appeared to be augmented by a "great number of od wordes of their [the rogues'] own devising."[78]

Whatever the constitution of their dialect, the "canting crew" was universally charged with creating an "unlawfull language,"[79] one indifferent to English rule. Harrison describes the language as "without all order or reason," and Dekker concurs:

> As touching the dialect or phrase itself, I see not that it is grounded upon any certain rules. And no mervaile if it have none, for sithence both the father of this new kind of learning and the children that study to speak it after him have been from the beginning and still are the Breeders and Norishers of a base disorder, in their living and in their Manners: how is it possible, that they should observe any Method in their speech, and especially in such Language, as serves but only to utter discourses of villanies?[80]

A linguistic accomplice to their crimes, the canting language was expressive of the disorderly conduct of its speakers. Moreover, cant was "unlawful" in its deliberate obscurity. As Robert Greene explained, "These quaint termes do these base arts use to shadow their villanie withal; for *multa latent quae non patent,* obscuring their filthie crafts."[81] Greene suggests that cant is best understood as a jargon, one that pertains to a specialized trade: "If you marvail at these misteries and queynt words consider, as the Carpenter hath many termes familiar inough to his prentices, that other understand not at al, so have the cony-catchers."[82] But the importance of preserving these "misteries" is so great that, according to Dekker, one of the ten articles of their fraternity explicitly prohibits translating the language, or teaching it to laymen: "Thou shalt teach no house-holder to cant, neither confess anything to them, be it never so true, but deny the same with oaths."[83] An "invented" language, derived from Latin and other foreign words, an obscure language, designed to mystify others, an "unlawful" language, that broke the rule of English – the contemporary description of thieves' cant might pass well enough for a contemporary account of neologisms and the "Babelish confusion" of early modern English. Indeed, cultural anxieties over neologism – that the practice was inimical to English society and to English law, that it constituted a mode of social exploitation – saw their fullest realization in contemporary accounts of underworld language. The earliest "authors" of thieves' cant expose what writers stood to gain or lose from illegal "coinings."

As Harman and his followers continually note, the canting language is otherwise known, in underworld parlance, as "pedlar's French." Harman explains that the phrase marks cant as a language of exploitive trade "where with they bye and sell the common people as they pas through the countrey."[84] Yet it is important to note that such "pedlars" have alternative linguistic means at their disposal; this is a society that chooses to use dialect as a conscious strategy of gain. Many of the rogues depicted in these pamphlets are proficient in a range of languages and a range of styles, and vary among them as it suits their purposes. The final volume of Robert Greene's series of rogue narratives, *A Disputation betweene a Hee Conny-Catcher and a Shee Conny-Catcher* (1592), is actually a learned debate between two practitioners of the trade, in which "hee" and "shee" boast of their respective skills in highly rhetorical prose: "Cyrces had never more charms, Calipso more inchantments, the Syrens more subtil tunes, then I have crafty slightes to inveigle a Conny."[85] The ranks of rogue society are filled with linguistic specialists. John Awdeley describes a rogue known in underworld parlance as the "Jack Man" as one who can "write and reade, and sometime speake latin. He useth to make counterfaite licences which they call Gybes, and sets to Seales, in their language called Jarkes."[86] Harman tells of the "Pallyards" who "goe about with counterfeate licenses; and if they perceive you wil straytly examen them, they will immeditly say they can speake no Englishe." "Dommerars," on the other hand, "wyll never speake, unlesse they have extreame punishment, but wyll gape, and with a marvelous force wylle hold downe their toungs doubled, groning for your charyty."[87] One Dommerar, Harman tells us, got his just deserts when a surgeon forced his tongue out with a knife. Robert Copland's *The Highway to the Spital-House* (c. 1535/6), reveals how rogues feign broken English:

> They ride about in many sundry wise,
> And in strange array do themselves disguise,
>
> . . .
>
> Counterfeiting their own tongue and speech,
> And hath a knave that doth him English teach.
> With "Me non speak English, by my fait;
> My servant speak you what me sayt.[88]

The rogues of Renaissance literature thus have numerous linguistic disguises – some of them requiring an understanding of foreign languages – at their command.

The authors of these works, in their zeal to expose the tricks of "such ill and licentious living persons as do *Ex alieno succo uiuere*, live of the sweat of other mens browes,"[89] claim to have done so at great personal risk. Dekker's Bellman chances upon a conclave of rogues while strolling in the woods and then eavesdrops while an elder rogue reveals the secrets of the fraternity to a novice. Greene presents himself as an English spy, attempting (as he puts it) to "decipher" the enemy.[90] Both authors make a great show of the fact that the publication of their works placed them in grave danger. Greene, for example, complains, "I am sore threatened by the hacksters of that filthie facultie, that if I set their practises in print, they will cut off that hande that writes the Pamphlet."[91] By reminding their readers of the perils of authorship, these authors turn the sensationalism of their subject-matter back onto the literary enterprise – writing, translating, and publishing. For Stephen Greenblatt, the cony-catching pamphlets represent printing as a form of social order, since they promise to aid in the detection of crime.[92] Dekker, to be sure, boasts of the fact that "under the conduct of the Bellman of London new forces were . . . levied against certain wild and barbarous rebels that were up in open arms against the tranquility of the weal public."[93] These authors pose as literary crimebusters, offering their texts in the service of the state. But this is just another cony-catching ploy.

Even as they are exposing the tricks of the cony-catching trade, the pamphleteers impart a sense of admiration for those who perpetrate them. Their works, in the jest book tradition, often present conies as fools taken in by their own ignorance and greed. The cony-catchers, on the other hand, are skilled professionals conducting a profitable business. Some of the cony-catchers' "business," in fact, involves the literary marketplace. Dekker describes some of the illicit operations involving the popular trade in books:

> Two sorts of madman trouble the Stationers' shops in Paul's Churchyard: they that out of a mere and idle vainglory will ever be pamphleting, though their books being printed are scarce worth so much brown paper. . . . Of the other sort are they that being free of wit's Merchant Venturers, do every new moon (for gain only) make five or six voyages to the press, and every term-time upon booksellers' stalls lay whole litters of blind invention; fellows yet, if they do but walk in the middle aisle, spit nothing but ink, and speak nothing but poem.[94]

He also describes a rogue known as the "falconer," who practices "a new kind of hawking, teaching how to catch birds [money] by books."[95] The falconer buys up editions of old sermons or other unsaleable work, adds new dedications, and presents a personalized copy to would-be patrons. The falconer and his associates, it seems, are thieves of a distinctly literary brand.

Thomas Harman hinted that beggars as well as thieves may exploit the business of popular literature. In his dedication to the *Caveat*, Harman, typically enough in works of this kind, pleads for the "charity" of his patronness. He begins by reminding her of the strict division between the sturdy and the impotent poor, calling for "the extreme punishment of all vagarantes and sturdy vacabons," and warning her of those that "through great hypocrisie do wyn and gayne great alms." He concludes by thanking his Lady for her patronage, "for such Almes so geven." Harman implies that he considers himself among the deserving poor, with "licence" to beg for his patroness' alms. But the image of the sturdy beggar, the very subject of the *Caveat*, casts its shadow over the author. Renaissance thieves and beggars may be portrayed as a foreigners, treacherous villains plotting to subvert English rule, but they also bear a striking resemblance to the authors who are privy to their secrets.

Greene, Dekker, and Rowlands continually stress the idea of a privileged and exclusive relationship between author and rogue. Greene invents a thief who declares that "R.G. hath so amply pend them downe in the first part of Conny-Catching, that though I be one of the facultie, yet I cannot discover more than hee hath layde open"; this author, it seems, has so completely mastered his subject that access to "real" rogues becomes superfluous.[96] The author of *The Defence of Conny-Catching*, who writes under the name of "Cuthbert Cunny-Catcher," criticizes Greene for pointing fingers at petty thieves and beggars; cony-catching, he argues, is only a symptom a larger social epidemic:

> For truth it is that this is the Iron age . . . and all conditions and estates of men seeke to live by their wittes, and he is counted wisest, that hath the deepest insight into the getting of gaines: every thing now that is found profitable, is counted honest and lawfull: and men are valued by theyr wealth.

Greene himself, he claims, is just another unscrupulous profit-seeker:

> But now Sir by your leave a littel, what if I should prove you a Conny-Catcher, Maister R.G., would it not make you blush at the matter? . . . Aske the Queens Players, if you sold them not *Orlando Furioso* for twenty Nobles, and when they were in the country, sold the same Play to the Lord Admirals men for as much more. Was not this plaine Conny-Catching, Maister R.G.?[97]

According to some scholars, it is likely that Greene wrote the *Defence* himself. In that case, he deliberately identified himself as a literary "cony-catcher" – perhaps as a joke.[98] Yet the relationship between hack writers like Greene and the beggars and thieves they describe is not entirely a matter for jest. As the prefaces to their works make clear, there was a real and vocal competition among the authors of these pamphlets, who vied for exclusive possession of the popular new genre. Dekker complains to his readers about Rowlands:

> There is an usurper that of late hath taken upon him the name of the Bellman, but, being not able to maintain that title, he doth now cal himself the Bellman's brother. His ambition is, rather out of vainglory than the true courage of an experienced soldier, to have the leading of the van.[99]

Rowlands, in turn, sought to expose Dekker as a fraud, a mere "pilferer" of Harman who had no inside knowledge of rogue society. Dekker, after all, explicitly solicited further information on their language: "If any that is more rich in this canting commodity will lend him any more or any better he will pay his love double."[100] Rowlands responded to Dekker's requisition:

> Because the Bel-man entreateth any that is more rich in canting, to lend him better or more with variety, he will pay his love double, I have thought good, not only to shew the errour in some places in setting downe olde wordes used forties yeeres agoe . . . but have enlarged his Dictionary (or Master Harmans) with such wordes as I thinke hee never heard of . . . and true englishing of the same.[101]

The underworld and its dialect, and the "true" englishing of the same, is truly a "commodity" on the new literary market, and each author sought a monopoly on its trade.

Dekker gives the game away when he offers up the canting language as a valuable new currency: "Many pieces of this strange coin could I show you." He presents his glossary to his readers as a means of redoubling their store: "Thus, I have builded up a littel mint where you may coin words for your pleasure."[102] The canting language, Dekker implies, is not only a commodity that may be acquired, but one that may be produced – for the profit of authors and readers alike. Rowlands bemoaned the way that "coin" had gained popular currency, in a way that devalued his wares: "These volumes and papers, now spread everie where, so that everie Jacke-boy now can say as well as the proudest of that fraternitie, 'will you wapp for a wyn, or tranie for a make?'"[103] The "canting commodity" was, it seems, just that: a language that generated profit not only for the rogues who allegedly spoke it, but for the authors who appropriated it. We don't know how many vagabonds there were in early modern England who were "rich" in canting, but there were certainly several contemporary authors who were. The authors of Renaissance rogue literature do not so much decipher the canting language as reproduce it for their own profit. If they denounce the underworld as foreign, threatening both social and linguistic rule, they also expose the nature of their own literary crimes. The enemy was nearer at hand than they ever let on.

* * *

Despite the popularity of the cony-catching pamphlets, they tended to share the status of their subject-matter, filling the lower ranks of the Renaissance literary hierarchy. In the drama of the period, however, we can trace the social climbing of popular rogue literature, the "raising" of the Renaissance underworld and its language, and the social transformation of popular pamphlets into an object of aristocratic pleasure – the court masque.

In three dramas of the first half of the seventeenth century, Thomas Dekker and Thomas Middleton's *The Roaring Girle, or Moll Cutpurse* (1604/10), Richard Brome's *A Joviall Crew, or The Merry Beggars* (1641), and Francis

Beaumont, John Fletcher, and Philip Massinger's *The Beggar's Bush* (1647), even the most debased of rogues undergoes some kind of social rehabilitation. *The Roaring Girle* offers a version of the story of Moll Cutpurse, perhaps the most notorious Renaissance rogue on record. In the early seventeenth century Moll was credited with heading a tightly-run criminal organization in London that included, for example, a warehouse for handling stolen property, which she returned to its former owners for a fee.[104] But according to Middleton and Dekker, Moll's reputation is undeserved. In the prologue to the play the authors explain that there are many corrupt "roaring girls" in both the suburbs and the city of London, but "none of these Roaring Girles is oures: shee flies/With wings more lofty."[105] The central plot involves Moll's efforts to reunite an upper-class young man, Sebastian Wengrave, with the commoner he wishes to marry, Mary Fitz-Allard. Sebastian's father, Sir Alexander, opposes the marriage. To elevate Mary's social status in his father's eyes, Sebastian pretends to fall in love with the disreputable Moll. Sir Alexander tries to expose Moll's infamy by proving her a common thief, but in vain. On his wedding day, Sebastian reveals that Mary, not Moll, is his bride, and Sir Alexander rejoices in the exchange.

In one scene, Moll exposes a pair of rogues, disguised as a poor soldier and a beggar respectively, the latter speaking fake Dutch (5.1). To an audience of spellbound aristocrats, Moll engages the two in a cant dialogue, providing her distinguished guests with translations: "Marry this my lord says hee; Ben mort (good wench) shal you and I heave a booth, mill a ken, or nip a bung? Shall you and I rob a house, or cut a purse?" (5.1.180–2). Although one of her auditors insists that "the grating of ten new cart-wheeles, and the gruntling of five hundred hogs comming from Rumford market, cannot make a worse noyse then this canting language does in my eares" (5.1.211–13), he urges her to teach him the language (5.1.163–4). When they ask her how she learned to cant, Moll explains that she has chosen to live of her own accord among the rogues. This Moll is no thief; like Harman, Greene, and Dekker, she has joined the underworld with the intention of one day publishing its secrets.

In fact, the Moll Cutpurse of Middleton's play is something of a social chameleon: A surrogate for Mary, whose name she shares, Moll descends in social status so that others may rise. Although Moll's services are enlisted by Sebastian, an aristocrat, it is not entirely clear that she acts in the interests of the upper classes generally. After all, she makes it possible for Sebastian to marry someone not quite his social equal, and she manages to make the bride's status seem higher than it is. *The Roaring Girle* is a middle-class fantasy that exploits the lower classes in pursuit of social respectability. Above all, the play informs us that the threat posed by the notorious Moll Cutpurse is no threat at all, and that the dangers of her criminal organization are an illusion. Moll gladly and openly reveals the secrets of the canting language to an upper-class public, whose natural distaste for the language quickly gives way to delight. The conspiracy theories of the cony-catching pamphlets gain little credence from the beneficent example of Moll. *The Roaring Girle* exorcizes the underworld of all its social demons.

In *A Joviall Crew* and *The Beggar's Bush*, the upper classes actually join the underworld; for a time, at least, beggars and aristocrats can hardly be distinguished. *A Joviall Crew* tells the story of a wealthy squire, Oldrents, who fears the fulfillment of a prophecy that his daughters will be beggars. Sure enough, his daughters – disguised as beggars – join the "joviall crew" as a lark. Other refugees include a young girl and her lover, who have run away from the tyranny of her father, and Springlove, Oldrent's steward. Formerly a vagabond, Springlove hearkens every spring to the call of the open road. The real beggars, along with their guests, are royally entertained by the squire himself, and all join in with the beggars' canting songs. Vagrancy, Brome would have us believe, is a lifestyle one chooses in order to escape the restrictions of aristocratic life, while cant is a medium of carefree song. In *A Joviall Crew*, beggars inhabit a romance greenworld, a haven of innocent misrule.

The Beggar's Bush goes one step further. Fletcher's underworld is not an alternative society, but a simulacrum of court life. The play centers on young Florez who, ignorant of his true status as heir to the earldom of Flanders, lives as a merchant in Bruges. In one encounter with the underworld, Florez questions a beggar on the nature of rogue society:

> *Flo.*: 'Troth thou mak'st me wonder: Have you a King and Common-
>   wealth among you?
> [*Beggar*]: We have, and there are States are governd worse.
> *Flo.*: Ambition among Beggars?
> [*Beggar*]: Many great ones
>   Would part with halfe their States, to have the place,
>   And credit to beg in the first file.[106]

In an effort to help his son regain his rightful social and political status, Florez's father, Gerrard, disguises himself as a beggar and gains the "throne" of the underworld kingdom. As monarch, he orders that the beggars continue to use the secret canting language, and Higgen, the official underworld orator, informs him:

> Sir, there is a table,
> That doth command all these things, and enjoyns 'em:
> Be perfect in their crutches: their fain'd plaisters,
> And their torn pas-ports, with the ways to stammer,
> And to be dumb, and deafe, and blind, and lame,
> There, all the halting paces are set downe
> I'th learned language.
>
> (2.1.131–7)

Higgen's description of cant as a "learned language" backed up by a learned "table" turns Dekker's description of the language as "unruly" on its head. The underworld has been transformed into a ruled nation, complete with a king who authorizes an official tongue. Better yet, that king is a court aristocrat.

To set his own world back in order, Gerrard appropriates the money of the beggars to save Florez from financial ruin, and, ultimately, elevates his son's status from middle-class merchant to aristocratic nobleman. So far he has co-opted the beggars' possessions only, but soon Gerrard seeks more. When the romance plot has seen its final revelation, the unmasked earl offers Higgen and his colleagues political posts in the Republic of Flanders. This time, however, Gerrard has gone too far; the beggars refuse him and choose, instead, the open road. They are heading, they say, for England.

Higgen and his fellow beggars may ultimately remain outside the bounds of courtly life, but they imitate it well enough throughout the play. Socially, politically, even linguistically, the beggars of Beaumont, Fletcher, and Massinger's play model their world according to the rules of court society. Where the cony-catching pamphlets emphasized the foreignness of cant, these three plays assimilate its strangeness to an elite standard. Despite Higgen's declaration of independence ("Shall we into England?" (5.2.221)), the rogues of Renaissance drama set their course straight for the English court.

In fact, they had already infiltrated the English court by 1621, with Jonson's *A Masque of the Gypsies Metamorphosed.* Performed three times that same year, *The Gypsies Metamorphosed* was held to be James's favorite court entertainment and may have been Jonson's as well.[107] The masque presents a band of gypsies, played by James's favorite, Buckingham, and other courtiers. The gypsies parade their exotic ways before the court, complete with colorful costumes, songs, dances, and fortune-telling. After a lengthy demonstration of gypsy practices that occupies the greater part of the masque, the gypsies remove their disguises and are "metamorphosed" into courtiers. The masque ends with songs in praise of the monarch, and an epilogue explaining the nature of the gypsies' change.

Jonson's gypsies are a composite of English rogues from the cony-catching pamphlets and actual "gypsies," a nomadic people from northern India. The gypsies spoke their own language, Romany, and were popularly associated with fortune-telling, thieving, and an ability to change shapes.[108] In essence, they were thought to be rogues with quasi-magical powers. Many Renaissance accounts of underworld life confused the "Egyptians" or gypsies with native rogues, and many, like William Harrison, assumed that the English variety, in creating their own language and taking up illegal activities, were attempting to "counterfeit" the gypsies.[109] Like the English underclass, the gypsies were subject to harsh legal restrictions during the period. Although there was no known social interaction between the two subcultures,[110] their social and legal status, their "foreign" language and nomadic way of life, helped associate them in the imagination of English Renaissance authors.

The Gypsies Metamorphosed begins with a prologue delivered by a porter upon the King's entrance.[111] The porter welcomes the King on behalf of all those present:

> If for our thoughts there could but speech be found,
> And all that speech be uttered in one sound,

> So that some power above us would afford
> The means to make a language of a word,
> It should be, Welcome! In that only voice
> We would receive, retain, enjoy, rejoice.
>
> (1–7)[112]

The porter declares that James's court, if it could, would speak in unison, a resounding political chorus. The prologue, in a sense, promises linguistic as well as political solidarity.

But that promise is broken as soon as the masque begins in earnest. The first gypsy on stage, and the first to speak, is the Jackman, the rogue famous for his erudition, especially his knowledge of Latin and other foreign languages. According to Jonson's stage directions, the Jackman enters leading a horse laden with five gypsy children. Other gypsies follow, leading horses bearing stolen goods. In a speech penetrated with cant terms, the Jackman describes the scene set before the court, relating, for example, the reason even the noblest born among the gypsy children must ride with the others:

> Till with his painful progenitors he be able to beat it on the hard hoof to the bene bowse [good drink] or the stalling ken [house receiving stolen wares], to nip a jan and cly the jark [to steal a purse and be whipped], 'tis thought fit he march in the infants' equipage.
>
> (73–6)

The Jackman follows with a brief canting rhyme:

> With the convoy, cheats [apples] and peckage [meat],
> Out of clutch of harman-beckage [constables],
> To their libkens [house] at the crackman's [hedge],
> Or some skipper [barn] of the blackman's [night].
>
> (77–80)

The Jackman's language turns a deaf ear to Jonson's own call for a language characterized by "perspicuitie, and nothing so vitious in it, as to need an Interpreter."[113] The masque's first spokesman, the most learned of the gypsies, actually flaunts the obscurity of the language recorded by Harman and his followers. Unlike Harman, Greene, and Dekker, who conscientiously translated all the difficult terms of the underworld, Jonson's Jackman resolutely refuses to play the interpreter: "If we be a little obscure, it is our pleasure; for rather than we will offer to be our own interpreters, we are resolved not to be understood" (97–9). Any who might question the legitimacy of the language are referred to a higher authority: "If any man doubt the significancy of the language, we refer him to the third volume of reports set forth by the learned in the laws of canting, and published in the gypsies' tongue" (99–102). Jonson, like the dramatists discussed earlier, depicts cant as a "learned" language authorized by laws inscribed in an official, published work. But unlike Massinger and Fletcher, for example, the

Jackman insists that the book of canting rules is composed "in the gypsies' tongue." The fact that the Jackman refers the court to a book written in a language utterly foreign to them seems deliberately coy. Jonson's Jackman defiantly preserves the obscurity of the gypsies' language and the impenetrability of their literary productions, excluding the King and his courtiers from a realm of privileged linguistic knowledge.

Like the English rogues of popular cony-catching works, Jonson's gypsies are not only versed in their own dialect. For practical reasons alone, Jonson could not have his rogues speaking cant exclusively without utterly alienating his audience; it was enough that members of the court were probably unable to follow the Jackman's opening speech.[114] Jonson's gypsies are multilingual, fluent in a range of literary forms. They are especially partial to dimeter couplets, reminiscent of Skelton's verse:

> Lay by your wimbles,
> Your boring for thimbles,
> Or using your nimbles
> In diving the pockets
> And sounding the sockets
> Or simper-the-cockets,
> Or angling the purses
> Of such as will curse us.
> (176–83)

The gypsies also experiment with more complex stanzas and more heightened diction:

> She [Henry's wife] is sister of a star,
> One the noblest now that are,
>   Bright Hesper,
> Whom the Indians in the east
> Phosphor call, and in the west
>   Hight Vesper.
> (355–60)

After their "metamorphosis" at the very end of the masque, the gypsies-turned-courtiers abandon humbler verse forms for formal panegyric:

> So we will take his praise, and hurl his name
> About the globe in thousand airy rings,
> If his great virtue be in love with fame,
> For, that contemned, both are neglected things.
> (1337–40)

But even before their social promotion, the gypsies prove capable of all manner of poetry.

Along with cant, the gypsies are privy to a second kind of secret language. The greater part of the masque is taken up with fortune-telling, the "reading" of palms. For Jonson, gypsy thieving is implicitly tied to palm-reading, a kind of underclass measure of literacy. When the gypsies read the palms of a troop of townspeople who appear in the middle of the masque ("You'll a' good luck to horse flesh, o' my life,/You plowed so late with the vicar's wife!" (776–7)), they perform a second sleight-of-hand, deftly stealing their nutmeg, hobnails, and thimbles. But just as the commoners become aware of the theft, the Patrico, the priest of the rogues, magically restores their goods. The Patrico claims that the thefts were merely "*deceptio visus*/Done *gratia risus*" (888–89). He even insists that

> We scorn to take from ye,
> We had rather spend on ye;
> If any man wrong ye,
> The thief's among ye.
>   (929–32)

Townshead remarks that the Patrico is "a most restorative gypsy. All's here again; and yet by his learning of legerdemain he would make us believe we had robbed ourselves" (933–5). The paradox of the "restorative gypsy" who is a thief and yet not a thief has proven to be the crux of modern critical interpretations of Jonson's masque.

Many critics have seen this paradox as an index of Jonson's covert criticism of the practices of the court. According to Dale Randall's convincing reading, Jonson's masque presents "an attractive but noxious band of gypsies who charm their way into the highest social circles"[115] – a comment on the insinuating social ambitions of Buckingham and other courtiers. Jonson, in other words, suggests that courtiers like Buckingham are rogues who, only by the grace of the King, are "metamorphosed" into courtiers. By having the gypsies return the stolen goods to the townspeople, in effect nullifying the charge that they are criminals, Randall argues, Jonson mitigates his critique of the court. Jonathan Goldberg concurs with Randall's identification of gypsies and courtiers in the masque, and goes further. Goldberg argues that the masque indicts the court as the "country's pickpocket," the royal favorites as a "band of stylish thieves." The way the gypsies relinquish responsibility for the theft is analogous, Goldberg suggests, to the way the King could deplete the game reserves of the country and maintain that, since he had a right to hunt (after all, the reserves were stocked for the purpose), he was committing no robbery.[116] For Goldberg, then, the gypsies' apparent "innocence" does not rescind their crime. On the contrary, it reveals the kind of crime it really is.

The many analogies that may be drawn between the gypsies and the courtiers make these readings very persuasive. One lingering problem, however, is that Jonson seems to hold back from conflating the two completely: The merging of gypsies and courtiers remains incomplete, even after the "metamorphosis." It seems more likely, indeed, that Jonson's gypsies are not courtiers, but more precisely, court poets such as Jonson himself. Like the Jackman at the very start of the masque, the gypsies always keep something for themselves. Randall has observed that the scene in which the gypsies tell the fortunes of the townspeople replays an earlier scene, occupying the better part of the masque, in which the gypsies tell the fortunes of the courtiers. When the gypsies steal the towns-people's property and promptly return it, the townspeople, awestruck, address the gypsies as "gentlemen" and beg to be taught the secrets of their trade. They have guessed that the gypsies "have other manner of gifts than picking of pockets or telling fortunes, if they would but please to show 'em" (1072–3). But the gypsies deny the townspeople that privilege, telling them that they "aim at a mystery" they can never fathom. This deliberate secrecy establishes a social distance between the gypsies and the townspeople: By reading their palms, the gypsies gain the upper hand in the relationship.

As Randall suggests, the juxtaposition of the two palm-reading scenes raises the unavoidable question of whether the gypsies, while telling the courtiers' fortunes, steal something of theirs as well. After all, the Patrico specifically orders the gypsies to rob them ("Strike fair at some jewel,/That mint may accrue well" (186–7)). But, as far as either we or the courtiers are aware, the gypsies read their palms and no more. The masque's narrative doubling, however, suggests irresistibly that a second theft has occurred, even if it has gone undetected by Jonson's audiences.[117] Rather than hobnails and thimbles, literary plunder no doubt includes financial gain through courtly patronage, and an attendant professional status. Once again, however, the gypsies' "trick" is to allow their gain to appear to revert to the courtiers. This is the ruse of gypsy fortune-telling: The courtiers hold out their "fortunes" to the gypsies, who apparently "read" or return those fortunes to its bearers. Like Moll Cutpurse, with her traffic in stolen goods, the gypsies give back what they have taken – but not without turning a profit on it first. The air of mystery surrounding these antics, once again, keeps the aristocracy at arm's length and ensures that the gypsy trade will remain in demand at court.

The political status of the gypsies, contrary to what some have suggested, is never entirely identified with that of the courtiers. The townspeople maintain that the gypsies are a part of the King's retinue, an entertaining crew whose license is ultimately subject to royal command: "The king has his noise of gypsies as well as of bear wards and other minstrels" (937–9). The gypsies, however, represent themselves as an independent nation analogous with, but not subordinate to, the English court:

> We preserved ourselves a royal nation,
> And never yet did branch of statute break
> Made in your famous palace of the Peak,
>
> . . .
>
> As being by our Magna Carta taught
> To judge no viands wholesome that are bought.
>> (236–8; 241–2)

It has surprised many critics that the gypsies, in full audience of the court, exult in the assertion that no representative of the law is present to restrict their activities:

> Here's no Justice Lippus
> Will seek for to nip us
> In cramp-ring or cippus
> And then for to strip us,
> And after to whip us.
> (207–11)

Despite the presence of the king himself, the "antimasquers" flagrantly deny his control over the masque. In Goldberg's scheme the gypsy-courtiers are above the law because their actions are royally countenanced.[118] But the gypsies' autonomous "government," complete with its own Magna Carta, does not suggest complicity with the court. Rather, Jonson portrays the gypsies as a separate nation beyond James's influence. They may appear to be a part of the King's retinue, their crimes contained by his rule; indeed, the gypsies stand to profit from that impression. As long as the gypsies – that is, court poets such as Jonson himself – merely reflect the bounty of their aristocratic audiences, they have license to steal where they will.

Even the gypsies' "metamorphosis" remains in their own hands. Despite the fact that *The Gypsies Metamorphosed* is, in Orgel's words, "substantially all anti-masque,"[119] the anti-masquers are never formally banished or compelled to change by any higher authority. From Randall's point of view, that is because they never do really change; the "metamorphosis" is something of a hoax.[120] In the epilogue, Jonson admits that he never actually described the metamorphosis:

> You have beheld, and with delight, their change,
> And how they came transformed may think it strange,
> It being a thing not touched at by our poet;
> Good Ben slept there, or else forgot to show it.
> (1381–4)

Needless to say, the poet did not fall asleep or forget to account for the metamorphosis, he simply chose not to. It is as if "good Ben" were deliberately withholding the kind of literary (i.e., linguistic) treatment that would solve the mystery. The poet goes on to explain that the gypsies' transformation "was fetched off with water and a ball/And to our transformation this is all" (1391–2). In other words, the "metamorphosis" was a visual, but not a poetic effect. Jonson excludes language from the process.

The gypsies' metamorphosis into courtiers, moreover, is not complete, never fully accomplished by the masque, even by means of water and the ball. The Patrico and, significantly, the Jackman, remain gypsies even after the metamorphosis has taken place. Jonson, once again, resists the complete integration of gypsies and courtiers. Like the Jackman, Jonson wraps his own literary practices in a veil of mystery, setting himself at once within and without court circles. By denying that poetry brought about the metamorphosis, Jonson excludes language from the general "translation" that rewrites the foreign as the familiar. The masque's initial promise of univocality is at the heart of Jonson's subterfuge. Implicitly, Jonson leaves poetry, and poetic language, to the keeping of the gypsies.[121]

By the time Jonson wrote *The Gypsies Metamorphosed*, the canting language had already experienced several stages of literary metamorphosis. The rogue literature of the sixteenth century emphasized the dangers of cant, and the crimes of its practitioners. These "crimes," however, often have literary overtones, and implicate authors such as Dekker and Greene in a similar kind of legerdemain. The dramatists, on the other hand, do not attempt any sensationalism; by this time, rogues are stock figures of the popular stage, almost entirely divorced from social reality. For Jonson's audiences, no doubt, the canting crew could never again inspire fear or awe. His gypsies, we can guess, were no more threatening to James than court jugglers or dancing bears.

If Jonson's gypsies could not inspire fear, however, they could still insist that the court regard them at a respectful distance. To achieve this, Jonson surrounds the gypsy language with an aura of mystery, a veil of secrecy which he refuses to rend. Even if thieves' cant no longer posed a threat to the established order, Jonson suggests, he is not obliged to reduce it to court terms. In Jonson's masque, the private dialect society of gypsies resembles the court but, crucially, cannot be contained by it. Although the canting language was culturally devalued by its association with the poor and the dispossessed, the dialect became, in Jonson's hands, one of the elite dialects of Renaissance English literature. The language of thieves proved a viable, if unlikely, contemporary model for a "poetic" dialect – "another kind of speech," hard and mysterious, the currency of a secret English society.

* * *

On Gadshill, Shakespeare's Prince Hal and his gentleman-in-waiting, Poins, devise another jest, this time at the expense of the cowardly Falstaff. When Falstaff and his company highjack money of the King's *en route* to the exchequer, Hal and Poins, disguised, ambush them and steal their booty. What Thomas Dekker, Robert Greene, and Ben Jonson share with Hal is a strategy of robbing the robbers – appropriating the tricks of the underworld trade as a means of personal enrichment. None of these authors evidence genuine interest in the plight of the beggars and thieves. None record lower-class language as a gesture of solidarity with the poor. Nor can we say that their interest in the Renaissance underworld is "sociological" in the modern sense, despite the ruse of empirical investigation commonly perpetrated in their works. Their interest, rather, is literary; that is, in producing something that belongs, exclusively, to authors and their fictional domains. The pamphleteers reproduce early modern vagabonds, and their criminal language, as literary property, and then fight for exclusive rights to its possession and distribution. But it is Jonson who most strongly intimates that literary authors and the rogues they portray speak, as it were, the same language.

Poets and thieves may seem to make odd bedfellows, yet the connection Jonson draws between them is not as anomalous as it may first appear. Thomas Randolph, in his play *The Muses' Looking Glass* (1638), has a rustic character observe that "there is a new trade lately come up to be a vocation, I wis not what: they call 'em boets: a new name for beggars, I think, since the statute against gipsies."[122] Still others compare the new linguistic authorities, early modern orthoepists and grammarians, to the secret fraternity of rogues. Thomas Smith, as I have already mentioned, draws an analogy between orthographers and gypsies; both, he suggests, deal in secret languages only understood by members of the guild. Thomas Nashe's character Winter, in his play, *Summer's Last Will and Testament* (1600), rails against "word-warriors" (poets) and others who pursue contemplative arts, asking how grammarians "differ . . . / From beggars, that profess the pedlar's French?"[123] Paradoxically enough, the criminal under-world provided a paradigm for a literary and linguistic enterprise based, in part, on the creation and the circulation of a "privileged" language. Thomas Nashe, Thomas Dekker, Robert Greene, William Shakespeare, and Ben Jonson all deal in new and unusual words, all venture across regional and beyond national linguistic boundaries, and "enrich" their works with the words of others. Some profess the trade to be a legal one; others (explicitly or not) condemn it as a crime. But in an age where the production of language was imagined as a potential crisis of the commonwealth, and as a challenge to royal prerogatives over the nation's treasure, how could they say with any certainty? The coinings of Renaissance literature – legitimate or counterfeit, worthy or base – bear only the effigy of their authors.

3

REGIONS OF RENAISSANCE ENGLISH I

South of the Border

Towards the end of Ben Jonson's *Bartholomew Fair*, a group of minor characters join together in a spirited game they call "vapours." The object of this game, according to Jonson's stage directions, is "Nonsense. Every man to oppose the last man that spoke: whether it concerned him, or no." The players include Puppy, a wrestler from southwestern England, Northern, a clothier from the northern shires, and Whit, an Irish bawd. The characters compete in their respective dialects:

> *Puppy*: Why, where are you, zurs? doe you vlinch, and leave us i' the zuds, now?
> *Northern*: I'll ne mare, I'is e'en as vull as a Paipers bag, by my troth, I.
> *Puppy*: Doe my Northern cloth zhrinke i' the wetting? ha?
> *Knockem*: Why, well said, old Flea-bitten, thou'lt never tyre, I see.
> *Cutting*: No, Sir, but he may tire, if it please him.
> *Whit*: Who told dee sho? that he vuld never teer, man?[1]

Jonson recreates the urban fair as a contemporary Tower of Babel, where linguistic differences do not cause "confusion" but the more innocuous "nonsense." Yet it is instructive that the playwright chooses a parley of dialects as the expression of a pure oppositionality, rendered comical here. Bakhtin notes the rise of dialect comedy in the Renaissance:

> Ridiculing dialectological peculiarities, making fun of the linguistic and speech manners of groups living in different districts and cities throughout the nation, is something that belongs to every people's most ancient store of language images. But during the Renaissance this mutual ridiculing of different groups among the folk took on a new and fundamental significance. . . . The parodying images of dialects began to receive more profound artistic formulation, and began to penetrate major literature.[2]

It is true that literary authors, from the early part of the sixteenth century, take an increasing interest in reproducing provincial language in their works. Bakhtin's formulation, however, is not entirely accurate. Although a variety of dialect speakers may participate in Jonson's game of vapours, the ridiculing

Bakhtin describes is not "mutual" at all in the English Renaissance, where provincial speakers are often an object of scorn, and have no opportunity to settle the score, at least not through the medium of print. The new linguistic relativism of the age was far from even-handed, and the "parodying images of dialects" are always projected by speakers of the King's English.

In his dialectology of early seventeenth-century England, as I note in the Introduction, Alexander Gill identifies four linguistic provinces of the "general" language – Northern, Southern, Eastern, and Western – along with the region of English he names the "Poetic." Literary authors of the period provide a simpler and more schematic map of the regional "difference of English," recreating dialects that are broadly southern or broadly northern in character. These will be the focus of this chapter and the chapter that follows, respectively. In each, I will show how Renaissance authors portrayed the "Babelish confusion" of English as a confrontation of provincial dialects. Like other contemporary "hard words," southern and northern English words are often invoked because they are deemed "uncommon," "foreign," or obscure. I include in these chapters a consideration of works where provincial language – however unfamiliar to "general" English speakers – constitutes the dominant idiom of the text; these may well be the earliest works of English dialect literature, in the modern sense.[3] Although provincial speakers often talk "nonsense" in Renaissance literature, they are sometimes rendered capable of articulating a more serious, oppositional relationship to a "common" culture. As an introduction to these chapters, I will begin by considering some of the ways that the notion of regionality – the particularity of place within the nation – was conceived and represented in the period. Just as the idea of a common English language was predicated on the notion of competing "Englishes," the idea of an English nation – a common national culture – depended, in part, on the articulation of the meaning of regional difference.[4]

It has long been a commonplace of Renaissance studies that nationalism – the celebration of the state as an embodiment of cultural identity – inspired much of the literature of the period. The revival of epic and the fascination with England's past, the elaboration of the masque and its "royal" perspective, the countless dedications and prefaces glorifying the Prince and the state he embodies, are often seen as just a few literary reflexes of the Renaissance spirit of nationality.[5] The literary endorsement of centralized power is often attributed, moreoever, to a collective memory of civil war. In addition to verse histories and popular ballads that treat the subject explicitly, the ghost of the fifteenth-century civil wars has been said to haunt such works as Sidney's *Arcadia* and Shakespeare's *Romeo and Juliet*. The idea of national unity seems to inform an ideal structure portrayed in a wide range of literary works throughout the period, so that the decentralization of power – as represented in Shakespeare's *King Lear*, for example – appears to identify regionalism as factionalism at best, cultural disintegration, even apocalypse, at worst.

There is no reason to assume, however, that the shadow of civil war in

Renaissance literature was cast solely by the memory of earlier political conflicts. The centralization of power heralded by the Tudor accession was not categorical, and the court was continually at odds with the claims of local authority through-out the sixteenth and seventeenth centuries. Recent historical studies of the period have increasingly emphasized the continuing conflicts between the regions and the London center. Alan Everitt, champion of the "county-community" school of Renaissance history, has demonstrated that the county and not the court represented the focus of political and social life for the majority of noble-men, gentry, and commoners; he concludes that "in some respects the England of 1640 resembled a union of partially independent county-states."[6] Anthony Fletcher, in his analysis of rebellions from the Yorkshire and Cornwall uprisings at the end of the fifteenth century to Wyatt's rebellion of the 1550s, registers the extent to which civil rioting continued well into the sixteenth century and, with it, the assertion of provincial autonomy. Regional allegiances contributed to tensions that ultimately led the nation once again to civil war, the "Great Rebellion" of the mid-seventeenth century.[7] The threat of national division, figured so prominently in the literature of the period, was no hobgoblin of the Renaissance historical imagination, but a living political reality.

The literary ratification of Renaissance nationalism was also encouraged, to be sure, by the politics of authorship in the period: The importance of court patronage and the localization of the publishing industry in London centralized the business of literature itself. For this reason alone, it is not surprising that regional literature, mapping out an autonomous imaginative space outside the capital, finds few representatives in the canon of Renaissance works. Yet the beginnings of literary regionalism – the localization of texts outside of London and its environs, the deliberate evocation of provincial settings and provincial practices – can, along with the new exploration of native dialects, be traced to the sixteenth century. While it would be centuries before England produced a genuine regional literature, providing a haven for distinctive political or cultural identities within the nation, two works of the period represent the first attempts to create a literature bounded geographically, and ideologically, by the English provinces. Both Michael Drayton's *Poly-Olbion* (1612/22) and Thomas Nashe's *Nashes Lenten Stuffe* (1599) begin as celebrations of the localities of England. Both works take their inspiration, in part, from the contemporary historical genre known as chorography. Beginning with John Leland's unfinished *Itinerary* (1535/43), English antiquarians began to compile county surveys that described the topography, demographics, laws, and customs of individual shires.[8] Richard Helgerson has identified Renaissance chorography as a genre that challenged royal centrism in its attention to particularities of the shires. Unlike Renaissance English histories, which were essentially chronicles of kings, chorographies, Helgerson argues, transfer the basis of national identity from the monarch to the land.[9] Renaissance chorography, I would add, provides an important generic paradigm for literary authors seeking to articulate the relationship between "center" and "region" in a nationalized culture.

National chorographers, such as John Leland, William Camden, and William Harrison, whose works offer a comprehensive survey of the English counties, portray England as a kind of internal empire of shires subordinate to the crown. Leland thus presents his work to Henry VIII as a description of "this your worlde and impery of Englande."[10] Harrison adds up the number of shires in Elizabeth's England to measure her power; counting fifty-three in England and Wales, Harrison rejoices "that under the Queen's Majesty are so many counties, whereby it is easily discerned that her power far exceedeth that of Offa, who . . . had so much of Britain under his subjection as afterward contained thirty-nine shires."[11] But in the fourth chapter of his *Description of England,* "Of the Partition of England into Shires and Counties," Harrison suggests that the division of the nation into counties, historically, was a means of containing the potential threat posed by internal differences among the regions. According to Harrison, King Alfred's England was besieged by years of Danish invasions, until Englishmen themselves were seduced:

> to fall to the like pillage, as practicing to follow the Danes in these their thefts and robberies. And the better to cloak their mischief withal, they feigned themselves to be Danish pirates. . . . The good King Alfred there-fore (who had marvelously travailed in repelling the barbarous Danes), espying this outrage and thinking it no less the part of a politic prince to root out the noisome subject than to hold out the foreign adversary . . . divided the whole realm into certain parts or sections, which (of the Saxon word *schyran,* signifying "to cut") he termed shires.[12]

The division of England was thus the monarch's way of rooting out subjects who, socially and politically, were "foreign" to Alfred's rule. The King further subdivided the shires into hundreds or tithings:

> Alfred caused each man . . . to be ascribed into some hundred . . . where he might always have such as should swear or say upon their certain knowledge for his honest behavior and civil conversation, if it should happen at any time that his credit should come in question.[13]

The hundreds were thus created as a kind of internal surveillance system, in which citizens were "bound for others' good bearing and laudable behavior in the commonwealth of the realm."[14] The shires and the hundreds, Harrison explains, were not established in order to provide representation for local interests but, rather, to contain the enemy within.

Michael Drayton, in his *Poly-Olbion,* also surveys the English shires as a way of containing the differences he delineates. Like contemporary chorographies on which it is patterned, *Poly-Olbion* is a glorification of England through a celebration of its parts. Although Drayton boasted in his dedication to Henry, Prince of Wales, that his poem was the "first in this kinde," *Poly-Olbion,* a 15,000-line poem in hexameter couplets, seems in many respects a versification of Camden's *Britannia.* Along with topographical description, Drayton's work incorporates a great deal of English history, from the legendary history of Britain to the civil wars of the fifteenth century. When he comes to contemporary civil history, however, Drayton is uncharacteristically brief. Drayton offers only the most summary inventory of some of the local uprisings of the sixteenth century:

> As for the Black-smiths rout, who did together rise,
> Encamping on Blackheath, t'annull the Subsidies
> By Parliament then given, or that of Cornwall call'd,
> Inclosures to cast downe, which overmuch enthrald
> The Subject: or proud Kets, who with the same pretence
> In Norfolke rais'd such stirres, as but with great expence
> Of blood was not apppeas'd; or that begun in Lent
> By Wyat and his friends, the Mariage to prevent,
> That Mary did intend with Philip King of Spaine:
> Since these but Ryots were nor fit the others straine,
> Shee [Drayton's narrator] here her Battles ends.[15]

Mere "ryots" rather than full-fledged wars, the local rebellions of the sixteenth century are, according to Drayton, unworthy of more elaborate poetic treatment.

Despite his restraint here, Drayton returns again and again to the theme of regional conflict; the idea of internal "war," as many of his commentators have shown, underlies the structure of the poem.[16] The very landscape is portrayed as a battlefield of competing rivers, mountains, and plains. The "argument" introducing the third song, for example, sets the tone:

> In this third Song, great threatnings are,
> And tending all to Nymphish warre.
> Old Wansdike uttereth words of hate,
> Depraving Stonendges estate.
> Cleere Avon and FaireWilly strive,
> Each pleading her prerogative.
> The Plaine the Forrests doth disdaine:
> The Forrests raile upon the Plaine.
> (Song 3.1–8)

The fourth song, setting the idea of topographical warfare on a grander scale, is devoted to a dispute between England and Wales over the possession of the Isle of Lundy. The idea of regional divisiveness is central to the poem, but rather than treating regional resistance directly, Drayton sublimates politics in a quasi-allegorical, quasi-mythical treatment of the landscape.

It is instructive, then, that Drayton rarely chooses to vary the language of his lengthy poem. In Song 23, the mountain Hellidon recounts the old, homely names the shires once bestowed on themselves, calling them "Clownish Blazons":

Kent first in our account, doth to itself apply,
(Quoth he) this Blazon first, Long Tayles and Libertie.
Sussex with Surry say, then let us lead home Logs.
As Hamshire long for her, hath had the tearme of Hogs.
So Dorsetshire of long, they Dorsers usd to call.
Cornwall and Devonshire crie, weele wrestle for a Fall.
Then Somerset sayes, set the Bandog on th' Bull.
And Glostershire againe is blazon'd, Weigh thy Wooll.
. . .
So Hartford blazon'd is, The Club, and Clowted Shoone,
Thereto, Ile rise betime, sleep againe at Noone.
(Song 23.237–41; Song 23.249–50)

When the shires, for the first and only time in the poem, speak for themselves, they apply the old epithets, including the colloquial "Dorsers" and the dialectal form *shoon*. Drayton includes this list, he claims, "to shew the Muse can shift her habit, and she now/Of Palatins that sung, can whistle to the plow" (Song 23.233–4). Although the poet alludes to a popular language of the plow, it is a language he chooses to avoid in the vast course of his work. Indeed, Drayton's difficult metrical form, his nearly invariable style, seem engineered to suppress the threat of difference posed throughout the poem. In the *Poly-Olbion*, poetic language aids in the containment of what may well be the emergent regional consciousness of the work.[17]

Numerous chorographies of the age, beginning with William Lambarde's ground-breaking *Perambulation of Kent* (1570), focus on specific regions and concern themselves, more explicitly, with political and economic conflicts among rival provinces. John Stow, in his *Survey of London* (1598), makes reference to such conflicts, especially, to the resentment of provincial Englishmen towards the capital, and the economic and political privileges Londoners seemed to enjoy at their expense. Stow's work thus ends with "An apology (or defence) against the opinion of some men, which think that the greatness of that city standeth not with the profit and security of this realm."[18] Although he admits that kings have traditionally granted the city special privileges (p. 202), Stow insists that:

in respect of the whole realm, London is but a citizen and no city, a subject and no free estate, an obedienciary and no place endowed with any distinct or absolute power; for it is governed by the same law that the rest of the realm is. . . . And in the assembly of the estates of our realm (which we call parliament) they are but a member of the commonality, and send two burgesses for their county, as every other shire doth; and are as straitly bound by such laws as any part of the realm is, for if contribution in subsidy of money to the prince be decreed, the Londoners have no exemption.

(p. 204)

Stow attempts to answer the accusation of those men who charge London "with the loss and decay of many (or most) of the ancient cities, corporate towns, and markets of this realm, by drawing from them to herself alone." He faults the decay of certain industries, like navigation, and the dissolution of religious institutions, for the decline of many provincial towns (p. 205). But despite these protestations, Stow finally concedes London's preeminence. He reminds his accusers that most of the shires, but especially Norfolk, Suffolk, Essex, Kent, and Sussex, "stand not so much by the benefit of their own soil" as by their proximity to London and its resources. Finally, Stow declares that London, of all cities in England, "is an ornament to the realm . . . and a terror to other countries" (p. 206). Stow's "apology," despite its efforts to sublimate regional assertiveness into national pride, exposes some of the economic and political asymmetries that set the towns at odds with London.

Nashes Lenten Stuffe, "containing the Description and first Procreation and Increase of the towne of Great Yarmouth in Norfolke: With a new Play never played before, of the praise of the Red Herring," highlights those asymmetries, in a work that is at once an imitation and a parody of the town and county chorographies. After the publication of the lost satirical comedy *The Isle of Dogs*, with its allegedly scandalous allusions to the contemporary political scene, Nashe was forced to flee London to escape censure. Nashe found refuge in Great Yarmouth, near his birthplace, and spent six weeks there in exile. *Lenten Stuffe*, which Nashe presents as his thanks to the town for granting him safe haven, was published in 1599, a short time before his works were officially banned.[19] Often hailed as Nashe's "quintessential performance,"[20] it is a landmark in the rise of regional literature in English.

Lenten Stuffe begins as a topographical description of the town of Great Yarmouth and its surroundings, focusing, in the chorographical manner, on the terrain, resources, industry, and customs of the locality. From the start, however, Nashe plays havoc with the conventions of the genre. Rather than dedicating the work to the local gentry and nobility, as the chorographers inevitably do, Nashe's title declares the work "Fitte of all Clearkes of Noblemens Kitchins to be read: and not unnecessary by all serving men that have short boord-wages, to be remembered."[21] Nashe's dedication, "To his Readers, hee cares not what they bee," disavows any concern that the work be received by readers holding positions of power. But Nashe's declaration of independence from the politics of patronage is just the starting point of a parody of regional chauvinism and "popular" pride. If he praises Yarmouth and its people, he does so, to be sure, in terms scarcely fit for the consumption of serving-men. *Lenten Stuffe* is no doubt the most outrageously neologistic work of the period, providing readers with what one critic has called "a linguistic experience unsurpassed in its kind in English literature."[22] Describing the landscape, for example, he writes:

> Forth of the sands thus struglingly as it exalteth and liftes up his glittering head, so of the neyboring sands no lesse semblably (whether in recordation

of their worn out affinitie or no, I know not) it is so inamorately protected and patronized. . . . In this transcursive reportory without some observant glaunce I may not dully overpasse the gallant beauty of their haven, which, having but as it were a welte of land, or, as M. Camden cals it, *lingulam terrae.* . . . A narrow channel or Isthmus in rashe view you would opinionate it.

(p. 157)

A local gentleman of Yarmouth praises the town and its herrings in a style that characterizes the language of the whole piece:

> Doe but convert, said hee, the slenderest twinckling reflexe of your eie-sight to this flinty ringe that engirtes it, these towred walles, port-cullizdgates, and gorgeous architectures that condecorate and adorne it, and then perponder of the red herringes priority and prevalence, who is the onely unexhaustible mine that hath raisd and begot all this. . . . The red herring alone it is that countervailes the burdensome detrimentes of our haven . . . that defrayes all impositions and outwarde payments to her Majestie. . . . Thou wilt commend thy muse to sempiternity, and have images and statues erected to her after her unstringed and silent interment and obsequies . . . chaunt and carroll forth the *Alteza* and excelsitude of this monarchall fluddy *Induperator.*

(pp. 174–5)

Nashe mockingly celebrates Yarmouth as a province that has overcome the "impositions" of the crown and set up a fish as its "monarchall . . . *Induperator*" – in language that only derides the town's claims to statehood. Nashe reveals, moreover, his contempt for chorographical work:

> I had a crotchet in my head, here to have given the raines to my pen, and run astray thorowout all the coast townes of England, digging up their dilapidations, and raking out of the dust-heape or charnell house of tenebrous eld the rottenest relique of their monuments, and bright scoured the canker eaten brasse of their first bricklayers and founders, & commented and paralogized on their condition in the present, & in the pretertense.[23]

(p. 167)

Nashe explains that the "crotchet" or whim entered his head "not for any love or hatred I beare them, but that I would not be snibd . . . that therefore I prayse Yarmouth so rantantingly, because I never elsewhere bayted my horse. . . . To shun spight I smothered these dribblements" (p. 167). While his ostensible purpose here is to demonstrate the sincerity of his celebration of Yarmouth, he exposes the satirical nature of his own treatise, devoted as it is, in part, to praising the "dilapidations" and rotten reliques of the town. His pseudo-archaisms ("tenebrous eld") and coinings ("paralogized" and "pretertense") only heighten the joke: If he praises Yarmouth, he does so "rantantingly" – in an exaggerated, entirely disproportionate manner.

As the title promises, *Lenten Stuffe* finds its ultimate theme in the red herring, the major product of the province. Nashe accounts the herring the most profitable commodity of the realm, surpassing all others in value, despite the claims of rival provinces:

> If you aske *Suffolke, Essex, Kent, Sussex,* or *Lemster,* or *Cotswold,* what marchandise that should bee, they will answere you it is the very same which Polidore Virgill calls *Vere aureum vellus,* the true golden fleece of our woll and English cloth. . . . Other engrating upland cormorants will grunt out it is *Grana paradisis,* our grain or corne, that is most sought after. The Westerners and Northerners that it is lead, tinne, and iron.
>
> (pp. 178–9)

Yarmouth's herrings are put forward as the national mascot, a fetish of patriotic fervor: "But to thinke on a red Herring, such a hot stirring meate it is, is enough to make the cravenest dastard proclaime fire and sword against Spaine" (p. 191). The fish is ultimately canonized, and set in in company with the patron saints of the great European powers: "Saint Denis for Fraunce, Saint James for Spaine, Saint Patrike for Ireland, Saint George for England, and the red Herring for Yarmouth" (p. 226). Yarmouth, by virtue of its herrings, is thus set forward not only as the preeminent province among others of the nation, but as a rival to the nation itself.

And there is more: Herrings put Yarmouth at the center of European literary culture, as well as national politics. Nashe hails Yarmouth's herrings as the very fountainhead of poetic inspiration, the wellspring of literary invention:

> the puissant red herring, the golden *Hesperides* red herring, the *Meonian* red herring, the red herring of red Herrings Hal, every pregnant peculiar of whose resplendent laude and honour to delineate and adumbrate to the ample life were a woorke that would drinke drie fourscore and eighteene Castalian fountaines of eloquence, consume another *Athens* of facunditie, and abate the haughtiest poeticall fury twixt this and the burning Zone and the tropike of Cancer.
>
> (p. 226)

Nashe pronounces the herring as matter surpassing that of the greatest of epics: "The Poets were triviall, that set up Helen's face for such a top-gallant summer May-pole for men to gaze at . . . our dappert *Piemont Huldrick Herring* . . . draweth more barkes to Yarmouth bay, then her beauty did to Troy" (pp. 184–5). He recreates a number of tales and myths, notably that of Hero and Leander, with herrings as protagonists. For example, Leander, in Nashe's version, is metamorphosed into a fish called the Ling, Hero into a Fabian fish (another kind of herring), and their nurse into mustard, to accompany the two fishes ever after (pp. 199–200). In several of his renderings of classical myths, an ordinary red herring is taken for a god because of its dazzling golden scales. Essentially, all of Nashe's revised tales are pseudo-myths of origin, giving the herring a host of impressive literary genealogies. In the same way, Nashe concocts numerous pseudo-etymologies to give the fish more luster, in a parody of the chorographers' fascination with the origins of place names and other local terms. The Persians who worship what they call *Mortus Alli*, actually worship, according to Nashe's fanciful derivation, a "*mortuum halec,* a dead red herring, and no other, though, by corruption of speech, they false dialect and misse-sound it" (p. 195). The key to all mythologies, Nashe reveals, is the Yarmouth herring.

Nashe admits from the start that his work is a satire, a mock-encomium whose terms are intentionally overblown. He finds plenty of literary precedents for such a practice: "I follow the trace of the famousest schollers of all ages, whom a wantonizing humour once in their life time hath possesst to play with strawes, and turne mole-hills into mountaines" (p. 151). The purpose of the satire, his critics have agreed, is to to create a work deliberately void of meaning, as a kind of mock-apology for his role in writing the *Isle of Dogs*.[24] Nashe protests his audience's tendency to overinterpret even the most innocuous of his works.[25] His detractors, he complains,

> have fisht out such a deepe politique state meaning as if I had al the secrets of court or commonwealth at my fingers endes. Talk I of a beare, O, it is such a man that emblazons him in his armes, or of a woolfe, a fox, or a camelion, any lording whom they do not affect it is meant by. . . . These bee they that use mens writings like bruit beasts, to make them draw which way they list.
>
> (pp. 214–15)

Nashe dares his readers to discover any covert political significance behind Yarmouth's herrings: "O, for a Legion of mice-eyed decipherers and calculaters uppon characters, now to augurate what I meane by this " (p. 218). *Lenten Stuffe* reveals, in fact, that the meaning of every tale, the allusion behind every reference, is – a red herring.[26] Nashe's chronicle of Yarmouth is, in a sense, deliberately meaningless – even as it baits its readers into interpretation.[27]

But Nashe's work, despite its self-proclaimed insignificance, is not entirely a concession to the authorities who damned his more substantial efforts. One of his most recent commentators has suggested that Nashe's parody is not really aimed at Yarmouth or its herrings, but rather at his own pretentions as a poet.[28] In fact, just the reverse is more likely the case: Nashe ridicules the subject of *Lenten Stuffe* as a way to exalt his own poetic powers. He defends his theme by anticipating critics who would accuse him of triviality:

> Alas, poore hungerstarved Muse, wee shall have some spawne of a goose-quill or over worne pander quirking and girding, was it so hard driven that it had nothing to feede upon but a redde herring? another drudge of the pudding house . . . sayes I might as well have writte of a dogges turde.
>
> (p. 225)

His verbose celebration of Yarmouth, he explains, is just

> a patterne or tiny-sample what my elaborate performance would bee in
> this case, had I a ful-sayled gale of prosperity to encourage mee . . . [there-
> fore] I take the paines to describe this superiminente principall Metropolis
> of the redde fishe.
>
> (p. 156)

Nashe goes to town on Yarmouth and its herrings, it seems, to announce what
he could do with a "greater" theme, had he "a ful-sayled gale of prosperity" to
carry him home. *Lenten Stuffe*, after all, commands attention, not because of
its diminished theme but because of the language Nashe devises to treat it. He
explains his extravagant use of new and unusual words at the start of his work:

> Let me speake to you about my huge woords which I use in this booke,
> and then you are your own men to do what you list. Know it is my true
> vaine to be *tragicus Orator* . . . not caring for this demure soft *mediocre
> genus*, that is like water and wine mixt togither; but give me pure wine of
> it self, and that begets good bloud, and heates the braine thorowly; I had
> as lieve have no sunne, as have it shine faintly, no fire, as a smothering fire
> of small coales, no cloathes, rather than weare linsey wolsey.
>
> (p. 152)

He only regrets that he cannot "marshall [his] termes in better array, and bestow
such costly coquery on the *Marine magnifico* as you would preferre him before
tart and galingale, which Chaucer preheminentest encomionizeth above all
junquestries or confectionaries whatsoever" (p. 176). Although some have
discovered in this language a foreshadowing of postmodern literary experiments,
a creation of a "pure rhetoric" that suspends meaning,[29] Nashe's contemporary
context provides another, more urgent explanation. Barred from topics that
might even be remotely associated with court politics, language is Nashe's only
recourse to recognition. Nashe, after all, succeeds in creating a work containing
nothing potentially incriminating, nothing provocative – except, crucially, his
language. If his "huge woords" are comical, and help bring home the marginality
of his theme, they also demonstrate the inventiveness of an author constrained,
by political circumstances, to say more.

The Thomas Nashe who writes of Yarmouth is not a regional author in the
modern sense. His literary chorography derides provincial chauvinism, the local
molehill turned mountain; he champions Yarmouth by necessity and not by will.
But the experience of exile (whether real or imagined), of alienation from
London or the court, continually finds Renaissance authors – so often allied
with, or dependent on, the King and "his" English – at home in the English
provinces. Although Nashe's "huge woords" are not provincial in any literal sense,
their example is instructive, for linguistic regionalism in early modern literature
takes root with those who, like Nashe, stand on the outside looking in.

* * *

And you that love the commons, follow me.
Now show yourselves men; 'tis for liberty.
We will not leave one lord, one gentleman:
Spare none but such as go in clouted shoon.
                    Jack Cade, *2 Henry VI* (4.3.175–8)

Shakespeare's Jack Cade, who in 1450 led an unsuccessful rebellion against King Henry VI, invokes a popular epithet – one of Drayton's "clownish blazons" – to describe the common people whose cause he promotes. Although Cade's commoners come from Kent and Sussex, he uses the dialect phrase *clouted shoon* (hobnailed shoes) to refer, metonymically, to the English peasantry as a whole, regardless of the region from which his followers hailed.[30] In Cade's speech, regional dialect is used to characterize a social class, the people Sir Thomas Smith, in his *De Republica Anglorum*, described as a "fourth sort of men" which "have no voice nor authorities in our common wealth, and no account is made of them but onelie to be ruled."[31] Yet when that voice is heard in Renaissance English drama, it is often enough in the accents of the southwestern shires. Alexander Gill described this language:

> Of all the dialects the western [i.e., southwestern] has the most barbarous flavour, particularly if you listen to the rustic people from Somerset, for it is easily possible to doubt whether they are speaking English or some foreign language.[32]

Similarly, a speaker of this dialect in Thomas Randolph's *The Muses' Looking Glass* (1638), is introduced as a rustic "whose discourse is all country; an extreme of [i.e., from] Urbanity."[33] Renaissance writers commonly portray southern English – as I shall refer to representations of this dialect, for convenience, throughout this chapter – as the most foreign of English dialects, from the standpoint of an elite social class, as the "extreme" of courtly language. At the same time, this "foreign" dialect is portrayed as the *vox populi* of early modern literary dialects, as a "common" language of the people.

Although aristocrats as prominent as Sir Walter Ralegh were said to have spoken with a broad Devonshire accent, and may have helped introduce southern features into the language at court,[34] literary southern English was reserved for the exclusive use of "clownish" characters. Southern English, of all Renaissance literary dialects, is rarely heard outside the domain of comedy. Yet sometimes the "extremity" of the people's language is given serious literary treatment, though not necessarily in support of popular causes. More often, southern English is adopted by those who, like Edgar in *King Lear*, borrow the forms of popular revolt, and leave the matter behind.

The dialects of Renaissance English, as we have seen, were often understood as languages of "misrule," and southern English is no exception. Andrew Boorde, in *The Fyrst Boke of the Introduction of Knowledge* (1542), describes the languages of Cornwall: "The Cornwal is two speeches, the one is *naughty englyshe*, and the other is Cornyshe speeche."[35] Renaissance dramatists reproduce the "naughty English" of the south by borrowing words and pronunciations largely derived from the dialects of the southwestern shires, especially Somerset, Devon, and Cornwall, although southeastern elements, from Kent and neighboring shires, are sometimes used as well. The signature features of literary southern English are the voicing of the consonants *f* and *s* to *v* and *z*, respectively; the southern form of the first person pronoun, *ich* (I) and the contractions *icham, chill, chwas* (I am, I will, I was) are also common. Other typical markers include the prefix *i* or *y* with past participles, as in *yvound* (found), and the ending *-th* in the third person plural of the present indicative. Some of Edgar's lines in *King Lear* – lines I will return to later in the chapter – may serve to illustrate this dialect:

> Chill not let go, zir, without vurther cagion. . . . Good gentlemen, go your gait, and let poor voke pass. An 'chud ha' bin zwagger'd out of my life, 'twould not ha' bin zo long as 'tis by a vortnight.[36]

Like all provincial speakers in Renaissance literature, southerners are also partial to elided forms (*ha* for have, *a* for he) and malapropisms. Thomas Wilson, in *The Arte of Rhetorique*, conflated dialect and malapropism in one of his anecdotes, in which (this time) it is a southern speaker who cannot command the "hard words" of a lettered class:

> When I was in Cambrige, and student in the kynges College, there came a man out of the toune, with a pinte of wine in a pottle pot, to welcome the provost of that house, that lately came from the court. And because he would bestow his present like a clerke, dwellyng emong the schoolers: he made humbly his thre curtesies, and said in this maner. Cha good even my good lorde, and well might your lordship vare: Understandyng that your lordeship was come, and knowyng that you are a worshipfull Pilate, and kepes a bominable house: I thought it my duetie to come incantivantee, and bryng you a pottell a wine, the whiche I beseche your lordeship take in good worthe. Here the simple man beyng desirous to amende his mothers tongue, shewed hymself not to bee the wisest manne, that ever spake with tongue.[37]

The connection that Wilson, among many others, draws between dialect and malapropism is an important one, for the implication is that provincial language, too, is an English misformed by the incapacity of its speakers.

Only one Renaissance writer, to my knowledge, spoke up for the distinctive qualities of southern English. Richard Carew, in his chorography *Survey of Cornwall*, called attention to the dialect as one of the "antiquities" of the region, and sought to promote the local language to a national status. Carew explains that some inhabitants of Cornwall – namely, those of Celtic stock – bear a cultural grudge against the rest of the nation:

> Fostering a fresh memory of their expulsion long ago by the English, they second the same with a bitter fellowship; and this the worst sort express

in combining against and working them all the shrewd turns which with hope of impunity they can devise.[38]

Their hostility towards the English is sometimes expressed linguistically. Although most of the inhabitants speak English and not Cornish,

> some so affect their own as to a stranger they will not speak it [English], for if meeting them by chance you inquire the way or any such matter, your answer shall be, Meea navidna cowzasawzneck, I can speak no Saxonage.
>
> (p. 127)

In general, Carew condemns the insubordination of the "worst sort" of Cornish, including the way they use a foreign language in defiance of their "Saxon" neighbors.

But the English dialect of Cornwall is another matter. According to Carew, the English spoken in Cornwall is actually the true descendant of the "Saxonage" repudiated by so many local residents. Southern dialect words like *pridy* (handsome), *scrip* (escape), *thew* (threaten), *shune* (strange) may sound "broad and rude" (pp. 127–8), he explains, but they "plead in their defence not only the prescription of antiquity but also the title of propriety and the benefit of significancy, for most of them take their source from the Saxon, our natural language." Carew insists that the southern dialect might one day be restored to its former status, for the dialect words of Cornwall "want but another Spenser to make them passable" (p. 127). Carew's idea, it seems, is that the southern dialect awaits a poet who will translate the "broad and rude" dialect to a language that meets courtly standards, just as Spenser had done for the "rude" language of the northern shires.[39] Carew is fond of citing popular rhymes, some composed in southern English, announcing a region that deserves a national hearing:

> Hengston downe, well ywrought,
> Is worth London towne, deare ybought.
> (p. 184)[40]

The southern dialect of Renaissance English never found a Spenser to promote the regional to the national. It never became a "passable" medium of literature. On the contrary, southern English is used again and again, by Renaissance authors, as a foil to "better" versions of the language. Columel, a simple plowman in John Ferne's *The Blazon of Gentrie* (1586), complains that he cannot understand the fancy language, replete with Latin and inkhorn terms, of the gentlemen in his company. Southern English and the neologistic language of the gentry both emerge as two mutually unintelligible dialects here; but it is Columel's incomprehension that is foregrounded: "By my vather's soule . . . I like not this gibberishe."[41] In early modern literature, southern English is the dialect of the unlettered, a language of ignorance. One of *Scoggin's Jests*, attributed to Andrew Boorde, tells how Scoggin tried to teach a poor youth how to read and write:

> The slovenly boy, almost as big as a knave, would begin to learne his A.B.C. Scogin did give him a lesson of nine of the first letters of A.B.C., and he was nine daies in learning of them; and when he had learned the nine . . . the good scholler said: am ich past the worst now? . . . Would God Ich were, for dis is able to comber any man's wits alive. Scogin then thought his scholler would never bee but a foole, and did apply him as well as he could to his learning; but he, that hath no wit, can never have learning nor wisedome.[42]

The forms *ich* and *dis* mark the regional origins of Scoggin's "scholler." The southern speaker can barely command an alphabet of nine letters, an abridged language that marks the limits of his intellectual powers. John Redford, in his mid-century play *Wit and Science*, includes a southern dialect speaker among his allegorical characters who is named, simply, "Ingnorance." His fellow, Idleness, attempts to teach him his name, syllable by syllable:

Idle.: Where was thou born?
Ingn.: Chwas i-bore in England.
Idle.: In Ingland?
Ingn.: Yea!
Idle.: And what's half Ingland? Here's Ing; and here's land.
   What's 'tis?
Ingn.: What's 'tis?
Idle.: What's 'tis? whoreson!
   Here's Ing; and here's land. What's 'tis?
Ingn.: 'Tis my thumb.
Ilde.: Thy thumb? Ing, whoreson! Ing, Ing!
Ingn.: Ing, Ing, Ing, Ing!
Idle.: Forth! Shall I beat thy narse, now?
Ingn.: Um-um-um —
Idle.: Shall I not beat thy narse, now?
Ingn.: Um-um-um —
Idle.: Say no, fool! say no.
Ingn.: Noo, noo, noo, noo, noo!
Idle.: Go to, put together! Ing!
Ingn.: Ing.
Idle.: No!
Ingn.: Noo.
Idle.: Forth now! What saith the dog?
Ingn.: Dog bark.
Idle.: Dog bark? Dog ran, whoreson! dog ran!
Ingn.: Dog ran, whoreson! dog ran, dog ran![43]

At last, Ingnorance manages to piece together the whole: "Ing-no-ran-his-I-s-s-s." But when Idleness asks him what he has learned, Ingnorance answers only "Ich cannot tell."[44]

If southern speakers are granted any virtues in Renaissance literature, they are those associated with hard labor, and, perhaps, what virtue comes of being poor. The anonymous play *The Contention between Liberality and Prodigality* (1602) makes southern English the language of the laboring classes – here, embodied in the character "Tenacity" – who work the earth and hoard their savings. Although the title promises to pit magnaminous Liberality against incontinent Prodigality, the story is devoted to the rivalry between Prodigality and Tenacity as they sue for possession of Money. Tenacity defends his frugality to his rival:

> Whilst thou dost spend with friend and foe,
> At home che hold the plough by the taile.
> Che dig, che delve, che zet, che zow,
> Che mow, che reape, che ply my flaile.[45]

The awkward repetitiveness of the dialectal *che*, a variant of *ich*, creates an impression of plodding dullness. Linguistic "tenacity" turns the southern dialect into a mere stutter, incapable of liberal expression. When Vanity asks Tenacity what he would do with Money if he possessed it, Tenacity can only stammer, "Chud [I would] chud, chud, chud." Vanity mimics him: "Chud, chud, what chud?" (4.3.808–9). At the end of the play, Prodigality robs and murders Tenacity, and although he is first sentenced to death by hanging, his penitence earns him the hope of a reprieve. Though the murder is never justified, it is not such a terrible crime, either: After all, Tenacity, too, must also be abandoned in favor of a more "liberal" attitude towards money.[46] But while Prodigality is implicitly reformed into Liberality, Tenacity's fate is fixed by his death. Perhaps it was simply unimaginable, for the author of this play, that the economic outlook of this class might be amenable to change. Or perhaps the implication is that Tenacity – as his southern dialect suggests – is incapable of reform, that he is, like Scoggin's scholar, uneducable.

At least Columel, in Ferne's *The Blazon of Gentrie*, has learned enough to know that he, as a plowman, will always remain ignorant of the ways of his betters. Listening to a dialogue between a learned Herald and a circle of gentlemen concerning the English gentry and the coats of arms that mark their degrees, in the second part of the treatise, Columel confesses his unworthiness to participate in the conversation. His southern dialect declaims that unworthiness:

> Heere is zutch a prattle of Lords and Earles, Kings and Queenes, Coates, and old quaint stories, that I was aferd to give eare . . . vor zutch as my selfe, are not worthy to hear this talke.

> (p. 99)

Although Ferne addresses his work to "all Gentlemen bearers of Armes, whome and none other this work concerneth," Columel is grudgingly included among the Herald's circle of auditors. His occasional comments are received with scorn by the others: "What scandalous speech is this to the state of Gentrie? and that from the mouth of a contemptible peysant" (p. 22). He consistently defers to his social betters ("vor zutch as my selfe, are not worthy"), yet his speech is deemed "scandalous" by the gentry. Columel's dialectal interruptions are berated throughout the work, but he is never silenced altogether. Why, then, is he allowed to speak this "scandalous speech" at all?

No doubt Columel functions simply as a point of contrast, a means of setting off the superior virtues, lineage, and language of the gentle classes. But Columel's uninvited commentary raises some questions that are not so easily answered. The latter half of Ferne's work is given over to an antiquarian exercise in local genealogy, an investigation of the lineage of one noble family, the Lacys, possessors of the earldom of Lincoln. Ferne traces their noble descent back to the time of King Alfred. After unifying the seven kingdoms of the ancient realm, Alfred, in the familiar story, divided the nation into shires, creating Lincoln, the seat of the Lacys. At this point in the narrative Columel interrupts:

> Is it possitable that this Countrey which I have heard bookish men to call but halfe an Island, to conteine within it seven kings? I perceive wel that old world is changed: for now I suppose we have some such Lords and Gentlemen by us, that be so covetous and gaping after earth, that I think this whole land would scarcely fill seven of their mouths.
>
> (p. 17)

If the "old world" of an England ruled by rival sovereign states has changed at all, it is hardly for the better, given the appetite of the provincial aristocracy for land. As if to make sure this point is understood, Ferne allows Columel to drop his southern idiom (although he is still prone to malapropism). Like many dialect speakers in Renaissance literature who are dispossessed of place in the politics of the work, Columel is allowed an occasional lapse into plain speaking.

"Plain speaking" is indeed the chief role of a southern speaker in Nicholas Udall's mid-sixteenth century court interlude *Respublica* (1553), a character whose provincial origins are never identified, but who is, rather, named simply "People." "Representing the poor Commontie" of the nation, People identifies himself as poor, "ignoram" (ignorant), and oppressed; his dialect, as well as his malapropisms, help to characterize his lot:

> Lett poore volke ha zome parte,
> vor we Ignoram people, whom itche doe perzente,
> Wer ner zo I-polde, zo wrong, and zo I-torment.
> Lorde Ihese Christ whan he was I-pounst and I-pilate,
> Was ner zo I-trounst as we have been of yeares Late.[47]

Respublica, a widow, is sorely oppressed by four evil counselors, Insolence, Adulation, Oppression, and Avarice. These four have disguised themselves to gain her favor, taking on the assumed names Authority, Honesty, Reformation, and Policy respectively. As they accomplish their schemes to enclose land, depreciate the currency, and steal bishoprics, Respublica's condition – as well as People's – grows steadily worse. While Respublica is duped by their disguises, only People is privy to their real names, and tries repeatedly to expose them. In answer to People's accusations, the counselors condemn him, "Canne ye naught els doe but rage and rave and crye out? . . . Crow against your betters! and murmoure against the Lawe!" (4.4.1143–6). The author treats People's "brode carping" (3.3.744) comically at times (ignorant of Latin, People calls Respublica "Ricepudding-cake" (3.3.637)), but his is also the lone voice of resistance, and of truth, for most of the play.

That is, until the character Verity (with an auspiciously Latinate name) arrives, at the end of the interlude, to redeem the republic. Verity, like People, reveals the true names of Respublica's ministers, but this time the truth does not fall on deaf ears. People's inability to convey his message to Respublica himself is surprising, considering that their relationship is described throughout as an intimate one; he is alternately her "man" or agent, her child or a beloved friend. Their interests, particularly where economics and religion are concerned, are the same. In fact, the relationship between Respublica and People is one of near identity, a relationship spelled out in the etymological derivations of their names: "People" is very nearly the English equivalent of the Latin "Respublica." Yet their difference, marked by the linguistic distinction between the English "People" and the Latin "Respublica," is one which the interlude ultimately refuses to translate, despite its sincere support for popular causes. When the goddess Nemesis, representing Queen Mary, arrives to punish the evil-doers, People shies away from her presence: "I namnot worthye to perke [thrust himself forward] with yowe, no I nam not" (5.10.1824). Nemesis makes People her minister, placing the villains in his custody, but despite the honor accorded him he refuses to approach her: "I will comme no nere; cha not bee haled up with states [the highest ranks of the realm]" (5.10.1821). The relation between People and the Respublica in the interlude is telling: People is the near-equivalent of the state, but still comes "no nere" to the site of political power.

"People" finds a new literary representative in Edgar, of Shakespeare's *King Lear*, who borrows southern English as part of a disguise he adopts while guiding his blind father from the "cliffs" of Dover. And, once again, real "people" do not stand to gain much from the exchange. Edgar's southern speech represents Shakespeare's only extended use of regional English in his works,[48] giving it a unique status in the canon. Yet Shakespeare seems to provide little motivation for its appearance here. As A.C. Bradley remarked in his famous list of the inconsistencies that beset the play generally, Edgar's father, the Earl of Gloucester, does not appear to notice when Edgar shifts from the language of a gentleman, to the southern dialect, and then back again to the King's English.[49] There is apparently no comedy intended, either; Shakespeare does not ask us to laugh at this outburst of provincial talk. What appears to be an unwarranted occurrence of the southern dialect in *King Lear* presents a puzzle worth unravelling.

Many critics of *King Lear* have suggested that Edgar's lapse into dialect is one of several examples of the play's preoccupation with the inadequacy of language.[50] According to this view, the play rejects the "glib and oily art" of courtly language in favor of a plain style more commensurate with feeling. Cordelia's refusal to adopt the insincere rhetoric of her sisters, Kent's brusqueness, and Lear's mad "language of the heart"[51] are, like Edgar's dialect, "unaccommodated" languages that aim towards authenticity. The sense that language is inadequate in the face of powerful experiences seems to culminate in Edgar's sorrowful injunction at the end of the play: "The weight of this sad time we must obey;/Speak what we feel, not what we ought to say" (5.3.324–5).

Many of Shakespeare's characters, in fact, have been said to confront the problem of a language which bears only an arbitrary relation to meaning,[52] to discover with Hamlet that "words, words, words" may be repeated endlessly without revealing one's intentions or compelling action. Margreta de Grazia, however, has argued persuasively that the "inadequacy of language" was an idea whose time had not yet come, that Shakespeare, along with his contemporaries, believed that any fault in language lay in speakers, not in the medium itself. "Words, words, words," de Grazia shows, are only ineffectual only for those who, like Hamlet, are unable to make adequate use of them.[53] De Grazia emphasizes the psychological and spiritual disposition of Shakespeare's speakers as the ultimate source of the efficacy of language. Hamlet's personal tragedy, in other words, cannot be passed off onto the tragedy of language as a whole.

I would take de Grazia's argument one step further in the case of *King Lear*, where so many characters deliberately and willfully choose their words, and discriminate among alternative varieties of speech. In *King Lear*, many speakers seem to exercise what Bakhtin calls a "literary linguistic consciousness":

> The actively literary linguistic consciousness at all times and everywhere
> . . . comes upon "languages" and not language. Consciousness finds itself
> inevitably facing the necessity of having to choose a language.
>
> (*Dialogic Imagination*, p. 295)

From the opening scene of the play, "choosing a language" is foregrounded, and every scene that follows traces the consequences of such an act.

The famous "love-test" that initiates the tragedy has generally been held to set up an opposition, productive throughout the play, between "true" and "false" language; the contrast between Cordelia's simplicity and the ostentatious praise that her sisters bestow on their father has prompted a typical approach to the play: "In *King Lear*, of course, the paramount linguistic idea is the difference between flattery and plain truth."[54] But this distinction is not as clear as it may seem. Goneril, the first to answer her father's challenge, claims that she loves Lear "more than [words] can wield the matter," but she manages to find a language designed to press her advantage over her sisters: "[I love you] dearer than eyesight, space, and liberty,/Beyond what can be valued, rich or rare,/No less than life" (1.1.56–8). Cordelia, no less than her sisters, faces the necessity of choosing a language, and asks herself, aside, "What shall Cordelia speak?" Her decision immediately follows: "Love, and be silent" (1.1.62). After Regan's speech, Cordelia reaffirms her commitment to verbal restraint: "I am sure my love's/ More ponderous than my tongue" (1.1.77–8). When Lear finally turns to his youngest daughter, asking, "What can you say to draw/A third more opulent than your sisters'?" Cordelia speaks these thoughts aloud: "I cannot heave/My heart into my mouth. I love your Majesty/According to my bond, no more nor less" (1.1.85–6; 1.1.91–3). Cordelia, by her own account, deliberately refuses to "heave her heart" in language; she claims to love her father "according to her bond, no more nor less," but she implies that her heart bears more than the legalistic term "bond" might suggest. Cordelia's speech is not ostentatious as her sisters' is, but that does not necessarily make it more truthful. Indeed, Cordelia tells her father, directly, that she is determined not to "speak her heart" at all.

It is critical to note that Kent, whom critics have cited as one of the play's pre-eminent "plain" speakers, admits that he has "borrow[ed] accents" and "defused" his speech as part of a purposeful disguise (1.4.1–2). Like Edgar later in the play, Kent deliberately cultivates plainness to certain effects. Even Cornwall recognizes this, describing Kent as

> some fellow,
> Who, having been prais'd for bluntness, doth affect
> A saucy roughness, and constrains the garb
> Quite from his nature. He cannot flatter, he,
> An honest mind and plain, he must speak truth!
> . . .
> These kind of knaves I know, which in this plainness
> Harbour more craft and more corrupter ends
> Than twenty silly-ducking observants
> That stretch their duties nicely.
> (2.2.95–9; 2.2.101–4)

If Cornwall misjudges Kent's motives, he is not wrong in his assessment of Kent's speech as a "garb." Kent, in fact, answers Cornwall's attack by mimicking the high style:

> Sir, in good faith, in sincere verity,
> Under th' allowance of your great aspect,
> Whose influence, like the wreath of radiant fire
> On [flick'ring] Phoebus' front . . .
> (2.2.105–8)

When Cornwall demands to know the meaning of this sudden shift in style, Kent replies, "To go out of my dialect, which you discommend so much" (2.2.109–10). Kent may identify "plainness" as his native dialect, but he proves that he is capable of adopting other "dialects" at will.[55] Both Kent and Cordelia choose a version of the plain style, but it is no less of a style for that. The problem of linguistic authenticity in *King Lear* is a red herring: from the very start of the play, versions of English – however elaborate or "plain" – are consciously selected to suit individual purposes. There are no "unaccommodated" languages in the world of the play, rather, all forms of speech are accommodations to specific social and political circumstances.

This account of the opening scene may seem to beg the question of why Cordelia chooses the particular language she does, if not to prove herself more sincere than her sisters. It is important to note that Lear's "love-test" is not primarily designed to discover, or even confirm his daughters' love. We know that Lear had already acted upon his knowledge of Cordelia's affection and granted her, in advance of the "test," the greater share of the kingdom. Her feelings were never in question; what mattered, instead, was the display of those feelings in words. Lear's "love-test" is more precisely a test of language, as he makes clear to his recalcitrant daughter: "Mend your speech . . . /Lest you may mar your fortunes" (1.1.94–5). As we learn a little later, Lear had reason to assume he still held the power to enforce the words of his subjects, who had previously "flatter'd me like a dog. . . . To say 'ay' and 'no' to every thing I said!" (4.6.96–9).

Cordelia's response, in turn, does not challenge the adequacy of words to represent her feelings so much as her father's right to command those words at all. Her stubborn refusal to comply with Lear's injunction, "Mend your speech," is not an expression of truth or honesty; she will not say what she truly feels. "Choosing a language," the opening scene of the play reveals, is a political act, for Cordelia's choice is conflated, dramatically, with the dissolution of the state which follows. Cordelia's revolt – that is, after all, how Lear sees it – is the first step towards the dismantling of Lear's monarchy, and the centralization of political power that he represents in the play. From this scene forwards, the England of King Lear will see a kind of "regionalization," a breakdown of centralized rule – including the rule of language.

King Lear has sometimes been read as a kind of antitype to James I, who pressed for the unification of England and Scotland despite the resistance of the Commons.[56] According to this view, James united, but Lear divided, occasioning his kingdom's fall to ruin. Whether or not Shakespeare had the union with Scotland in mind, the revolution that shakes Lear's kingdom is one that explicitly sets regional powers against the crown. Regan and Goneril have married members of a provincial aristocracy whose names refer to the geographical extremities of the nation. Albany, according to Holinshed, was originally the name of the northern part of the realm, including Scotland, and Cornwall represents the southernmost portion of the kingdom.[57] For Lear's Fool, at least, his tragedy is the direct result of an injudicious decentralization of authority: "Thou hast par'd thy wit o' both sides, and left nothing i' th' middle" (1.4.187–8). Lear's fall, however, does not come about because he divides his power, but because he abuses it; there is every reason to assume that, had there been no "love-test," Cordelia would have received the greater portion of the kingdom and preserved the nation.

Shakespeare's regionalism is not about advancing the claims of the regional powers as against a strong, central monarchy, but rather limiting the kinds of authority that monarchy legitimately may wield.

The relationship between political dissolution and linguistic dissolution in the play is further reinforced by the tragicomical scenes that occur beyond the bounds of the various courts, where the mad Lear, the Fool, and poor Tom O'Bedlam wander the hostile countryside. These characters speak in idiolects, distinct, mutually unintelligible languages. As de Grazia describes it:

> The Fool riddles and equivocates, largely about the storm's afflictions; Poor Tom wildly rants about sin and hysterically confesses to myriad vices; Lear's sporadic snatches and rambling disquisitions revolve loosely around themes of revenge and justice. . . . The confusion extends beyond the confines of the play; to a great extent, we are unable to understand these three speakers.[58]

The heath is Shakespeare's recreation of the biblical Tower of Babel, the original story of political disintegration and linguistic anarchy.[59] The apocalyptic landscape of the heath represents the fall of unified rule and with it, the fall of ruled language. Lear imagines the end of the world in his broken phrases: "There's hell, there's darkness/This is the sulphurous pit, burning, scalding/ Stench, consumption. Fie, fie, fie! pah, pah!" (4.6.127–9).

While one may attribute Lear's ravings on the heath to psychological causes – to madness, conceived as an entirely subjective experience – it is important to note that Lear's idiolect also participates in the politics of language of the play as a whole. His speeches do not only reflect a broken mind, but a man cut off from his family and his people; it is a language conditioned by social extremity:

> In such a night
> To shut me out? Pour on, I will endure.
> In such a night as this? O Regan, Goneril!
> Your kind old father, whose frank heart gave all –
> O, that way madness lies, let me shun that!
> . . .
> Poor naked wretches, wheresoe'er you are,
> That bide the pelting of this pitiless storm,
> How shall your houseless heads and unfed sides,
> Your loop'd and window'd raggedness, defend you
> From seasons such as these? O, I have ta'en
> Too little care of this!
>
> (3.4.17–21; 3.4.28–33)

As many have noted, Lear's experience leads him to feel compassion for others who are homeless and oppressed; indeed, he seems to develop a remarkably democratic sensibility on the heath. Both Lear and the Duke of Gloucester, the mighty who have fallen so low, rhapsodize on the inequalities of the social and political system. Lear demystifies political power:[60] "A dog's obey'd in office" (4.6.158–9). Gloucester seems to call for the radical redistribution of wealth and power: "Let the superfluous and lust-dieted man,/That slaves your ordinance, that will not see/Because he does not feel, feel your pow'r quickly;/So distribution should undo excess,/And each man have enough" (4.1.67–71).[61] Lear identifies himself, and his condition, with that of all "unaccommodated" men: "I am mightily abus'd; I should e'en die with pity/To see another thus" (4.7.52–3).

Yet for all this, *King Lear* is a play that concerns itself exclusively with the affairs of the aristocracy; with the possible exception of the Fool, who is part of the royal retinue, common "people," on whom Lear and Gloucester bestow so much good feeling, find no representatives in the play. Even the subplot of the play, concerning Gloucester and his sons, revolves around the local aristocracy, and their preoccupation, so manifest in contemporary chorographies, with the succession of property. The characters dispossessed of power in the play, collectively, assume the status of an underclass, but the "real" underclass remains behind the scenes. Dispossession, in other words, is an upper-class plight in *Lear*: The loss of status, property, and "place" defines the extraordinary fate of the aristocrat in exile, rather than the ordinary condition of commoners. What, then, is the relationship between "unaccommodated man" and the class referred to collectively in the interlude *Respublica* as "People"?

Although they never appear on stage, "People" sometimes appear to be moving events in the play from behind the scenes. Albany, on the eve of the French invasion, claims that "The King is come to his daughter,/With others whom the rigor of our state/Forc'd to cry out" (5.1.21–3). Albany continues, "It touches us as France invades our land,/Not bolds the King, with others, whom, I fear,/Most just and heavy causes make oppose" (5.1.25–7). These "others" never cry out against the abuses of the present rule loud enough for us to hear, yet they appear to pose a serious threat to the new regime. Edmund leads Albany to believe that he has imprisoned Lear, "Whose age had charms in it, whose title more,/To pluck the common bosom on his side,/And turn our impress'd lances in our eyes/Which do command them" (5.3.48–51). The "common bosom," Edmund warns, is in danger of turning in violence against the new rule, but once again, this occurs on a level of action suppressed in the play. Goneril urges her husband and their cohorts to "Combine together 'gainst the enemy;/For these domestic and particular broils/Are not the question here" (5.1.29–31). Although it is forgotten in the diversion of a foreign war, a popular uprising seems to be brewing in the corrupt reign of Cordelia's sisters.

Yet it is important to note that every mention of popular unrest is made by aristocrats, that "People" are always re-presented by the upper class. In Act 4, scene 4, the common people find a new representative in Edgar when, for a brief time, he adopts the peasant dialect of the southern shires. Edgar, destined to be Lear's heir, shares the King's fate: Edgar, too, is dispossessed of title and land; he, too, seeks refuge in the wilderness. And Edgar, like Lear, speaks a language of exile, a dialect that marks his estrangement from a former life at court. N.F.

Blake, noting that Shakespeare's lower-class characters do not typically use dialect, and that "Katherine [in *Henry V*] who mangles her English is a princess,"[62] concludes that Shakespeare used dialect in service of characterization only. Yet Edgar's dialect – no less than Lear's – is one determined by his relation to others, by his social and political status. Lear may no longer be able to choose his words, but Edgar can, and (for the space of ten lines, at least), he chooses the language of the people.

After saving his father from himself at Dover, Edgar is confronted by Oswald, who has come to murder Gloucester at Regan's command. Edgar advances into a remote region of language:

> Chill not let go, zir, without vurther cagion. . . . Good gentleman, go your gait, and let poor voke pass. And 'chud ha' bin zwagger'd out of my life, 'twould not ha' bin zo long as 'tis by a vortnight. Nay, come not near th'old man; keep out, che vor' ye, or Ice try whither your costard or my ballow be the harder. Chill be plain with you. . . . Chill pick your teeth, zir. Come, no matter vor your foins.
>
> (4.6.235; 4.6.237–42; 4.6.244–5)[63]

There is no apparent reason why Edgar should choose to shift from Tom O' Bedlam's language of madness to provincial language in this encounter, why the people's dialect should serve as a prologue to his murder of Oswald. But it is important to observe that the confrontation between Edgar and Oswald re-enacts an earlier scene, in Act 3, in which a servant tries to stop Cornwall from blinding Gloucester. Where the servant fails (Regan stabs him in the back), Edgar succeeds: He may play the part of a commoner, but he is truly the match for a courtier. Like Cordelia's language in the first scene of the play, Edgar's dialect is represented as "plain" speech ("Chill be plain with you"), and once again, "plainness" represents an expression of protest, not of sincerity. He "talks back," and he kills – fulfilling, indirectly, the promise of popular revolt held out in the latter part of the play.[64]

Edgar's dialect may be representative of popular resistance, but, crucially, it is not the genuine article. Gloucester, who earlier remarked upon Edgar's shift from the language of Poor Tom to the language of a gentleman ("Methinks thy voice is alter'd, and thou speak'st/In better phrase and manner than thou didst" (4.6.7–8)), does not acknowledge Edgar's rustic speech. The aristocratic leaders of the state, despite their new-found sympathies with the poor, cannot, it seems, fully recognize their voice. In the political logic of the play, however, Edgar, in effect, *is* "People"; *he* is the "unaccommodated man" who has been dispossessed of status, and who will benefit from the "new" social order. Edgar's (temporary) social descent makes it possible for the play to make good on the promise of political reform, and without posing any threat to the old system of aristocratic privilege.

Like the theme of social criticism, the southern dialect surfaces only to be submerged again, disappearing, in this case, from Shakespeare's canon altogether.

It was clearly not a language, or a cause, Shakespeare wished to champion in any systematic way. Thus, Gloucester's revelation of social inequity is never fully incorporated into the ideology of the drama. Edgar reports at the end of the play that Kent "having seen me in my worst estate,/Shunn'd my abhorr'd society" (5.3.210–11) and only embraced him when Edgar revealed his true, noble identity. Yet as many commentators have noted, the succession of Edgar to the throne of England seems strangely anticlimactic; after Lear, Cordelia, Albany, and even Kent are no longer available to rule the nation, it is as if he gains the crown by default. And Edgar, to be sure, lacks Lear's commanding presence, and with it, some of his authority. Edgar restores the center to a world torn by regional conflicts, but the abdication of a succession of potential rulers – Lear, Albany, and finally Kent – somehow qualifies the impact of the restoration.

The center, it seems, will never again hold the kind of absolute authority represented by Lear. If Lear characteristically speaks in imperatives, even on the heath,[65] then Edgar establishes a new relationship between the king and the language of his subjects. When Edgar enjoins the survivors of the tragedy to "Speak what we feel, not what we ought to say" (5.3.325), he asks only that his subjects' words obey the "weight of this sad time" (5.3.324), not his own linguistic strictures. In his first act as monarch, Edgar is not only levying sincerity or decorum, but the kind of linguistic discretion Cordelia was denied. Edgar's refusal to enforce "what we ought to say" may be, indeed, the only genuine political reform that survives the play.

King Lear, then, is not about the inadequacy of language; on the contrary, it is a testimony to the power of language, in all its many forms.[66] Goneril's rhetorical flourishes gained her a kingdom, or almost did; Cordelia's reticence brought one to ruin. Even the meanest dialect, Shakespeare shows, can inspire violent action: it is all a question of making an effective choice. And it is precisely that ability to choose – as Edgar would have it – that Shakespeare upholds in this play. Shakespeare does not condone regional insurrection; the treachery of the provincial powers in *Lear* remains undisputed. Edgar's tenure as a peasant is surely not intended to incite popular revolt. The regionalism – or more precisely, the anticentrism – of *King Lear* rests, at least in part, in its view of language, and its insistence that even a King should not have the power to prescribe another's words. In *Lear*, Shakespeare invoked contemporary discourses of regionalism, and popular protest, just as he borrowed the forms of southern English, but he emptied them of much of their social content and applied them to the needs of an elite. If the play ultimately reneges on its promise to champion the cause of social and political change, however, it never fails the cause of linguistic freedom.[67] And for a poet and playwright, that was surely a battle worth fighting to the end.

* * *

Shakespeare took southern English seriously enough to apply its forms to tragedy, but Ben Jonson returned the dialect to the province of comedy and farce. Jonson selected the "people's" dialect as the primary language for his last completed play, *A Tale of a Tub* (performed 1633, published 1640). *A Tale of a Tub* is one of the earliest examples of dialect literature in English, one of a handful of works of the period in which provincial English is systematically employed throughout.[68] The phrase "a tale of a tub" was proverbial in Jonson's day for a silly, nonsensical story.[69] Like *Nashes Lenten Stuffe*, or one of his own games of vapours, Jonson's play intentionally sets forth the impression of dealing in trifles. In the Prologue, Jonson insists that the play is devoid of political content:

> No State-affaires, nor any politique Club,
> Pretend wee in our Tale, here, of a Tub.
> But acts of Clownes and Constables, to day
> Stuffe out the scenes of our ridiculous Play.
> . . .
> Wee bring you now, to shew what different things,
> The Cotes of Clownes, are from the Courts of Kings.[70]

Jonson equates the absence of "State-affaires" or court politics in his play with insignificance; a work that eschews the court is by definition a "ridiculous" one. But rather than foregoing politics entirely, Jonson's play distances itself from London as part of a real, if comical, protest to audiences who, by his account, have failed to hear him. Like Nashe in *Lenten Stuffe*, Jonson creates a regional world that is "ridiculous" by court standards, yet finds there grounds for dramatizing some of his rivalries back home.

The main plot of *A Tale of a Tub* concerns the blundering attempts of a succession of suitors for the hand of Awdrey Turfe, daughter of the local constable. In an effort to break Awdrey's engagement to John Clay the tile-maker, Squire Tub, a member of the local gentry, has Clay accused of theft. While Constable Turfe raises the hue and cry for his would-be son-in-law's arrest, another suitor, Justice Preamble, finds a pretext to have Squire Tub detained. In these and further intrigues, Awdrey Turfe is led off by four potential husbands, any one of whom would have contented her, although she resists Tub's advances ("Hee's too fine for me; and has a Lady/Tub to his Mother" (2.3.69–70)). In all the confusion, Pol-marten, Lady Tub's usher, woos Awdrey and marries her before the others realize what has happened. The play ends with a wedding masque, also entitled "A Tale of a Tub," an abbreviated version of the larger play that rehearses the twists and turns of the first.

Though Jonson sets the play in Middlesex, the "Clownes and Constables" speak a version of literary southern English. Constable Turfe, for example, answers the accusations against Clay in this way:

> I doe convesse, 'twas told me such a velonie:
> . . .
> Now I (the halter stick me, if I tell,

You worships any leazins) did fore-thinke 'un
The truest man, till he waz run away.
I thought, I had had 'un as zure as in a zaw-pit,
Or i' mine Oven.

. . .

But now, I zee 'un guilty,
Az var as I can looke at 'un. Would you ha' more?
(4.1.32; 4.1.37–41; 4.1.43–4)

The dialect of the play relies heavily on the voicing of *f* and *s*, ellisions like *'un* for him and *ha'* for have, and occasional lexical items like the dialectal *leasins* (lies). Turfe and his countrymen are also prone to mistaking "hard words," and their speeches are full of malapropisms: "Sir, we that are Officers/ Must 'quire the speciall markes, and all the tokens/Of the despected parties" (2.2.115–17). "Yes, I doe know, I vurst mun vee a Returney,/And then make legges to my great man o'Law" (4.1.58–9). The sense that the residents of Finsbury-hundred speak nothing but "nonsense" is reinforced by Squire Tub, who uses a word with no apparent meaning for no apparent reason:

Tub: Hee will ha' the last word, thought he talke Bilke for't.
Hugh: Bilke? what's that?
Tub: Why nothing, a word signifying
    Nothing; and borrow'd here to expresse nothing.[71]

(1.1.60–2)

Tub may not speak in the local dialect, yet his words confirm that the natives of this region, regardless of class, have little of substance to say.

Yet Jonson's provincials are not exactly "unlettered" – at least, not in the sense that Scoggin's scholar is. Jonson's Middlesex is a region in which "ignorance" is elevated to a science. A great deal of the dialogue of *A Tale of a Tub* is taken up with debates about language, and the locals' arguments over the proper form and meaning of words. The fact that the amorous events of the play occur on Saint Valentine's day gives them opportunity to debate the meaning of the word "saint" – or rather, their own peculiar dialectal variants of it. Clench, a petty-constable, thinks in terms of infractions of laws: "*Zin Valentine* /Hee was a deadly *Zin*" (1.2.7–8). Scriben, the local scholar, disagrees: "Did he not write his name, *Sim Valentine*? /Vor I have met no *Sin* in Finsbury bookes" (1.2.13–14). Turfe, caught up in expectation of a new son-in-law, is certain that "*Zonne Valentine*" is the proper expression (1.3.60). When Scriben recalls Turfe's interpretation to the others ("There's another reading now:/My Mr. reads it *Sonne*, and not *Sinne Valentine*"), another concurs: "Nor Zim: And hee is i' the right: He is high Constable/And who should read above un, or avore 'hun?" (1.4.44–7). The source of all the confusion, of course, is their ignorance of "common" pronunciation; not one of these locals recognizes the word as "saint." Jonson's dialect speakers, instead, imbue words with meanings that have relevance to their own situations, translating them to their private domains, although they occasionally defer to the malapropisms of their betters.

The dialect of Jonson's play is thus presented as felicitous error, a creative "mistaking" of words that affords a kind of social empowerment. The locals, for example, repeatedly exploit their fanciful etymologies to assert claims to status. Turfe refers to John Clay as a clown, and when asked why, he explains that Clay is "a *Midlesex* Clowne; and one of *Finsbury*: They were the first Colons o' the kingdome here" (1.3.34–5). Scriben confirms Turfe's derivation of the word "clowne" from the Latin "colonus": "Sir, *Colonus* is an Inhabitant:/A Clowne originall: as you'ld zay a Farmer/A Tiller o' th'Earth./Ere sin' the *Romans* planted their Colonie first,/Which was in *Midlesex*" (1.3.40–3). In the same spirit, Clay is hailed as "Originous Clay" (1.1.4). Jonson, like Nashe, parodies contemporary chorographies which, in addition to providing local genealogies that traced the ownership of property manor by manor,[72] offered linguistic "genealogies" of the place names of the region, making language witness to the property claims of provincial landholders. Jonson's locals similarly engage in an ongoing discussion of the word "constable," and the proper role of the constable in the political life of the county. Medlay, the headborough of the tithing, boasts that he can gage the physical measurements of all officials on the political hierarchy of the state:

> A Knight is sixe diameters; and a Squire
> Is vive, and zomewhat more: I know't by compasse,
> And skale of man. I have upo' my rule here,
> The just perportions of a Knight, a Squire;
> With a tame Justice, or an Officer, rampant,
> Upo' the bench, from the high Constable
> Downe to the Head-borough, or Tithing-man.
>
> (4.1.43–9)

Although Medlay literalizes the "diminutive" status of the constable and other local officials, etymology is once again invoked to enhance the constable's political importance. As Scriben explains, "Two words,/ *Cyning* and *Staple*, make a Constable:/As wee'd say, A hold, or stay for the King" (4.1.54–6). The word "constable," in Scriben's derivation, contains the word "cyning" (king); the two, his linguistic genealogy bears out, share common grounds for authority. Scriben informs the others that in Roman times, "Dictator, and high Constable/Were both the same" (3.6.20–1), listing Pompey, Caesar, and Trajan among Turfe's noble ancestors. Turfe sighs over the weight of his office: "High Constable! The higher charge/It brings more trouble, more vexation with it" (3.1.7–8). By fixing the history of words, Jonson's "Clownes and Constables" elevate their status to colonizers and kings.

The winner of the local competition for "Turfe," Pol-marten, was in fact born Martin Polcat, and remained so until Lady Tub took it upon herself to christen him anew:

When I heard his name first, Martin Polcat,
A stinking name, and not to be pronounc'd
Without a reverence, in any Ladies presence;
My very heart eene earn'd, seeing the Fellow
Young, pretty, and handsome,

. . .

           [I] made it my suit
To Mr. Peeter Tub, that I might change it;
And call him as I doe now, by Pol-marten,
To have it sound like a Gentleman in an Office.
           (1.6.23–7; 1.6.29–32)

The translation is complete, for Pol-marten's status as a gentlemen is granted by all the others, including the mother of the bride, who rejoices in her new son-in-law: "Nay, an' he be a Gentleman, let her shift" (5.4.20). Justice Preamble, on the other hand, is renamed "Bramble" by the provincial population; by means of this translation he, too, belongs to the soil or local "turf." In the provinces, all discourses associated with education (like "preambles") are summarily dismissed. Law, along with poetry, is scorned as "vlat cheating" (1.2.43), and Turfe mocks what little knowledge the "great Writer" Scriben possesses of his craft:

Hee'll vace mee down, mee my selfe sometimes,
That verse goes upon veete, as you and I doe:
But I can gi' 'un the hearing; zit me downe;
And laugh at 'un; and to my selfe conclude,
The greatest Clarkes, are not the wisest men
Ever.

           (1.3.10–15)

The rhetorical figure "metaphor" is reduced to the name of a character who serves as clerk for Justice Preamble; on one of his miscarried errands he is seized and, in his words, "beaten, to an Allegory." (3.7. 40). Rhetorical language, in turn, has no place in the provinces. Tub courts Awdrey in language that only confuses her:

Tub: Hath the proud Tiran, Frost, usurp'd the seate
       Of former beauty in my Loves faire cheek;
       Straining the rosest tincture of her blood,
       With the dull die of blew-congealing cold?
    . . .

Awdrey: I ha' seen much o' your words, but not o' your deeds.
           (2.4.52–5; 2.4.68)

Metaphore – himself – makes no sense to her:

Met.: Let not the mouse of my good meaning, Lady,
      Be snap'd up in the trap of your suspition,

> To loose the taile there, either of her truth,
> Or swallow'd by the Cat of misconstruction.
> *Awdrey*: You are too finicall for me; speake plaine Sir.
>
> (4.4.25–9)

In Jonson's dialect comedy, the matter of courtly power and of eloquence must be fully translated, and rendered in regional terms.

What does matter in Middlesex, we might say, is "turf" – of one kind or another.[73] Awdrey Turfe is the unlikely object of the desires of most of the male characters of the play, from Squire Tub to Puppy, the High Constable's man. Tub admits that Awdrey Turfe is hardly worth the trouble:

> Troth I could wish my wench a better wit;
> . . .
> Faine would I worke my selfe, from this conceit;
> But being flesh, I cannot. I must love her,
> The naked truth is: and I will goe on,
> Were it for nothing, but to crosse my Rivall's.
>
> (2.4.86; 2.4.92–5)

This "Turfe" has no intrinsic value; like a game of vapours, the contest for Awdrey is about competition for its own sake. But Jonson, perhaps, has at least a small stake in the regional rivalries he portrays in this play.

Like Nashe in Yarmouth, Jonson does not dismiss the value of his regional "turf" altogether. At the end of the play, Squire Tub decides he wants a masque produced to celebrate Awdrey's marriage: "I'ld have a toy presented,/ *A Tale of a Tub*, a storie of myself, / . . . / . . . to shew my adventures/This very day" (5.2.43–4; 5.2.50–1). Tub thinks of commissioning Scriben, but the writer explains that the "artificer," In-and-In Medlay, refuses to collaborate:

> Hee'll do't alone Sir, He will joyne with no man,
> Though he be a Joyner: in designe he cals it,
> He must be sole Inventer: *In-and-In*
> Drawes with no other in's project, hee'll tell you,
> It cannot else be feazeable, or conduce:
> Those are his ruling words.
>
> (5.2.35–40)

Yet despite a rather elaborate set with a tub at its center, In-and In's version of "*A Tale of a Tub*" is no match for the larger play that contains it; it has aptly been called "an incompetent rendering by an incompetent artist."[74] Medlay's incompetence, no doubt, is a stroke in Jonson's parodic portrait of Inigo Jones, Jonson's sometime collaborator, and a strike against him in their notorious debate over the rival claims of poetry and the visual arts. Jonson's epilogue, spoken by the Squire, thus returns the play to the domain of the poet: "This Tale of mee, the *Tub* of *Totten-Court*/A Poet, first invented for your sport" (1–2). Jonson added the final masque, he explains

That you be pleas'd, who come to see a Play,
With those that heare, and marke not what wee say.
Wherein the *Poets* fortune is, I feare,
Still to be early up, but nere the neare.

(13–16)

Jonson's epilogue claims indifference to his audience's preference to bad spectacle over good poetry, but it is an act he does not make especially convincing. Like Nashe, Jonson directs some of his parody outward, here, to those who would damn or slight his more substantial literary efforts. In *A Tale of a Tub*, Jonson circumscribes his writing within the bounds of a regional space and a regional language, as if to underscore the insignificance of his art, to dismiss the importance of his own play, as set by court standards. Yet even in the provinces, Jonson grants language the power to confer authority and to create social status. Jonson's use of the southern dialect in this play has nothing at all to do with a defense of popular interests, as it had in the interlude *Respublica*, and, *pro forma*, in *King Lear*. *A Tale of a Tub*, as advertised by Jonson's prologue, does not concern itself with court politics, and even less with social unrest. Rather, finding himself, with "People," "nere the neare" to getting the hearing he believes he deserves, the playwright revels in the regions, and makes a provincial "turf" his own. In *A Tale of a Tub*, Jonson manages to make dialect an advantage, and to get provincials to speak, albeit in broken forms, for the power and prestige of words.

The contingencies of Renaissance literary politics may have ensured the centrist loyalties of Renaissance authors, and their dependence on the aristocracy, if nothing else, biased their works against the interests of commoners. But the new, literary interest in southern English, the *vox populi* of early modern literary dialects, sometimes speaks to the alienation of Renaissance English authors from the audiences – often, aristocratic audiences – that they, inevitably, served. The Renaissance appropriation of popular language, however, has nothing, finally, to do with "people" at all; like Edgar, these authors borrow accents, briefly, to serve their turn. Because Renaissance authors had a stake in the license to voice opposition or resistance, they continually found themselves in company with people for whom, otherwise, they had little to say.

4

REGIONS OF RENAISSANCE ENGLISH II
The North Country

Of all writers, only poets are permitted to use dialects, yet they abstain from using them . . . unless they use the Northern dialect, quite frequently for the purpose of rhythm or attractiveness, since that dialect is the most delightful, the most ancient, the purest, and approximates most nearly to the speech of our ancestors.

Alexander Gill, *Logonomia Anglica*[1]

Despite the recommendations of Richard Carew, who spoke for the literary qualities of the dialect of Cornwall, Renaissance authors reproduce southern English as a stage dialect or, in narrative literature, as a transcript of popular speech. Northern English was often assigned to provincial speakers as well, but not exclusively: For some sixteenth- and early seventeenth-century writers, northern dialect words were "passable" within the bounds of poetic diction more generally. With Gill, several Renaissance linguists concurred that the language of the northern shires represented an older, "purer" English, uncontaminated by foreign influence; northern words were thus identified with old words, or archaisms,[2] and an early modern project of cultural restoration through language. But the literary use of northern words and archaisms remained controversial throughout the period, for both remained, for many contemporaries, dialects of English that had no place in a "common" national culture. Numerous studies have been devoted to Renaissance archaism, especially in Spenser's poetry, but its place among other early modern varieties of English has not been fully explored. A traditional language, yet one invoked by writers for its novelty, a "pure" English that was foreign to native readers, archaism highlights the complexities of the Renaissance "question of the language" – especially, the question of which version of the vernacular was truly "English."

From the early part of the sixteenth century, old words, culled from Chaucer and other Middle English authors, were set forward as a native alternative to inkhorn and foreign words as resources for enriching the language. T. Berthelette hoped that his edition of Gower's *Confessio Amantis* (1532) would revive and advance

the plenty of englysshe wordes and vulgars, besyde the furtheraunce of the lyfe to vertue, whiche olde englysshe wordes and vulgars no wyse man, bycause of theyr antiquite, wyll throwe asyde. For the wryters of later dayes, the which beganne to loth and hate these olde vulgars, when they them selfe wolde wryte in our englysshe tonge, wcre constrayned to brynge in their writynges, new termes (as some calle them) whiche they borowed out of latyne, frenche, and other langages, whiche caused that they that understode not those langages, from whens these newe vulgars are fette, coude not percyeve theyr wrytynges.[3]

The older language was acclaimed, by some, as "unmixt and unmangeled" in comparison with the "Babelish confusion" of modern English.[4] By the beginning of the following century, English antiquarians had begun to investigate the Anglo-Saxon roots of the vernacular, and "English Saxon" came to be associated with the idea of an authentic national culture.[5] Early seventeenth-century writers cite the difference of "nature" that distinguishes Saxon and "foreign" forms. Verstegan, arguing against the use of "oversea" language, emphasizes the cultural necessity of privileging "natural" English words:

> For myne own parte I hold them deceaved that think our speech bettered by the abundance of our dayly borrowed woords, for *they beeing of another nature*, and not originally belonging to our language, do not, neither can they in our toung, beare *their natural and true deryvations*, and therefore as well may we fetch woords from the Ethiopians, or East or West Indians and thrust them into our language, and baptise all by the name of English, and those which wee dayly take from the Latin, or languages thereon depending; and heer hence it cometh . . . that some Englishmen discoursing together, others beeing present and of our nation, and that *naturally speak the English toung*, are not able to understand what the others say, notwithstanding that they call it English that they speak.[6]

Verstegan thus identifies true English with that "originally belonging to our language," as opposed to languages, of alien derivation, that bear "another nature" entirely. Gill professed a similar idea, naming inkhorn language the "illegitimate progeny" or "monstrous" birth of the mother tongue.[7]

The idea of a "natural" English was also often associated, rhetorically, with the preservation of an original – and threatened – national identity. William Camden, in his *Remaines*, especially admired the Saxons for their "steadfastness in esteeming and retaining their own tongue," noting that their conquest of England was so complete that no Celtic or Latin words were able to penetrate the language.[8] When Gill entreats his countrymen to avoid Latinisms and to "retain what hitherto remains of your native tongue," he invokes the ancient struggle over possession of the island: "Will you whose forbears despised the Roman arms make your language a Roman province?"[9] Extremists went as far as proposing that "our Language be cleared of the Normane and French invasion upon it, and deprevation of it, by purging it of all words and termes of that descent, supplying it from the old Saxon."[10] The rhetoric of conquest and inheritance (explored further in Chapter 5), of an "invasion" of foreign words on English territory, implicitly linked the revival of archaic words to the resurgence of the "true" nation.

Yet, alongside those who celebrated their nativeness, others deemed archaisms quite the contrary, too "foreign" for use in contemporary writing. The idea of a "natural" English was also exploited, after all, to promote the King's English; Puttenham, as I have noted earlier, deemed the elite dialect of London "naturall, pure, and the most usuall of all [the poet's] countrey."[11] Those who proposed limits on linguistic innovation often cited archaisms, right along with neologisms, as examples of objectionably "hard words." Caxton, as noted earlier, explained that he avoided using old words because "In my Judgement the comyn termes that be dayli used ben lyghter to be understonde than the olde and auncyent englisshe."[12] P. Ashton, in 1556, wrote of the importance of avoiding both old and new words:

> Throwghe al this simple and rude translation I studyed rather to use the most playn and famylier english speche, then either Chaucers wordes (which by reason of antiquitie be almost out of use) or els inkhorne termes (as they call them) whiche the common people, for lacke of latin, do not understand."[13]

George Gascoigne, in his *Certayne Notes of Instruction Concerning the Making of Verse* warns poets to use unfamiliar words, including archaisms, sparingly: "Asmuche as may be, eschew straunge words, or *obsoleta et inusitata*."[14] Ben Jonson prescribed limits on all words, old or new, that hampered understanding:

> Wee must not be too frequent with the mint, every day coyning. Nor fetch words from the extreme and utmost ages; since the chiefe vertue of a style is perspicuitie, and nothing so vitious in it, as to need an Interpreter.[15]

More than a century after Caxton, the lexicographer Edward Phillips, in the preface to his dictionary, *The New World of English Words* (1658), judged that "It [is] an equall vice to adhere obstinately to old words, and fondly to affect new ones."[16] Archaism, for many early modern writers, was just another example of linguistic "extremity," an unwarranted departure from the common language.

It is critical to note, however, that many who objected to archaisms allowed that poets – and poets alone – were licensed to break the general law prohibiting their use. Archaisms, after all, had in their favor a venerable literary tradition to support their use, especially in poetry, and Renaissance proponents of reviving old words often cited Quintilian, who wrote that archaisms conferred dignity and majesty upon a verse.[17] George Gascoigne made an exception for the use of "unnatural" words, including archaisms, in poetry:

> You shall do very well to use your verse after theenglishe phrase, and not after the maner of other languages. . . . Therefore even as I have advised you to place all wordes in their naturall or most common and usuall

pronunciation, so would I wishe you to frame all sentences in their mother phrase and proper Idioma, and yet sometimes (as I have sayd before) the contraries may be borne, but that is rather where rime enforceth, or *per licentiam Poeticam*, than it is otherwise lawfull or commendable.

This poeticall licence is a shrewde fellow, and covereth many faults in a verse; it maketh wordes longer, shorter, of mo sillables, of fewer, newer, older, truer, falser, and to conclude it turkeneth all things at pleasure, for example, *ydone* for *done*, *adowne* for *downe*, *orecome* for *overcome*, *tane* for *taken*, *power* for *powre*, *heaven* for *heavn*, *thewes* for *good partes* or *good qualities*, and a numbre of other whiche were but tedious and needelesse to rehearse, since your owne judgement and readying will soone make you espie such advauntages.[18]

Poets are licensed to make words "newer, older, truer, [or] falser", according to Gascoigne, although he apparently favors archaisms, noting that the use of old forms such as "*ydone* for *done*" and "*thewes* for *good partes* or *good qualities*" may sometimes prove an advantage in verse. Nashe, taking Gabriel Harvey to task for his neologistic diction, allowed that "antique" words may be suited to poetry: "I would teach thy olde Trewantship the true use of words, as also how more inclinable verse is than prose, to dance after the horizonant pipe of inveterate antiquitie.[19] While Nashe granted that some neologisms, such as his own "horizonant," and "inveterate," might be acceptable in prose writing, he relegates archaisms, specifically, to the domain of verse.[20]

Indeed, by the middle of the sixteenth century, Thomas Wyatt had initiated a fashion for archaic language in poetry, composing, perhaps, under the influence of Italian debates over the vernacular. Wyatt's archaisms may have been inspired by the recommendations of Castiglione's Federico who, following Quintilian, stated that old Tuscan words give grace and authority to writing, and that it was the duty of a gentleman to preserve the mother tongue from decay.[21] Archaism was certainly the most conspicuous feature of the language of the poems that appeared in *Tottel's Miscellany* (1557); Thomas Wilson's complaint that "the fine Courtier will talke nothyng but Chaucer" no doubt speaks to the prevalence of old words in courtly poetry of the period. Later in the century, Thomas Sackville, George Turberville, and William Warner are among those who continue to incorporate archaisms into their works.[22] As Veré Rubel has suggested, archaisms, though associated with a literary past, helped announce a new generation of Renaissance poets: Wyatt, she notes, "was able to evolve a poetic diction that was new because it was deliberately old."[23] Gill concurs that old words were valued, in part, for their novelty, "for they . . . possess the authority of antiquity and because neglected, add a charm similar to freshness."[24]

The "freshness" and unfamiliarity of archaisms was implicitly granted by poets who provided translations of old words in glosses appended to their works. Gascoigne, who confessed a poetic preference for old words over new ("I have more faulted in keeping the olde English wordes (*quamvis iam obsoleta*) than in borowing of other languages, such Epithets and Adjectives as smell of the

Inkhorne") glossed the archaisms that he used in his play *Jocasta*, explaining that "I did begin those notes at request of a gentlewoman who understode not poetically wordes or termes."[25] In 1573, Ralph Lever wrote a treatise on logic, *The Arte of Reason, Rightly Termed, Witcraft*, which put forward the case for "antique" words:

> We therfore, that devise understandable termes, compounded of true and auncient english woords, do rather maintain and continue the antiquitie of our mother tongue: then they, that with inckhorne termes doe change and corrupt the same, making a mingle mangle of their native speache, and not observing the propertie thereof.[26]

Yet despite his insistence on "understandable" native terms, Lever added a glossary to his text to translate all the "true" English words he devised.

Edmund Spenser also supplied glosses to his *Shepheardes Calender* (1579);[27] his editor, E.K., presumes that old words are "strange" and unfamiliar, and require interpretation by a specialist. E.K. called attention to his glosses as he does to Spenser's "hard words": "Hereunto have I added a certain Glosse or scholion, for thexposition of old wordes and harder phrases: which maner of glosing and commenting, well I wote, wil seeme straunge and rare in our tongue." Each of these glosses participates in the politics of early modern lexicography generally, where "understanding" must be mediated by a master of words.

The association of old words with a "natural" idiom, and with a national identity – something "common" to English culture – was only part of their appeal to poets such as Spenser. Spenser, I will suggest, was interested not only in the native quality of archaisms, but in their foreignness, not only in the antiquity of old words, but in their "freshness" as well. These contradictions are endemic to the idea of "poetic diction" itself, as it emerged in this period.

One of the "fresh" aspects of Spenser's diction in *The Shepheardes Calender* is no doubt his use of northern English, an experiment he did not choose to repeat in his later works, including *The Faerie Queene*. Northern words make up only a part, and a relatively minor part, of Spenser's composite diction, which includes numerous archaisms and a smaller number of foreign borrowings and invented words. The significance of Spenser's use of northern English lies not only in its relation to his use of archaisms, although that identification, as I will demonstrate in the section that follows, is an important one. The presence of northern English in *The Shepheardes Calender* calls attention, more generally, to the way that the poet selected among the contemporary variety of "Englishes" – the dialects of English – in his construction of a poetic language. The language of *The Shepheardes Calender*, as a whole, is predicated on the idea of dialect, of contested boundaries within the national language.

* * *

Renaissance representations of northern English are generally more elaborate than those of southern English, and invoke a greater variety of linguistic markers.

Some of the more typical features of literary northern include the use of *a* for *o* in words like *ane* (one), *bath* (both), and *fra* (from). This is especially common before the cluster *ng*, as in *wrang, amang,* and *lang*. The sound represented orthographically by *ae* or *ea* often replaces the standard *o*, as in *frae* (from), *wae* (woe), and *heame* (home). Before *n*, however, *o* usually appears instead of *a* (*ony, mony*). The vowel represented by double *o* in good or book occurs as *u* (*gude, buke*). With consonants, typical phonological markers include the metathesis of *r* in words like *brast* (burst) and *brunt* (burned), the velarization of *ch* in *sic* (such), *whilke* (which), *kirk* (church), and *carl* (churl), the vocalization of *l* to *u* in *fause* (false) and *caud* (cold), and the loss of final consonants, as in *sel* (self). Common morphological cues include the first- and second-person singular forms of the verb *to be*, in *I is* (or *I'se*) and *thou is* (or *thou's*). Finally, the literary northern lexicon includes words such as *barn* (child), *bonny, deft* (neat, trim), *derne* (dismal), *dight* (to prepare, arrange), *gang* (to go), *gar* (to make, cause), *gif* (if), *mickle* (much), *mun* (must), and *til* (to). The following passage from William Warner's *Albion's England* (first part, 1586) illustrates some of these features:

> Robinhood, liell [little] John, frier Tucke, and Marian deftlie play,
> And Lard and Ladie gang till kirke with Lads and Lasses gay.
> Fra Masse and Eensong so gud cheere and glee on erie [every] Greene,
> As, save our Wakes twixt Eames [uncles] and
> Sibbes [cousins, kinsmen], like gam was never seene.[28]

From the viewpoint of the capital and the court, northern English was in many ways indistinguishable, in social if not in formal terms, from the southern dialect. Both were provincial languages, specimens of marginal speech; the regional differences they embodied, from the standpoint of many "common" English speakers, were incidental. In the *Merie Tales of Master Skelton*, the mid-sixteenth-century jest book attributed to the poet laureate, Skelton travels to London with a foolish "Kendalman" whose language confirms his northern origins: "Ise wrang; I bus [must] goe tyll bed. . . . In gewd faith, Ise bay your skott [charge] to London."[29] Skelton tricks the Kendalman into believing he has the sweating sickness by placing a stick of butter under his hat, and magically "cures" him by drying it off. Like Shakespeare's Francis the drawer, the Kendalman owes his infirmity to a Londoner, on whom all hope of advancement to the capital depends. Richard Verstegan tells an anecdote about a London courtier who orders a northern man to "equippe" his horse. The northerner, confounded by the Londoner's pronunciation, believes that the courtier desires him to "whip" the animal.[30] Like Skelton's jest, Verstegan's comedy is heightened by the harsh tones of broken English, but one does not need to identify the dialect in question as specifically northern or southern to get the joke.

Many theoretical accounts of northern English in the period, in turn, offer the dialect as another exhibit in the case against provincial language generally. Peter Levins listed 200 northern words in his *Manipulus Vocabulorum* (1570), apparently to discourage their use, for in the preface he remarks that he included words such as *kirke, myrke* and *ken* as negative examples, so that "the rude may reforme their tong."[31] In *A Methode or Comfortable Beginning*, John Hart writes of those of

> the farre West, or North Countryes, which use differing termes from those of the Court, and London, where the flower of the English tongue is used. If some such one come to any good learning . . . and putteth some worke in print, his authoritie maketh many a rude English worde to be printed.[32]

Twenty years later George Puttenham denounced the poetic use of northernisms: "Neither shall he [the poet] take the termes of Northern-men, such as they use in dayly talke, whether they be noble men or gentlemen, or of their best clarkes all is a matter."[33] While both men acknowledged that even courtiers use dialect freely in their "dayly talke," neither would tolerate the presence of northernisms in the language of literature.

For some of Spenser's contemporaries, however, the north country was associated with a modest literary tradition of its own, and one that potentially conferred the type of authority Hart had denied to the dialects. Northern versions of certain medieval texts, like *Amis and Amiloun*, were available to poets like Spenser, and probably provided sources for his *Faerie Queene*. Some of the poets who contributed to *Tottel's Miscellany* used a few northern terms in their poems, setting a precedent, perhaps, for Spenser.[34] Nicholas Grimald's poetic idiom includes northernisms like *naamkouth* (famous), *grysely* (fearful to see), *shinand* (shining), *ugsoom* (horribly), and four northern dialect words for "man" – *freke, goom, renk*, and *seg*. George Turberville, too, is credited with an occasional northernism.[35] But these "northernisms" have no provincial flavor at all:

> By heavens hye gift, in case revived were
> Lysip, Apelles, and Homer the great:
> The most renowmd, and ech of them sance pere,
> In gravyng, painting and the Poets feat:
> Yet could they not, for all their vein divine
> . . .
> So grave, so paynt, or so by style expresse
> . . .
> As, in the famous woork, that Eneids hight,
> The *naamkouth* Virgil hath set forth in sight.[36]

There is no way to determine, moreover, whether Grimald was aware that such words had regional origins. But it seems clear, at least, that the poet had no intention of striking a rustic note.

It is more likely that Grimald and Turberville were simply confusing northern terms with archaisms, old words that had the sanction of literary history. By the middle of the sixteenth century, Renaissance language scholars had hypothesized just such a relationship between old words and local expressions. In 1565 Lawrence Nowell began to compile the first Old English dictionary, the

Vocabularium Saxiconum. Observing a resemblance between Anglo-Saxon vocabulary and terms that occurred exclusively in provincial speech, Nowell included in his dictionary 173 words from his home county, Lancashire, as well as a handful from other shires.[37] Nowell noted northern survivals of older words as follows:

> Adreogan. To endure, to suffer, to abide. Lanc. to dree.
> Aetwitan. To blame, to reproache, to laye the fawte on. Lanc. to wite.
> geDaeft. Clenlinesse. Lanc. deft.
> Derian. To hurt, to harm. Lanc. to deere.[38]

Nowell's pioneering work confirmed the idea that the rubble of northern English could be mined for fossils of the older language.

A careful philologist, Nowell made a significant contribution to English language study when he deduced that older elements of the language, long out of use in standard written English, sometimes survive in nonstandard speech. But the enthusiasm of the early Saxonists generated the notion that northern English was the oldest of the regional dialects, and therefore bore a privileged relation to the ancient language.[39] Implicitly, northern English was wed to a nationalistic bias towards Saxon and a xenophobic zeal for linguistic purity.[40]

But the union of northern English and Old English was not an entirely felicitous one. Despite recent advances in the field of linguistic history, and the new claims of northern English, traditional theories of poetic diction simply made no provision for provincial speech. Although the use of archaisms was widely known to have classical precedents, even Quintilian himself specifically denounced the use of dialect words as well as other, "foreign" forms, in poetry.[41] The Renaissance search for a purer English led theorists such as Puttenham and Gill face-to-face with the "barbarisms" of regional language.

Gill, for his part, did his best to integrate northern English into an orthodox poetics, despite his insistence that proper poetic language "will have to conform not to the pronunciation of ploughmen, working girls, and river-men, but to that used by learned and refined men." After describing the pronunciation of ploughmen, including that of northern ploughmen, he cements the alliance between poetic English and the King's English by reminding his readers:

> What I say here concerning the dialects, you must realise, refers only to country people, since among persons of genteel character and cultured upbringing, there is but one universal speech.

Poets, he continues, should therefore draw their materials from the "universal" speech of the genteel. But Gill qualifies the identification with one exception:

> Unless they [poets] use the Northern dialect, quite frequently for the purpose of rhythm or attractiveness, since that dialect is the most delightful, the most ancient, the purest, and approximates most nearly to the speech of our ancestors.

It is very likely that Gill had Spenser in mind when he made this allowance for northern English in poetry, for he cites Spenser continuously throughout this work. Gill also cites a fragment of a popular northern ballad, transcribed in his reformed spelling: "And so that we may not always quote the Sidneys and Spensers, note the epilogue of a story written in the Northern dialect entitled 'Machiavelli the Villain':

> Machil iz hanged,
> And brened iz his bvks.
> Doh Machil iz hanged,
> Yit hi iz not wranged . . ."[42]

The difficulty here is that Gill never denies that northern English, like the other regional dialects, is the language of ploughmen and working girls. At the same time, he hails the northern dialect for its poetic qualities, its "rhythms" and its "attractiveness." His apology for northern English leads him to assimilate Spenser's poetic diction, implicitly, to the language of provincial balladeers.

Puttenham, on the other hand, had managed to avoid this situation by adhering to a consistent appraisal of the English dialects. He simply refused to make an exception for the language of northerners, even "though no man can deny but that theirs is the purer English Saxon at this day," on the grounds that the northern dialect "is not so Courtly nor so currant as our Southerne English is." The relative coherence of Puttenham's views on northern English owes a great deal to the fact that he disapproved of old words as well. In addition to proscribing provincial words, he decreed that poets "shall not follow Piers Plowman nor Lydgate nor yet Chaucer, for their language is now out of use with us."[43] By avoiding the entangled relations of archaisms and northern words, Puttenham's promotion of London English as the exclusive medium of literature remained free of equivocation.

The profile of northern English that emerges from the writings of Nowell, Puttenham, and Gill is a difficult and inconsistent one, a jumble of classical doctrine, English chauvinism, and the new prescriptivism, a chief by-product of Renaissance language reform. At once the rude dialect of ploughmen and an ancestral English, the northern dialect was prosecuted as provincial and defended as the wellspring of the national language. Literary authors took up the case.

* * *

Comedy prevails in early modern literary representations of northern provincialism. Thomas Heywood and Richard Brome, in *The Late Lancashire Witches* (1634), show their contemporaries how funny it would be – and, perhaps, how dangerous – if northerners came to power. Basing their material on an actual scandal said to have occurred in contemporary Lancashire, the playwrights tell of a northern village in which the proper order of things has been rendered "topsie turvy" by a bevy of malevolent witches, disguised as ordinary housewives.[44] In this bewitched English region children command their parents and servants lord it over their masters. Two peasants named Lawrence and Parnell, the only dialect speakers of the play, usurp the role of their employers. Lawrence describes his new-found authority:

> Heres sick an a din . . . he mainteynes me to rule him, and i'le deu't, or ma' the hear weary o' the weambe on him. . . . A fine World when a man cannot be whyet at heame.

He and his fiancee, Parnell, settle their plans to marry and seize full control of the household:

> 'Tis all as true as booke, here's both our Masters have consented and concloyded, and our Mistresses mun yield toyt, to put aw house and lond and aw they have into our hands. . . . And we mun marry and be master and dame of aw.
>
> (1.1)

This preposterous state of affairs is made all the more outrageous by the rustic language of the reigning servants.

Although the witches themselves do not speak in dialect, the social promotion of dialect speakers, the authors imply, can only be the work of the devil. Fortunately, the witches' sorcery is readily contained by the application of ordinary Lancashire law: "Witches apprehended under hands of lawfull authority, doe loose their power;/And all their spells are instantly dissolv'd" (5.1). The apprehension of the witches restores Lawrence and Parnell to their working-class status, and their commitment to servitude: "Yie han pit on your working geere, to swinke and serve our Master and Maistresse like intill painfull servants agone, as we shudden" (5.1). These provincials return, at last, to the station in life to which their language properly conscribes them.

In his romance of the Renaissance cloth trade, *Thomas of Reading or the Sixe Worthie Yeomen of the West* (1612), Thomas Deloney glorifies the clothing industry and its representatives, long since associated with the northern counties of England. The opening chapter idyllically relates "How King Henry sought the favour of all his subjects, especially the clothiers" and a series of episodes describing "the sundry favours which he [King Henry] did for them [the clothiers]."[45] In Deloney's account, the clothiers periodically gather at the capital from all corners of the nation, but not primarily because they are dependent on the London market. The clothiers, at the King's request, come to court to air their grievances. A northern man called Hodgkins explains to the King that he has incurred great losses at the hands of thieves, a problem endemic to economic life at the Scottish border. When King Henry assures him that harsher measures will be taken against such villainy, Hodgkins is not satisfied. Deloney narrates:

> With that Hodgkins unmannerly interrupted the King, saying in broad Northerne speech, Yea gude faith, mai Liedge, the faule eule of mai saule,

giff any thing will keepe them whiat, till the karles be hanged by the cragge.

(p. 227)

The King greets this "unmannerly" interruption with paternal amusement, but he also redoubles his promise and decrees even stricter penalties for Hodgkins's assailants. "Broade Northerne speech" may be amusing to London ears, but the comic effect of Hodgkins's speech serves only to mitigate a serious appeal to royal power. Deloney, a silk-weaver by trade, had a great deal at stake in the idea that northern tradesmen have every right to converse with kings, even to "interrupt" their authority.

Still other works exploit contemporary dialect theory and the idea that northern English was somehow purer than other varieties of the language. Playwrights attracted to the supposed purity of the northern dialect, however, had to surmount the contradiction of a language deemed to be at once provincial and somehow superior to London English. Francis Beaumont and John Fletcher, in their play *Cupid's Revenge* (1615), pose an imaginative solution to the problem. *Cupid's Revenge* is the tragedy of Duke Leontius, who courts disaster by destroying all the images of Cupid in the dukedom. Outraged at the vandalism, Cupid plots a hideous revenge. The Duke's daughter throws herself at the feet of a misshapen dwarf, and the Duke falls in love with an evil prostitute named Baccha. When Leucippus, the Duke's son, spurns the advances of the prostitute, Baccha plots the boy's death, and prepares her daughter Urania to take Leucippus' place as heir to the dukedom. But Urania is horrified at her mother's treachery, and assures Leucippus in her northern dialect:

> I, but ne'r Sir be afred;
> For though she [Baccha] take th' ungain'st weas she can,
> I'll n'er ha't [the Dukedom] fro you.
> And though she be my Mother,
> If she take any caurse to do you wrong,
> If I can see't, youst quickly hear on't Sir.[46]

Urania disguises herself as a boy and enlists herself as Leucippus' page, in a desperate attempt to preserve his life. Her efforts are in vain: Cupid's revenge continues unabated until the Duke and his children are dead at the hands of Baccha and her bloody schemes.

Beaumont and Fletcher create a radical, if unlikely, linguistic scenario in this play. While Baccha speaks nothing but the King's English, Urania, her own child, speaks in a northern idiom, "the pretlest and innocentlest" of dialects, according to one of the play's characters (3.1.17–18). The playwrights never explain how Urania acquired her northern speech; the dukedom, we can assume, has its borders far beyond the English sea. In order to show that Baccha's sins are not visited upon her daughter, Beaumont and Fletcher strip northern English of its own lineage, and with it, the taint of provincialism; in their usage, dialect is a matter of essence, not genealogy. In this way, Beaumont and Fletcher adapt the complexities of contemporary linguistic theory to the moral exigencies of their drama.

In *The Northern Lass* (1632), Richard Brome combines Deloney's aggressive provincialism with the linguistic purism promulgated by Beaumont and Fletcher. For Brome, the regionality of northern English was as essential to his literary aims as the dialect's purity. Brome's northern lass is a peasant girl named Constance who journeys south to marry the prodigal Sir Philip Luckless, to whom she has been promised. When her prudish governess asks how often she has seen Sir Philip, Constance answers in her northern dialect: "Feath but that bare eance nother, and you seln were by too. Trow yee that Ide not tell yee an twere maer. By my Conscience Mrs. Trainewell I lee not."[47] Their engagement, Constance assures her, was consummated with a single kiss: "As I live Mrs. Trainewell, all that ere he had o'me, was but a kiss. But I mun tell yee, I wished it a thoosand, thousand till him" (2.2). The Londoners await the arrival of their northern guest and the language she will bring to them with great anticipation: "You said, she spoke and sung Northernly. I have a great many Southern Songs already; but Northern Ayres nips it dead. York, York, for my money," exclaims one of her enthusiasts (2.1). The northern dialect, it seems, has become a saleable commodity, more attractive, and more highly valued, than London speech.

Where *The Late Lancashire Witches* relied on the sensationalism of its subject-matter to lend interest to its rustic characters, Brome's *Northern Lass* attempts to sell the novelty of "northernness" itself to its audience, exploiting the fact that the dialect, despite its casual appearance in a variety of works throughout the period, was foreign in the eyes of most London readers. In a dedicatory letter affixed to the play, Brome describes his protagonist:

> A Countrey Lass I present you. . . . Shee came out of the cold North, thinly clad, but wit had pity on her, Action apparrell'd her. . . . She is honest, and modest, though she speake broad; And though Art never strung her tongue; yet once it yeelded a delightful sound.

Without warning, Brome's description of the northern girl's journey south becomes an account of his own literary odyssey. Constance's northern dialect, he writes,

> gain'd her many Lovers and Friends, by whose goodliking she prosperously lived, until her late long Silence and Discontinuance (to which she was compell'd). . . . Wherefore she, now, desirous to settle herself in some worthy service and no way willing . . . to return from this Southern Sun-shine, back to her native Air; I thought it might become my care (having first brought and estrang'd her from her Countrey) to sue, with her, for Your noble Patronage. . . . Northern spirits will soon wax bold. If you be pleased to accept of her, shee will travaile no further.[48]

The northern lass, it is clear, has much in common with the man who has authored her: Constance's enforced "long Silence" apparently refers to Brome's own frustrated attempts to write or produce his works. The northern girl, Brome claims, desires nothing more than to remain in the south; the author has "estrang'd her from her Countrey" to sue for a southern patron. Whether or not Brome literally made a trip to the capital at this time is not as important as the fact that he figures himself as a northerner yielding a new "delightful sound" to the southern literary market. If Brome's scheme succeeds, his patron will recognize the value of northern commodities. "York, York, for my money."

Constance's story strengthens the analogy between the playwright and his protagonist. The plot turns on Sir Philip's fear that the Constance who seeks to marry him is Constance Hold-up, a prostitute with whom he had dallied in his youth. This second Constance exploits Sir Philip's confusion by disguising herself as the northern lass. When the whore assumes the dialect of her rival, she does not shrink from asserting her sexual claims on Sir Philip: "You have getten a Barn by me, I is sure o' that" (4.4). The resemblance between the two women becomes so strong that a rogue named Widgin disguises himself as Sir Philip to gain the hand of the strumpet, whom he has mistaken for the "real" Constance. Sir Philip gradually comes to recognize the legitimate suit of the northern lass, and their marriage is carried out as originally intended.

But the pairing of the two Constances creates a tension that takes the play beyond a comedy of mistaken identities. If the northern lass has something in common with the whore who seeks to ensnare a wealthy lord, Brome, too, has a hand in the seduction. As Brome says in his dedication, "Northern spirits will soon wax bold" in the pursuit of their desires. Assuming the status of a northerner, an outsider who speaks the "pretlest" language, Brome, in his own account, "estranges" his work in an effort to attract a bountiful southern patron.

Brome's play was written fifty years after Spenser composed his *Shepheardes Calender*. But it is not impossible that Brome borrowed the idea of exploiting linguistic novelty, and northern "boldness," from his predecessor. I turn now to Spenser's brief foray into the north country, and the place of dialect in the English he devised for his early pastoral poetry.

* * *

What is striking about the prefatory material that accompanies *The Shepheardes Calender* – the author's own dedicatory poem and E.K.'s *Epistle* to Gabriel Harvey – is how persistently the poet is characterized as "unknown." Spenser never identifies himself directly, choosing, instead, to pass under an Italian pseudonym, "Immerito." In the dedicatory verses to the eclogues, Spenser underscores the mystery by describing his work as a child "whose parent is unkent" ("To His Booke"). E.K. immediately reinforces the idea of the poet's obscurity in his *Epistle* to Harvey, which begins by presenting the author of the eclogues as "uncouthe, unkiste," a phrase attributed to "the olde famous poete Chaucer." The archaic words "uncouthe" (unfamiliar, unknown), and "unkiste" (literally, "unkissed," hence, untried or unknown) resonate with Spenser's self-identifying epithet "unkent" (also, unknown). Despite the morphological similarities of the three terms, Spenser did not borrow them all from Chaucer or other sources of archaic English. "Unkent" is a northern dialect term, and since Spenser's dedicatory verses to *The Shepheardes Calender* mark its first appearance in print,[49] it is unlikely that the word would have been widely familiar to a courtly audience. Spenser's refusal to name himself is not an act of self-effacement, a plea for anonymity; when he calls himself "uncouthe" and "unkent" he is calling attention to the mystery surrounding the poet and his unknown language.

Most important of all, E.K.'s *Epistle* to Harvey, an extended explanatory gloss that offers strategies for understanding Spenser's design, centers on a discussion, or rather a defense, of the "uncouthe" language of the poem. E.K. admits to Harvey that much about the eclogues will seem unfamiliar to readers, but "of many things which in him be straunge, I know [the language] will seem the straungest". He attributes the strangeness of Spenser's language to the fact that the poet borrowed so many words from Chaucer, words that have since become "something hard, and of most men unused". Like the early Saxonists, E.K. defends archaizing as an effort to recover a purer English; the poet, he says, "hath laboured to restore, as to theyr rightfull heritage such good and naturall English words, as have ben long time out of use and almost cleane disherited." This "disinheritance," he notes, has caused writers to make up the difference with "peces and rags of other languages, borrowing here of the French, there of the Italian, every where of the Latine," making contemporary English "a gallimaufray or hodgepodge of al other speches."[50] Spenser's language, on the other hand, is pure English, however unrecognizable it might be to his readers. E.K. forestalls the criticism of his countrymen who "if they happen to here an olde word, albeit very naturally and significant, crye out streight way that we speak no English, but gibbrish" with some ideological wrist-slapping: "[Their] first shame is, that they are not ashamed, in their own mother tonge straungers to be counted and alienes." Critics who attack Spenser's old words as "strange" or "alien," E.K. asserts, are strangers to their own native tongue. E.K. thus represents what seems most foreign in Spenser's diction as what is most native, his borrowings from literary sources as an expression of the natural "mother tongue."

E.K.'s apology for Spenser's poetry also appeals directly to the precedents set by earlier authors who made use of archaic diction. He assures his readers that Spenser's antique language is "both English, and also used of most excellent authors and most famous poetes", and notes the archaisms of Livy and Sallust as examples. Quintilian, he reminds Harvey, said that archaisms bestow majesty and dignity upon a verse. He predicts that Spenser will succeed Chaucer as "the Loadstarre of our language," taking English to new literary heights. According to many twentieth-century critics, in fact, E.K. could have found numerous literary precedents for Spenser's use of archaisms a lot closer to home. As I have already noted, archaisms appeared in both pastoral and courtly poems of the earlier sixteenth century. Bruce McElderry, using the *OED* to search for other contemporary examples of the words E.K. glossed, concludes that E.K., in a frenzy of "overzealous editing not unlike the bristling annotations of many a modern text . . . at times explained the obvious or the near-obvious."[51] E.K., in other words, had no need to "apologize" for the strangeness of Spenser's diction at all.

Yet these accounts beg the question of why E.K. chose to highlight the unfamiliarity of Spenser's language, both in his *Epistle* to Harvey and in his glosses, which are predicated on the idea that Spenser's diction required translation. The reception of the *Calender* among Spenser's contemporaries, if nothing else, refutes the claim that E.K. was merely explicating "the obvious or the near-obvious" for readers already in the know. Everard Guilpin, in 1598, records the immediate controversy generated by Spenser's language:

> Some blame deep Spencer for his grandam words
> Others protest that, in them he records
> His maister-peece of cunning giving praise,
> And gravity to his profound-prickt layes.[52]

Samuel Daniel deemed Spenser's archaisms "untimely," and Ben Jonson, fulfilling E.K.'s prediction that many would find Spenser's English "gibbrish," denied that his diction was English at all: "Spenser, in affecting the Ancients, writ no Language."[53] Long after the publication of Spenser's eclogues, they remained a repository of "hard words"; Bathurst's publication of *The Shepheardes Calender* (1653) included a glossary; and John Ray included words from Spenser in his dialect dictionary, *A Collection of English Words Not Generally Used* (1674). Clearly, E.K. was not alone in his judgment of the strangeness of Spenser's language – or in his sense that such a language, given the controversial status of "hard words" in Renaissance culture, required a defense.

Although Spenser's use of northern English might have seemed strangest of all to some of his readers, E.K. says nothing about it to Harvey, or at least, nothing explicit. We know that he observed the presence of dialect in the poem, since he marks several words as northern in his glosses, but he makes no mention of them in his prefatory remarks. As far as one can tell from E.K.'s *Epistle*, the only unusual thing about Spenser's poem is a preponderance of old words. One might conclude that E.K. did not distinguish Spenser's northern words from his archaisms, that he simply understood both as examples of an older, purer English. Indeed, E.K. confirms the theories of Renaissance linguists who perceived that old words may survive in contemporary dialects, suggesting that Spenser used archaisms "because such olde and obsolete words are most used of country folke."

Modern philologists have confirmed that it is difficult to distinguish dialect words from archaisms in the poem. Moreover, there is no consensus among them as to how many dialect words Spenser employs. The most conservative count of dialect in the *Calender* cites twenty-one words and phrases from the northern counties (with many appearing multiple times, so that there are seventy-five instances of dialect in the poem).[54] But certain words that appear in the *Calender*, such as *cragge, dight, hale, hent, kirke, narre, mister, steven, tydes,* and *wae,* among others, existed in Middle English as well as in provincial dialects of the period; because they were rare in medieval texts that would have been available to Spenser, it is likely that the poet derived them from native speech.[55] If so, the *Calender* includes more than seventy-five separate dialect words.[56] Yet a third study settles on forty-one terms from the northern shires.[57] Although the dispute over the number of dialect words that appear in the *Calender* has not been settled, the most conservative estimate still represents a significant addition to Spenser's pastoral diction. The question remains whether E.K. and his contemporaries would have simply conflated them with the hundred or more archaic words used throughout the poem.[58]

First, it is essential to note that E.K. does not praise Spenser's archaisms unreservedly, as so many commentators seem to assume. Along with the recommendation of Quintilian, the precedent of Livy and Sallust, and the nationalistic virtues of ancient Saxon, E.K. offers another explanation – perhaps Spenser intended his archaic diction to set off another, better kind of language:

> But all as in most exquisite pictures they use to blaze and portraict not only the daintie lineaments of beautye, but also rounde about it to shadow the rude thickets and craggy clifts, that, by the basenesse of such parts, more excellency may accrew to the principall. . . . Even so doe these rough and harsh termes enlumine and make more clearly to appeare the brightnesse of brave and glorious words.

In a marked shift of terms, E.K. determines that Spenser's "strange" words are neither "brave" nor "glorious," but rather "rude," "base," and "rough." He adds that Spenser may have been following Horace's dictum of poetic decorum, prescribing a "low" language for low characters and kinds; the poet used old words "as thinking them fittest for such rusticall rudenesse of shepheards, . . . for that theyr rough sounde would make his ryme more ragged and rustical". These last hypotheses are in themselves coherent accounts of the poet's intent, but they are somewhat inconsistent with Quintilian's ideas of poetic majesty, or the legendary conquests of Saxon English.[59]

E.K.'s characterization of Spenser's language as at once majestic and low, authoritative and rude, points obliquely to the contemporary association of old words and words from the provinces – and to the contradictions produced by that association. Renaissance theories of northern English, in all their equivocality, penetrate E.K.'s commentary and confound his efforts to motivate Spenser's choice in a consistent way. Most critics, like McElderry, have assumed that E.K. simply granted northern words the cultural authority of archaisms, and otherwise disregarded them. But E.K. was clearly aware of the "rustic" qualities of Spenser's diction, and of the problem of authorizing rustic language. Because of the association of old words with provincial speech, E.K. is compelled to characterize Spenser's archaisms as "rough," "base," and "rude" – almost as if they were dialect words themselves.

The early reception of the *Calender* offers additional evidence that Spenser's contemporaries recognized that the diction of the eclogues was, at least in part, provincial in origin. Although many Renaissance critics, such as Ben Jonson, fixed their attention on Spenser's archaisms exclusively, Sidney censured Spenser's choice of words in his well-known remark: "That same framing of his style to an old rustic language I dare not allow."[60] For Sidney, the fault in Spenser's language lay in the fact that it was not only old but "rustic" as well. Indeed, Sidney, in the same context, praises not only Chaucer's *Troilus and Criseyde* but also contemporary experiments in archaism such as Surrey's lyrics and Sackville's *Mirror for Magistrates*, so it appears that he disapproved of Spenser's dialect words more than he did his archaisms.[61] Gill, as I mentioned earlier, seems to have had Spenser in mind when he made an exception for northern terms in poetry. We can be certain, at least, that Spenser was conscious of the varieties of diction he was employing in the *Calender*: Although he occasionally used northern pronunciations for the purposes of rhyme in *The Faerie Queene* (1590/6),[62] the presence of dialect words in works outside *The Shepheardes Calender*, including his late pastoral *Colin Clouts Come Home Again* (1595), is negligible.[63] The concentration of northern English in the *Calender* underscores the choice that the poet made in his inaugural work.

But why did Spenser make this choice at all? The question has been debated since E.K. first confessed his own uncertainty about the poet's intentions in choosing his diction. Although he comes out in favor of "old rustic" words, E.K. cannot say for sure "whether [Spenser] useth them by such casualtye and custome, or of set purpose and choyse, as thinking them fittest for such rusticall rudenesse of shepheards." The first explicit theory of Spenser's use of dialect was espoused by John Dryden, who referred the "strangeness" of Spenser's language to the influence of "our northern dialect," along with "Chaucer's English."[64] Dryden proposed that Spenser used northern English in imitation of the Greek pastoral poet Theocritus. By the middle of the seventeenth century, it was widely understood that Theocritus had composed his *Idylls* in an artificial Doric dialect that came to be associated with rustic literature. Alexander Pope compared Spenser's "Doric" unfavorably with his supposed original:

> Notwithstanding all the care he [Spenser] has taken, he is certainly inferior in his Dialect: For the Doric had its beauty and propriety in the time of Theocritus; it was used in part of Greece, and frequent in the mouths of many of the greatest persons, whereas the Old English and country phrases of Spenser were either entirely obsolete, or spoken only by people of the lowest condition.[65]

It was a reasonable theory, but no doubt a mistaken one. It is unlikely that Spenser or other sixteenth-century readers were familiar with the *Idylls* in the original or had experienced Theocritus' Doric at first hand. There were no editions of Theocritus published in England in the sixteenth century, and only one translation, published eight years after the appearance of the *Calender*.[66] In fact, Sidney censured the diction of the *Calender* precisely because it had no Greek or Latin precedent; he cannot allow Spenser's "old rustic language," he writes, "sith neither Theocritus in Greek, [nor] Virgil in Latin . . . did affect it."[67] Surely E.K., who cited the archaisms of Sallust and Livy, would have mentioned Theocritus if he had believed Spenser was drawing on Greek practice. Although northern English made a small but significant showing in dramatic and prose works of the period (in the speech of northern characters), the idea that a provincial dialect might be an appropriate medium for pastoral poetry was unheard of in Spenser's day.[68]

With regard to the sources of Spenser's use of dialect, however, E.K.'s idea that old words survive in the speech of contemporary rustics bears further consideration. By using the present tense, saying that such words "are," and not "were," used of country folk, E.K. asserts that Spenser deliberately meant to evoke the language of contemporary provincials. E.K. was suggesting, in other words, that Spenser was applying the use of dialect to the problem of pastoral decorum. If E.K. was right, it is essential to note that there was nothing in pastoral theory to give Spenser (or E.K.) the idea that shepherds in pastoral poems should speak like real, contemporary provincials. Nor is there is any evidence to suggest that Spenser's readers would have expected this kind of linguistic verisimilitude.[69] George Turberville had prescribed common diction for the language of shepherds: "For as the conference betwixt shephierds is familiar stuffe and homely: so have I shapt my stile and tempred it with suche common and ordinarie phrase of speach as Countreymen do use in their affaires." Before the publication of the *Calender*, "common and ordinarie phrase of speach as Countreyman do use" had never included provincial dialect. Later in the same passage, Turberville explains that the shepherds figured in literary pastorals are not "such siellie sottes as our shephierdes are now a dayes. . . . But these felowes . . . had reason to know the difference twixt Towne and Countrey."[70] The shepherds of courtly pastoral might be expected to speak in a low or "ordinarie" manner, but not like the "siellie sottes" who inhabited the countryside of contemporary England.

Spenser's more immediate contemporaries were not any more inclined to identify literary shepherds with sixteenth-century provincials.[71] Philip Sidney, for example, uses little in the way of unusual diction in his *Arcadia*. But one of the work's interpolated lyrics, the "Ister Bank" song, contains more archaisms than occur in all the other songs and eclogues combined:

> The welkyn had full niggardly inclosde,
> In coffer of dymme clowdes his sillver groates,
> (Yclipped starres), eche thing to rest disposde.[72]

The "Ister Bank" song is composed by Philisides, the exiled courtier whose name has identified him as a figure for the poet Sidney. While native shepherds like

Dametas and Mopsa do not speak or sing in archaic English, courtly "shepherds," like Philisides, may. For most sixteenth-century poets, in other words, archaic diction is an idealized speech, a literary idiom that has nothing to do with the "rustical" language of sixteenth-century northerners. Further, if dialect words were widely understood to be interchangeable with archaisms (i.e., both were simply "old") one might also expect to find them scattered among the archaisms of songs like "Ister Bank," or in contemporary sonnets, which also employed archaic words. Spenser's inclusion of northernisms was surely an innovation: As far as Spenser's English contemporaries were concerned, at least, the "unkent" poet was treading on unknown literary territory.

Although Spenser may have departed from native tradition here, his choice of dialect may have been inspired by continental theory and practice. The midsixteenth-century circle of poets known collectively as the Pléiade set forth a program for enriching and expanding literary diction that made provision for regional words. Du Bellay's *Deffence de la langue francoyse* (1549) and Ronsard's expanded version, the *Abbregé de l'art poetique françois* (1565) encouraged poets to search out new sources of diction in order to promote an expanded vernacular. To that end, Du Bellay championed archaisms and neologisms, and Ronsard proposed a more radical poetic language that would draw on the technical fields, like founding and metallurgy, and the provincial dialects. Spenser was familiar with Du Bellay's poetry (some of Spenser's earliest literary endeavors were translations of Du Bellay) and the literary theory espoused in the *Tears of the Muses* suggests he knew Du Bellay's theoretical writings as well. There is no evidence that Spenser had read the *Abbregé* of Ronsard, but Puttenham's writings, among others, seem to bear traces of Ronsard's treatise.[73] None of Ronsard's English enthusiasts, it should be noted, mentioned his ideas concerning dialect.

If he did not discover Ronsard's ideas for himself, Spenser may have gleaned something from his teacher at the Merchant Taylors' School, Richard Mulcaster, whose rather unusual linguistic views have been traced directly to Ronsard.[74] Mulcaster, of border descent, may also have provided Spenser the knowledge of specific northern words.[75] A vocal champion of introducing foreign words into English as a way to enrich the vocabulary, Mulcaster outlines a scheme for passing foreign words off as native in *The Elementarie*:

> If the strangenesse of the matter do so require, he that is to utter . . . use the foren term, by waie of premunition, [he might say] that the cuntrie peple do call it so, and by that mean make a foren word, an English denison.[76]

In his sole reference to provincial language, Mulcaster suggests that regional dialects form a kind of bridge between foreign words and "common" English, allowing new words access into English. Although Mulcaster betrays no further interest in the English dialects than can be inferred from the citation above, he seems to include "cuntrie" words as "denisons" or citizens of the language.

Mulcaster's idea of linguistic citizenship, however, was not a pluralistic one: He strongly favored acclimating strange-sounding language to English standards. He characterizes this process in political terms, and names it "enfranchisement":

> by which verie name the words that are so enfranchised, becom bond to the rules of our writing . . . as the stranger denisons be to the lawes of our cuntrie. . . . If we mean to make them ours, then let them take an oath to be trew to our tung, and the ordinances thereof.[77]

In Mulcaster's scheme, the English language would grow by naturalizing foreign words, subjecting them to English rule.

But if Spenser was inspired by the theories of the Pléiade, either directly or through Mulcaster's teachings, his motives for using native words widely diverged from his masters'. At least, he did not seem concerned that the provincial dialect of the *Calender* gain general currency; if he had been, he surely would have carried the project into his later works, especially *The Faerie Queene*, an epic dedicated to the glory of England and her prince. Most importantly, Spenser made not the slightest effort to adapt his diction to the "ordinances" of English, as Mulcaster charged him to do. Rather, he let them remain "strange."

There is no doubt that Spenser favored archaisms, in part, because they represented a language already authorized by both classical and native tradition. E.K., after all, openly acknowledges Spenser's debt to Chaucer, whom Spenser himself would later call a "well of English undefiled."[78] But it is essential to note that Spenser did not only use "undefyled," native words to produce the English of *The Shepheardes Calender*.[79] He also incorporated foreign loanwords (words such as *faytours*, *peregall*, and numerous words ending in the French suffix *-ance*, such as *jouyssance* and *miscreance*) along with several neologisms, the most famous of which is *derring-doe*.[80] Spenser's incorporation of dialect, foreign words, and neologisms in his diction suggests that the "unfamiliarity" and the novelty of Spenser's archaisms – the fact that they were, as Puttenham observed, "now out of use with us"[81] – was just as important to him as their antiquity. Their "strangeness" apparently met Spenser's unusual specifications for a newly authorized English.

The "September" eclogue offers further evidence that Spenser judged old words and dialect words as examples of a "foreign" diction. "September" introduces a character named Diggon Davie, a traveler, like Colin, "devised to be a shepherd that, in hope of more gayne, drove his sheepe into a far countrye," who seems to be identified with a particularly "strange" language. E.K. calls attention to it in his gloss: "The Dialecte and phrase of speache in this dialogue, seemeth somewhat to differ from the comen." Diggon's opening speech, addressed to Hobbinol, is barely comprehensible: "Her was her while it was daye light/But now her is a most wretched wight./For day, that was, is wightly past,/And now at earst the dirke night doth hast" (3–6). The conspicuous repetition of the pronoun "her," according to many critics, confirms that Diggon Davie is Spenser's figure for Richard Davies, a well-known bishop of Wales. The stage

Welsh of Shakespeare, Jonson and Dekker also relies on the substitution of "her" for other pronouns, and the name "Diggon" for "Diccon" (a contemporary nickname for Richard) is typical of Welsh pronunciation of the period.[82] Diggon's description of the poverty of the "far countrye," and the abuses of the clergy there, provide further evidence for the identification. The strange dialect of "September," for these critics, is Spenser's attempt at providing enough linguistic verisimilitude to reveal the Welsh origins of the foreign shepherd.

Yet the linguistic evidence for identifying Diggon Davie as a Welshman is not as compelling as many have suggested. After his opening speech, Diggon uses the pronoun "her" for the possessive plural "their" five times in the eclogue, a Middle English usage. "Her" is used again in this sense in the "May" eclogue, although neither Palinode nor Piers has been credited with a knowledge of Welsh. Critics have also ignored the fact that Hobbinol opens the eclogue with a greeting that includes the "Welsh" usage: "Diggon Davie, I bidde her god day/Or Diggon her is, or I missaye" (1–2). Assuming Hobbinol is not revealing his own, hitherto concealed, Welsh lineage, why would Hobbinol imitate Diggon in this way? It is important to note that when E.K. describes the uncommon dialect of "September," he does not associate it with Diggon Davie exclusively. It is as if Diggon's foreign travels had colored the dialect of the eclogue as a whole: "The cause whereof [the dialect differs from the common] is supposed to be, by occasion of the party herein meant, who . . . had bene long in forraine countryes."

In fact, the most salient aspects of Diggon Davie's speech have been largely overlooked by critics seeking to make a strong case for his Welsh origins. With the single exception of the use of the word "her" for I, you, and he, Diggon's "uncomen" dialect consists entirely of northern and archaic words. Of the former, Diggon uses *dirke, wae, garres, cragge, han, gange, war, ligge,* and *wagmoires.* Hobbinol, a native of the southern dales, shares Diggon's propensity for northernisms, using *myster, leasing, han, sike, ligge, vetchie,* and the phrase *hidder and shidder.*[83] The language of the "September" eclogue differs from the language of the poem as a whole, if it differs at all, only in degree: "September" includes more northern dialect words than any of the other eclogues. I am not suggesting that Diggon Davie has been wrongly identified as a Welshman, but the dialect of the eclogue does not seem primarily to serve a representative function. What is striking in "September" is that Spenser uses archaic words, and even English dialect words, to enhance the "foreign" character of the eclogue; for all E.K.'s talk about their national character, the poet accounted these "native" forms "strange."

The Shepheardes Calender does not, finally, represent a project of linguistic reconstruction but of linguistic innovation, an effort to produce an "original" English – at once old *and* new – that would have even greater claims to a national status than the "common" vernacular of London and the court. This linguistic project, for Spenser, was also an essentially literary one. Although Spenser's ideas about poetic language have often been traced to those of Du Bellay and Ronsard, they are far closer in spirit to Italian theories, especially those of Pietro Bembo and even of Dante. E.K., after all, recapitulates Bembo's strategies by turning to literary archaisms as the best hope for a national linguistic renaissance. Spenser's work, E.K. claims, will bring Englishmen home, as he puts it, to "their own mother tonge . . . their owne country and natural speach, which together with their Nources milk they sucked." Dante began with a promotion of the "natural" speech of his countrymen, and ended up with the art of the *canzone*. Spenser, too, implicitly substitutes a poetic language, of his own design, for the native tongue.

What remains to explore here is how the composite, poetic "dialect" of *The Shepheardes Calender*, which incorporates the dialect of northern provincials, participates in the fiction of the eclogues. In the opening eclogue, the winter lament of "January," Colin Clout – the figure E.K. identifies with Spenser himself – tells how the earth had once been full of hope: "Whilome thy fresh spring flowrd, and after hasted/Thy sommer prowde with Daffadillies dight" (*daffadilies* is northern, *dight* is both archaic and northern, and *whilome* is archaic) (21–2). But ever since Rosalind rebuffed his amorous advances, the frost has destroyed the summer flowers and Colin, dramatizing the brittleness of the winter landscape, breaks his pipes.[84] While Colin's hanging up his pipes in the "December" eclogue may represent a gesture of farewell, that is not where the singer begins: The broken pipes of the "January" eclogue characterize the peculiar nature of Colin's song, not its suppression.[85] After all, Colin continues to sing in the "June," "November,"and "December," eclogues, after he has allegedly destroyed the instrument of his music. Implicitly, Colin composes his "rurall musick" on pipes he has purposefully broken, not as an act of futility or resignation, but as a deliberate poetic strategy. In the opening eclogue, Spenser establishes the figure of the broken pipe as the emblem of a poet who sings, from afar, of what he desires. The interpenetration of unusual words throughout *The Shepheards Calender* creates the impression that the language of the eclogues, altogether, is a kind of dialect, a regional language set at a distance from the common language. Spenser thus applied the pastoral tradition of distancing oneself from worldly affairs to language, using words to map out his poetic domain.

E.K., in fact, pinpoints Colin's whereabouts rather precisely: in the north country. In "June," Hobbinol and Colin debate whether Colin is better off in staying in the "hylls" or migrating to Hobbinol's "dales." Hobbinol describes the dales as a kind of paradise, "where shepheards ritch,/And fruictfull flocks bene every where to see" (21–2). He invites Colin to "forsake the soyle, that so doth thee bewitch" (18) and join his community of prosperous shepherds. E.K. fills in the eclogue's sketchy geography when he explains in the glosses that

this is no poetical fiction, but unfeynedly spoken of the Poete selfe, who for special occasion of private affayres (as I have bene partly of himselfe informed) and for his more preferment removing out of the Northparts, came into the South.

He further glosses the "hylles" as "the North countrye" and the "dales" as the "Southpartes . . . whiche . . . in respecte of the Northpartes they be called dales. For indede the North is counted the higher countrye."

The regional identification of Colin's hills (north) and Hobbinol's dales (south) centers on the determination of their relative height. As the eclogue continues, however, the issue of height, the elevation of the north country with respect to the south, takes on a broader meaning. When Hobbinol praises the songs that Colin was "wont on wastfull hylls to singe" (50) he is still referring to the "wastful hylls" in the north. But suddenly the "hylls" become charged with professional significance: The poet's place (where he sings) and the poet's ambitions (why he sings) become deeply implicated as the eclogue develops. Colin swears he has never ascended any hills: "I never lyst presume to Parnasse hyll,/But pyping lowe in shade of lowly grove,/I play to please my selfe" (70–2). "Pyping lowe" is the activity of the singer without professional aspirations: "Nought weigh I, who my song doth prayse or blame,/Ne strive to winne renowne, or passe the rest:/ . . . /I wote my rymes bene rough, and rudely drest" (73–4; 77). As a poet, Colin claims, he has no ambition to climb; his rhymes, "rough and rudely drest," are not songs of self-promotion. But the glosses give Colin the lie: E.K. tells us outright that Colin, representing Spenser, travels south in search of preferment. Why does the poet deny his desire to gain professional advancement, even as he contemplates joining Hobbinol's southern paradise of "ritch" and "fruitfull" shepherds?

This is the central paradox that defines Spenser's poetic strategy: Colin sings in the north to please himself (in the fiction of *The Shepheards Calender*, he never actually migrates south) yet succeeds in pleasing his southern audiences. His fame, in fact, is a foregone conclusion among his southern peers: "O Colin, Colin, the shepheards joye,/How I admire ech turning of thy verse" (Perigot, "August," (190–1)). For Spenser, there is no contradiction in the idea the North country is "higher" than the South, and yet a wasteland for poets seeking fame. Colin does not deny the accuracy of Hobbinol's description of the hills "where harbrough nis to see,/Nor holybush, nor brere, nor winding witche" ("June," (19–20)). Like Richard Brome in *The Northerne Lass*, Spenser characterizes his protagonist as a northerner, an outsider attempting to gain entry to the south, but the key to that entry, in part, is his northern language. Like Brome, Spenser hints that the north country is really the higher poetic region, even as he presses his suit for southern patronage. "Pyping lowe," the poet has discovered, is an effective way to scale the literary heights; being "unknown" may provide fertile grounds for recognition.

Spenser continues his discussion of poetic height, and the proper "place" of the poet, in "July." The "July" eclogue, close on the heels of "June," stages a debate between Thomalin, a shepherd, and Morrell, a goatherd, concerning the relative merits of life on the hill and on the plain. At the start of the eclogue, Morrell urges Thomalin to exchange the lowly plain for the mountain, calling him from above, "Come up the hyll to me" (7). But Thomalin refuses, saying,

"Ah, God shield, man, that I should clime" (9). He warns the goatherd to "learne to look alofte;/This reed is ryfe, that oftentime/Great clymbers fall unsoft" (10–12), and suggests that Morrell "come downe" instead (31). Morrell accuses Thomalin of ungodliness, cursing his denigration of the hills: "In evill houre thou hentest in hond/Thus holy hylles to blame" (37–8). He reminds Thomalin of all the glorious mountains of history – St. Michael's Mount, Mount Parnassus, Mont Sinai – but Thomalin persists: "He that strives to touch the starres/Oft stombles at a strawe" (99–100). Thomalin concludes by telling the moral tale of Algrind who, sitting on top of a hill, was struck with a shell-fish on his bald pate, and endured terrible pain the rest of his days.

E.K. stacks the deck in Thomalin's favor when he tells us, in the glosses, that goatherds represent the wicked and the reprobate, and shepherds worthy priests. But though E.K.'s judgement (like Colin's in "June") falls with Thomalin and the plain, the case is not yet closed. The two emblems that appear below the "July" eclogue read, respectively, *In medio virtus* and *In summo felicitas*, presenting the two positions in even-handed, positive terms. E.K. explicates the emblems this way:

> By thys poesye Thomalin confirmeth that, which in hys former speach by sondrye reasons he had proved. For being both hymselfe sequestred from all ambition and also abhorring it in others of hys cote, he taketh occasion to prayse the meane and lowly state, as that therein is safetie without feare, and quiet without danger; according to the saying of olde philosophers; . . . whereto Morrrell replieth with continuance of the same Philosophers opinion, that albeit all bountye dwelleth in mediocritie, yet perfect felicitye dwelleth in supremacie.

According to Spenser's editor, Morrell's pursuit of "perfect felicitye" is a "continuance," not a contradiction, of the "same philosophers' opinion" that "mediocritie," is the superior mode of life; Morrell, it appears, merely does Thomalin one step better. Once again, Spenser appears to champion the humble life of the "lower" country, only to end up at the summit of his pastoral terrain. As "June" gives way to "July," Spenser further unsettles our ability to distinguish which is ultimately "higher," the hill or the plain, the heights or the grove, denying any necessary link between what is apparently "low" and a lack of ambition or achievement.

When Piers in "October" cries out "O pierlesse Poesye, where is then thy place?" (79) he asks a central question posed by the *Calender*: Should poetry be the art of "pyping low in lowly grove" or should poetry strive, in Piers' words, to "climbe so hie/And [lift] him [the poet] up out of the loathsome myre"? (91–2). It has generally been assumed that the answer lies in Spenser's self-conscious imitation of Virgil's career, in which the successful poet begins by piping low and ends with higher kinds.[86] With the hindsight of Spenser's subsequent achievement, culminating in the epic *Faerie Queene*, it seems a reasonable solution to the problem. But had there been no *Faerie Queene*, the testimony of the *Calender* alone would not have convinced so many critics. There is no conclusive textual evidence to support the idea that the poet is presenting *The Shepheardes Calender* as a low form that will be superceded by a higher one. Critics have relied on the "October" eclogue to support the Virgilian model, where Cuddie seems to foretell his literary future: "O if my temples were distaind with wine,/And girt in girlonds of wild Yvie twine,/How I could reare the Muse on statey stage,/And teache her tread aloft in buskin fine,/With queint Bellona in her equipage" (110–14). It takes Piers to return Cuddie to matters conventionally associated with pastoral, and to dialect as well: "And when my *Gates* shall *han* their bellies layd,/Cuddie shall have a Kidde to store his farme" ((119–20), emphasis added). But the effect of Cuddie's "poetical fury," and the shepherds' references to tragedy and epic, is not to defer higher forms, but to incorporate them within the literary space of pastoral. The tremendous range of styles that occur throughout the eclogues, from the ballad measures of "March" to the "poetical fury" of "October," are not incidental variations of kind, but a testimony to Spenser's expansive notion of appropriate forms for the "lowest" of genres, the pastoral eclogue. In *The Shepheardes Calender*, the poet transsects the boundaries between high and low diction, and high and low kinds, in order to present himself, impossibly enough, as an untried poet at the height of his literary powers, as a "northern" poet deserving of southern fame. Using a provincial dialect as a medium of courtly song, Spenser transforms a lowly grove into a hill – and better yet, a hill his southern readers cannot climb without his instruction. Spenser's first poem indeed plots the path of his literary career, but not in terms of future achievement. *The Shepheardes Calender* did not merely presage the arrival of an eminent poet, for that poet, the eclogues tell us, had already arrived.

There have been numerous scholarly efforts to assimilate Spenser's poetic diction to sixteenth-century literary practice, but these, perhaps, have, overlooked a simpler way to understand his purpose: Spenser estranged his language from more traditional forms of courtly discourse in an effort to solicit the very attention that his diction immediately received. Like any poet new to the London literary scene, Spenser began as something of an outsider, but this newcomer pushed the idea that he was unknown to his readers beyond the usual charade of authorial modesty. In this regard, the "unkent" poet may be characterized as one of the first dialect writers in English, a "regional" author who defined his language and his work, in part, in terms of the provinces. If it is an exaggeration to compare Spenser with a modern dialect poet such as Robert Burns, perhaps one can allow this much: Both distinguished their poetic worlds by means of a marginalized variety of English, using linguistic difference as a way to set themselves apart from a "common" (i.e., dominant) culture – in Spenser's case, as a means of gaining entry there. Both implied that their works were only apparently "low," in fact, they invited us to recognize the superior values, both aesthetic and ideological, that their poetic language embodied. Charles Gildon, writing sixty years before the publication of Burns's early poetry, remained uneasy about the presence of dialect in *The Shepheardes Calender*, although he allowed that the poetic use of northernisms represented a new departure for English literature:

> He gives us a Northern Dialect, which renders his Pastorale unintelligible, without the help of Spelman, or some other Glossarist. . . . No body before this extraordinary Poet ever writ in any of our own Country Dialects, whether Western or Northern.[87]

Gildon's characterization of the language of *The Shepheardes Calender* as a "northern dialect" is inaccurate, from a strictly formal perspective. But in terms of Spenser's intentions, he is not so far off: *En route* to becoming the pre-eminent poet of London, and of the nation at large, Spenser, like his protagonist Colin Clout, began his literary journey in the north country.

Spenser's poetic diction had no material effect on the development of a national language in sixteenth-century England, despite E.K.'s rhetoric of linguistic recovery and inheritance.[88] Instead, the language of *The Shepheardes Calender* became a model for *literary* diction, for a specialized language that belonged, exclusively, to the realm of poetry. George Peele, in his "Eclogue Gratulatorie" (1589), was among the many poets who borrowed directly from Spenser's idiom:

> Herdgroom, what gars thy pipe to go so loud?
> Why bin thy looks so smicker and so proud?
> Perday, plain Piers, but this couth ill agree
> With thild bad fortune that aye thwarteth thee.[89]

Whatever his designs on the national vernacular, Spenser did not change the language so much as he reformed it for poetry. The diction of *The Shepheardes Calender* is probably the best example, in all, of Renaissance writing, of Gill's "Poetic" dialect, an original "mingle mangle" of forms authorized as English; for E.K., the one true language. Yet literary history had the last word, for future readers would judge it as an example of the strangeness and artificiality of poetic language – the "difference" of literary English.

LANGUAGE, LAWS, AND BLOOD
The King's English and His Empire

It hath been ever the use of the conqueror to despise the language of the conquered, and to force him by all means to learn his. So did the Romans always use, insomuch that there is almost no nation in the world but is sprinkled with their language.

Edmund Spenser, *A View of the Present State of Ireland* (1596)[1]

And this communion or difference of language hath always been observed a special motive to unite or alienate the minds of all nations; so as the wise Romans as they enlarged their conquests, so they did spread their language with their laws, and the divine service all in the Latin tongue, and by rewards and preferments invited men to speak it, as also the Normans in England brought in the use of the French tongue in our Common Law. . . . And in general, all nations have thought nothing more powerful to unite minds than the community of language.

Fynes Moryson, *An Itinerary* (1617–*c.* 1626)[2]

The dominion of Latin, enduring in the predominance of Latin elements in so many modern European vernaculars, was widely envisioned by Renaissance writers not only as a historical consequence of the Roman conquest of England and the continent, but as a means by which that conquest was achieved. Linguistic unity, levelling the "difference of language" across national borders, was understood to be a powerful weapon in service of attaining and consolidating imperial claims. The author of one of the earliest European vernacular grammars, Antonio de Nebrija, is often credited as the first writer explicitly to link linguistic rule with imperial rule, reminding his sovereign that language had always been the "companion of empire," and that those brought under Spain's sovereignty "must necessarily accept the laws the conqueror imposes on the conquered, and together with them our language."[3] In England, John Hare, writing of England's "Mother Nation," Germany, saw the "communion" of language shared by her modern descendants as the foundation of a greater empire that might one day rule the world:

Doubtless were all the foresaid limbs of the Teutonick Nations as united in the political association of one head and heart, as they are in the naturall

126

ligaments and communion of bloud, lawes, language, and situation, that Empire would not only be head of the West as now it is, but also able to wrastle with the Orientall Competitor, for the command of the world.[4]

For each of these early modern writers, "language" goes hand in hand with "law" as the basis not only of exercising power at home, but, potentially, throughout the world. And for each, the communion of language and laws represented a "natural" rule conjoined by ties of blood.

The conquests of English in the early modern period were thus often rhetorically "naturalized," that is, both the language and the laws of the conqueror were represented as already given by nature or as destined to restore an original or "native" condition of a people. Several English writers, from the end of the sixteenth century, began to cite the natural superiority of English over other languages.[5] As I have already noted in Chapter 1, Alexander Gill was able to imagine the time when English, once ruled by grammar, might extend that rule to other nations. He may be the first to suggest that English would serve well as a "universal" language:

Since in the beginning all men's lips were identical, and there existed but one language, it would indeed by desirable to unify the speech of all peoples in one universal vocabulary; and were human ingenuity to attempt this, certainly no more suitable language than English could be found.[6]

Gill thus places English in an originary position with respect to other languages and other cultures; in his account, a universal English fulfills the dream of recreating the original "unitary" language of mankind. The poet Samuel Daniel dreamed of an English conquest of new worlds yet to be discovered:

> And who in time knows whither we may vent
> The treasure of our tongue, to what strange shores
> This gain of our best glory shall be sent,
> T'enrich unknowing Nations with our stores?
> What world in th' yet unformed Occident
> May come refin'd with th'accents that are ours?[7]

Daniel adapts a familiar economic metaphor – language as treasure or coin – to the imperial scenario, so that the English language "enriches" "unknowing" nations with the gift of speech. Even more dramatically, the "English" of Daniel's fantasy gives form to the very world it conquers: In his imperial creation story, the English "word" creates the new world out of a cultural void.[8] For many early modern writers, the imposition of English abroad was understood not only as an act of political reformation – uniting political systems – but one that would also reform men, "uniting minds" by uniting words. In the Renaissance, the English language became part of a cultural recreation myth according to which, by translating foreign languages into English, the early modern world would be "reborn" as the British empire.

Levelling the "difference of English" was often an implicit goal of early modern language reformers who favored a "common" language. The internal conquest of English was a matter of discriminating among forms of speech and of writing, a process that helped consolidate the status of the "King's English" as the unitary language of the nation. But the triumph of the King's English was only achieved by means of an ongoing redefinition and re-articulation of the social and regional borders that set it apart from other varieties of the language – and from other, foreign languages that bordered on its domain. Throughout the period, writers were testing the bounds of what Spenser referred to as "a kingdom of our own language"[9] – not only among the local shires, but among the nations that fell within England's imperial sphere. By 1603, England's most immediate neighbors, Wales, Scotland, and Ireland, had all been the object of English efforts towards annexation or union, and it is no coincidence that along with the native English dialects, "British" languages, from Irish Gaelic to Lowland Scots, make their first appearances in English literature in this period. In this final chapter, I will examine the ways that Renaissance English writers incorporate the speech of the Welsh, the Irish, and the Scottish into the province of English letters, and how these authors dramatize the differences in language that, in the political sphere, were often marginalized or suppressed.

The linguistic analogue of Renaissance English attempts to annex or unify the British Isles is generally referred to as Anglicization, the process by which English forms began to infiltrate foreign languages abroad. Like the progress of linguistic centralization within England, Anglicization proceeded largely without intervention, as a reflex of cultural evolution rather than a consequence of deliberate reform. And yet, along with the process of levelling "the difference of English" at home, Anglicization found its first crusaders among writers and lawmakers of the sixteenth century. As Spenser suggests in the citation that opens this chapter, the dissemination of language abroad was not always left to political chance, but at times "enforced" by law. Acts were promulgated to suppress the surviving Celtic languages of the British Isles – Cornish, Welsh, Irish, and Scottish Gaelic – generally viewed as vestiges of tribal societies inimical to English civilization. Some of these acts will be detailed later in this chapter. But despite contemporary efforts to silence them, Celtic languages make occasional appearances in English literature of the period, revealing a fairly widespread familiarity with at least some of the neighboring British tongues.[10] Far more often, however, the language of the Welsh, Irish, or Scottish is represented as a kind of "broken English" associated with each of these peoples respectively. Welsh characters, for example, are generally represented speaking English with a Welsh "accent." Irish characters also use a broken English characterized primarily by phonological deviation from a "common" English. Some literary Irishmen, however, approximate a dialect associated with the "Old English," the descendants of the original English settlers of Ireland. The Scottish speech recorded in English literary works, finally, is not a "broken English" at all (except, perhaps, as perceived by Renaissance Englishmen) but rather a rendering of Scots, a dialect of Anglo-Saxon and the dominant language of the Scottish Lowlands. In Scotland, Anglicization in the early modern period was primarily directed towards bringing Scots, closely related to the northern dialect of English spoken across the border, in line with the language of London and the English court.

The broken English of the Welsh, Irish, and Scottish often provided nothing more than additional grist for the mill of Renaissance dialect comedy. Welshmen, for example, are stock characters in the collection of jests entitled *A Hundred Merry Tales* (1526). One tale complains of Welsh "babbling":

> God of His goodness soon after His passion, suffered many men to come to the kingdom of heaven with small deserving – at which time there was in heaven a great company of welchmen, which with their craking and babbling troubled all the others. Wherefore God said to Saint Peter that He was weary of them, and that He would fain have them out of heaven. . . . Wherefore Saint Peter went out of heaven's gates and cried with a loud voice – "Cause bob" – that is as much to say as "roasted cheese," which thing the welchmen hearing, ran out of heaven a great pace.[11]

The jest seems to rest on the assumption that God shares the perspective of Englishmen on the problem of Welsh "craking and babbling"; their speech alone makes their expulsion from the neighborhood desirable. The Irish and their language, to be sure, were no more welcome. John Shank, composer of songs, jigs, and dance rounds wrote a character song, "The Irish Exile's Ochone," in which the English only laugh at the poor man's efforts to express his pain:

> I was so crost
> That I was forc't
> To go barefoot
> With stripes to boot,
> And no shoes on,
> None English could I speake
> My mind for to break
> And many laughed to hear the moan I made.[12]

When Lady Percy tells Hotspur to "Lie still, . . . and hear the lady [Mortimer's wife] sing in Welsh," Hotspur mocks, "I had rather hear Lady, my brach [bitch], sing in Irish." (*1 Henry IV*, 3.1.233–6).[13] Hotspur's primary target may be Mortimer's wife, but he strikes out at Welsh and Irish as well, which are both likened to the bayings of a dog. Many jokes made at the expense of Welsh, Irish, and Scottish characters rest on the confusion caused by the "diversitye of language" in an England infiltrated with their speeches. In one of these a Welsh-man, having been instructed by his English master to hunt male (deer), ignores the animals in his path and threatens to shoot a man with a "male" (wallet) at his side. He explains his actions to his master in broken English: "Master, by Cot's bloot [God's blood] and her [his] nail I have stand yonder this two hours and

I could see never a male but a little male that a man had hanging at his saddle bow."[14] In one of the *Merie Tales of the Mad Men of Gotam* (1565) we are told of a Scottish man who is building an inn, but lacks a boar's head for the sign. The jest continues:

> He dyd come to a Carver . . . saying in his mother tonge, I saye spek, kens thou meke me a Bare [boar] Heade? Ye said the Carver. Than sayd the skotyshman, mek me a bare head anenst [by] Yowle, an thowse bus [must] have xx pence for thy hyre. I wyll doe it sade the Carver. On S. Andrewes daye before Chrystmas (the which is named Yowle in Scotland, and in England in the north) the skottish man did come to London. . . . I say speke said the skotish man, haste thou made me a Bare head? Yea said the Carver. Then thowse a gewd fellow. The Carver went a did bryng a mans head of wod that was bare and sayd, syr here is youre bare head.[15]

These tales, like those that involve southern or northern provincials, show the difficulty (and, occasionally, the danger) of conducting business with people whose language is not current in England.

Despite the participation of these languages in a tradition of early modern English dialect comedy, the Welsh, Irish, and Scottish of Renaissance literature sometimes speak with a very different cultural accent, and command a very different kind of attention from their English audiences. For some writers, the broken English of such speakers was an expression not only of a cultural difference (in the sense of a difference in forms or customs alone) but of a racial difference embodied in words; the claims of their speeches were the claims of blood. My focus here will be on the rhetoric of blood, descent, and derivation in the early modern discourse on British languages and cultures, the "naturalization" of language and law, two chief forms of cultural "rule."[16] Renaissance ideas about linguistic difference across cultures, and the idea of Anglicization – that is, the erasure of those differences through linguistic union – were fundamentally concerned with the "nature" of language – its deepest ties not only to the nation as polity but to the nation as people or race. What was at stake, finally, was the determination of who, according to the "law of nature and of nations"[17] should inherit the earth.

* * *

> Faire Wales her happy Union had,
> Blest Union, that such happinesse did bring.
> R.A., Gent., *The Valiant Welshman*[18]

From the perspective of Renaissance Englishmen, the Welsh were no doubt, as one recent scholar has put it, "the most remote and strange of provincials and the nearest and most intimate of foreigners."[19] The political border between Wales and England was abolished in 1536, when Wales was officially assimilated into its eastern neighbor. Wales was the first and most successful of English efforts to colonize or incorporate the remainder of the British Isles, contrasting sharply with less felicitous enterprises in Scotland and Ireland. There were several reasons why the English sought union with Wales in this period. Economically, the union promised the English certain resources, especially exported foods; politically, English national development depended on crushing the independent principalities that controlled the border regions between the two states. Along with the north country, the most notorious border region, the Welsh border provided sanctuaries for criminal activity, and the decentralizing influence of the powerful Marcher lords.[20]

The union with Wales was achieved without bloodshed, but not without certain cultural sacrifices. In addition to imposing English religion and English law, the Act of Union of 1536 made specific provisions for the Welsh language. The Act banned Welsh speakers from pursuing justice in their native tongue, or from holding municipal office of any kind:

> All Justices commissioners Shireves Canoners Eschetours Stewardes and their lieutenauntes and all other officers and ministers of the lawe shall proclayme and kepe the sessions courtes hundredes . . . and all other courtes in the Englisshe Tonge and all othes of officers juries and enquestes and all other affidavithes verdictes and wagers of lawe to be geven and done in the Englisshe tonge. And also that frome hensforth no personne or personnes that use the Welshe speche or langage shall have or enjoy any manner office or fees within the Realme of Englonde Wales or other the Kinges dominions upon pain of forfaiting the same offices or fees onles he or they use and exercise the speche or langage of English.[21]

Many forms of political and legal representation were thus denied to the Welsh unless "they use[d] and exercise[d] the speche or langage of English." The Anglicization of Wales proceeded apace with the help of the Welsh gentry, many of whom sent their sons to be educated at Westminster and other English schools.[22] As George Owen's provincial chorographies, the *Survey of Wales* and *Survey of Pembrokeshire* (1603) show, however, Welsh remained the dominant form of speech of the region, despite the progress of Anglicization in writing. Thus, Owen tells us that his countrymen "usuallye speche the welshe tongue, yett will they writte eche to other in Englishe, and not in the speache they usually talke."[23] According to Owen, English was widely spoken only in Pembrokeshire, which was often called "Little England beyond Wales." Owen depicts Pembroke as a kind of cultural oasis, another English island encircled by a (Welsh) "sea"; for entering the region would thus prompt a traveller to "imagine he had travelled through Wales and come into England againe." Yet even in Pembrokeshire, the Welsh language persisted, even in the courts, where it was prohibited:

> Soe that often tymes it is founde at the Assizes, that in a Jurye of xii men there wil be the one half that cannot understand the others wordes; and yett must they agree upon the truth of the matter, before they departe.[24]

Owen's chorography, bringing Wales into the province of English regional writing, openly celebrates the union with England, including, implicitly, the progress of

Anglicization there. Yet the second volume of his work, entitled *Cruell Lawes against Welshmen*, is devoted to detailing the "unnatural" laws enacted against the Welsh during the reign of Henry IV.[25] Owen does not say why he decided to interrupt his narrative with a chronicle of English efforts to suppress Welsh culture, but it surely points again to the ways that Renaissance regional writing begins to articulate distinctive – and sometimes recusant – cultural positions.

Welsh linguists and grammarians, writing after the union, may be considered some of Wales' most vocal "regional" writers, and their response to Anglicization was notably mixed, even contradictory at times. William Salesbury, author of an English–Welsh dictionary and a guide to Welsh pronunciation, openly embraced English nationalism, pledging his commitment to the dissemination of English across Wales. The title page of his *Dictionary in Englyshe and Welshe* (1547) directs his work towards "all suche Welshemen as wil spedly learne the engelyshe tongue thought unto the kynges majestie very mete to be sette forth to the use of his graces subjectes in Wales," and declares the acquisition of English as a necessary condition of obedience to the crown:

> I would fayne wyth all industry endever my selfe to helpe and further all Waleshemen to come to the knowledge of Englysche, as a language most expediente, and most worthiest to be learned, studied, and enhaunced, of al them that be subjectes, and under the obeysaunce of the imperiall dideme, and triumphante Sceptre of Englande.

He applauded the standardizing efforts of Henry VIII, referring explicitly to his language policy:

> Your excellent wysdome (as you have an eye to every parte and membre of your Dominion) hath caused to be enactede and stablyshede by your moste cheefe and heghest counsayle of the parlyament, that there shal hereafter be no difference in lawes and language betwyxte youre subjectes of youre principalytye of Wales and your other subjectes of your Royalme of Englande moost prudently consyderynge what great hatred debate & stryffe hathe rysen emongeste men by reason of dyversitie of language and what a bonde and knotte of love and frendshyppe the comunion of one tonge is, and that also by the judgment of all wyse men it is moost conveniente and mete that they that be under dominion of one most gracious hedde and kynge shall use also one language and that even as theyr hertes agree in love and obedience to your grace so may also they tongues agree in one kynd of speche and language.[26]

Invoking the idea of the incorporation of the realm within the body of the King, which is its "hedde," Salesbury celebrates the "union" of laws and language as an expression of a "unity" of hearts.

Three years after the publication of his dictionary, however, Salesbury turned his attention to preserving the Welsh language for its own sake, attempting to reintroduce Welsh into England with his "playne and a familiar Introduction, teachyng how to pronounce the letters in the Brytishe tong, now commonly called Welshe, whereby an Englysh man shall . . . wyth ease read the sayde tonge rightly."[27] Exploiting the popularity of British history and legend spurred by the Tudor succession, Salesbury favored the term "British" over "Welsh" to describe his native vernacular: By "the studye of Brytyshe" he wrote, "I meane the language that by continuall misnomer . . . is called Walshe."[28] By promoting the "British" tongue to English readers, Salesbury still paid lip service to union, while at the same time invoking the original, sovereign claims of the Welsh language. He abandoned, moreover, his earlier stand on the "hatred debate & stryffe" caused by the "dyversitie of language," and intended his book to be read not only by Englishmen, but by Welshmen raised abroad "who thought it reproch to be utterly ingnoraunt in their mother tonge . . . whereby they myght rather (semyng lesse straung) renewe friendshyp and familiaritie with their contrye folke and frendes."[29] For other Welsh linguists, as well, preserving the "comunion" of tongues among Welsh nationals became paramount. Thomas Wiliems, whose work was incorporated into John Davies's dictionary, spoke of the importance of retaining Welsh, and called on loyal countrymen "to shame those Judases who desire to see the death of this polished tongue."[30] The native grammarians ultimately advanced the native Celtic language as a "British" language with ancestral claims to pre-eminence on the island, and reasserted the status of Welsh as the sovereign language of the Welsh people.

The preservation of the Celtic vernacular was also promoted by Welsh clergymen, who, like their Cornish neighbors, sued to retain religious observances in their own vernacular as a means of facilitating the Reformation of Wales. John Penry claimed to see the value of "linguistic comunion" but argued that retaining Welsh in the short run would advance the cause of Anglicization in the long run:

> Al should be brought to speak English . . . [but] shal we be in ignorance until wee all learne English? This is not hir Majesties will wee are assured. Raise up preaching even in welsh, and the uniformity of the language wil be sooner attained.[31]

In Elizabeth's reign, the Act of Uniformity finally took precedence over actions enforcing uniformity of language. In an Act of 1563, Elizabeth granted leave to have the Bible and the Prayer Book published in the Welsh language, with the stipulation that they be accompanied in churches by English versions. New dictionaries and grammars of Welsh appeared in the years following the Act, including John Davies's *Antiquae Linguae Britannicae* (1621) which recorded the language of Welsh poets throughout history.[32] By the early part of the seventeenth century, Robert Holland suggested that King James's son should study Welsh: "A taste of the tongue . . . would verily hereafter please and satisfie him, as being thereby made able both to speake unto his people, and also to understand them speaking to him."[33] Just as Salesbury had insisted on the term "British," Holland worked to return the Welsh language to the English throne.

Although the native vernacular retained a stronghold within Wales, Welsh claims for the nobility and prestige of the "British" tongue only gained limited acceptance, even among Welshmen. English clearly remained a cultural standard, and the "broken English" spoken by Welshmen confirmed, for some, their inferiority as a people. In 1598, Thomas Madryn, a captain in the company of the Earl of Essex, apologized to Essex for his manner of speaking: "If I have in any wise offended you, either in speaking false English or otherwise in my simple manner of speech, I beseech you to consider that I am a Welshman." Welshmen are unable to speak English, according to another early seventeenth-century observer, "without any corruption from [their] mother-tongue, which doth commonly infect our country, so that they cannot speak English but that they be discovered by their vicious pronunciation or idiotisms." In 1622, John Brinsley declared Wales to have remained an "ignorant country . . . along with Ireland and Virginia" because of the people's inability to read English.[34] "Broken English" thus remained, even within Wales, a sign that this people still shared the barbarousness of other subjects who continued to resist "Englishing."

Many Welsh characters who appear in Renaissance English literature reflect contemporary debates over the nature and the status of the Welsh language. In Thomas Dekker's *The Welsh Embassador* (1624), the title character, really an Englishman in disguise, tells the English court "Welse tongue I can tell you is lofty tongue/And prave sentill men [brave gentlemen] as are in the urld [world] tawge [talk] it."[35] Yet the broken English of the ambassador, typical of Renaissance stage Welsh, makes something of a mockery of his "prave" words, as well as his social status as a "sentill" man. The "Anglo-Welsh" that appears in Renaissance English literature is composed of a handful of distinguishing features, several of which occur in the line just cited. The most common phonological features of the literary dialect include the devoicing of *b, d,* and *g,* when they appear at the start of a word, to *p, t,* and *k,* respectively (as in *prave* for brave, above). If they occur medially or in final position, however, *p, t,* and *k* become voiced *b, d,* and *g* (e.g., *tawge* for talk, also above). Other sounds that undergo devoicing are *v* and medial *z* (Shakespeare's Fluellen, for example, says *falorous* for valorous, *asse* for as). The three sounds represented in London English by *sh, ch,* and *j* become *s* (as in the Welsh ambassador's *Welse* and *sentilman*); *ch* and *j* also occur as *sh* (*Shesu* for Jesus is common in Anglo-Welsh oaths). Initial *w* is often silent (cf., the ambassador's *urld*). Morphological features of Anglo-Welsh, which occur more sporadically, include the use of the plural form for singular nouns. Fluellen, for example, says, "the mines is" and "there is not better directions." One of the most peculiar features of literary Anglo-Welsh is the use of *her* as a kind of universal pronoun.[36] The Welsh that appear in Renaissance English literature, finally, use characteristic tags and expressions, including *look you, mark you, great deal,* and *out of cry* (extremely), and tend to favor words in pairs (Shakespeare's Hugh Evans, for example, says *pribbles and prabbles*). As further examples, here are two additional passages of literary Anglo-Welsh, the first from Thomas Dekker's *Patient Grissill* (1603), the second from Ben Jonson's masque *For the Honor of Wales* (1618):

> As God udge mee, her thinke the prittish shentelman, is faliant as Mars that is the fine knaves, the poets, say the God of pribles and prables.

> Is a great huge deal of anger upon yow from all Wales and the nation that your ursip would suffer our young master Sarles, your ursip's son and heir . . . to be pyt up in a mountain. (Got knows where!)[37]

English audiences, it seems, may have been accustomed to Welsh characters who though incapable of London English were bilingual; Dekker's ambassador, for example, is introduced to a lady of the English court this way: "Hee will court you in welsh and broken english, hee speaks both" (3.1.127–8).

Shakespeare spoke his mind about the languages of the expanding British empire in two plays, *The Merry Wives of Windsor* (1597) and *Henry V* (1599), both of which portray the broken English of foreigners, including a couple of plucky Welshmen, living in England or under English rule. In *The Merry Wives*, several versions of broken English come under fire from native speakers. Mistress Quickly announces Dr Caius, a Frenchman, with the warning: "Here will be an old abusing of God's patience and the King's English" (1.4.4–6). Nym, one of Falstaff's low-life followers, is described as "a fellow [who] frights English out of his wits" (2.1.138–9). Sir Hugh Evans, a Welsh parson, gets more than his share of jibes. Aping Evans's dialectal pronunciations of "cheese" and "butter," Falstaff mocks " 'Seese' and 'putter'! Have I liv'd to stand at the taunt of one that makes fritters of English?" (5.5.142–3). The Host of the Garter Inn claims that Sir Hugh "gives [him] the proverbs and the no-verbs" (3.1.104–5). Turning over a new leaf at the close of the play, Falstaff promises Evans "I will never mistrust my wife again, till thou art able to woo her in good English" (5.5.133–4) – a day, he knows, that will never dawn.

The running joke at the expense of Evans's dialect is pressed even further by the fact that the Welshman professes himself a teacher and a scholar. When Evans recites a sampling of contemporary poetry, for example, including bits of Christopher Marlowe's pastoral lyric "Come Live with Me," his broken English makes fritters of it: "There will we make our peds of roses . . . " (3.1.19). Dekker's Welsh ambassador explained that

> In Wales . . . wee have noe universities to tawge in uplandish greekes and lattins, wee are not so full of our rethoriques as you are heere, and therefore your greate and masesticall eares was not to looke for fyled oratories and pig high stiles.

(3.2.43–7)[38]

But Evans seems entirely unaware that his manner of speaking might interfere with his literary aspirations. By vocation, Evans is a language instructor, and he zealously corrects the linguistic foibles of Falstaff ("*Pauca verba*; Sir John, good worts" (1.1.120)) and schoolboys alike. An entire scene is devoted to a Latin lesson he provides William, Anne Page's young son, and his comic enunciations ("*Nominativo, hig, hag, hog*" (4.1.42)).

Like Holofernes in *Love's Labors Lost*, Evans is a pedant, and Shakespeare is no doubt using dialect as a device to expose his pretentions as a scholar. If Evans were Shakespeare's only "learned" Welshman, we could rest with the assumption that Evans's broken English is intended to drive home the fact he is not in a position to teach others how to speak. But Shakespeare created a second Welshman in *Henry V*, a captain in the English army leading the invasion of France. Shakespeare's Fluellen is another purveyor of knowledge, and he professes himself an expert on a subject he calls "the disciplines of war." Fluellen is part of a circle of dialect speakers that includes Jamy, a Scotsman, and Macmorris, an Irishman.[39] But it is Fluellen, and his professed knowledge, that presses the function of these characters in *Henry V* beyond dialect comedy. Like Evans before him, Fluellen provides a language lesson, of a kind, to the new, multilingual British society that emerges in the play. When Fluellen translates English, and the English King, into Welsh, the result is not a comic deformation of words, but a kind of reformation – not just of words but of men.

The one scene that brings together Henry's international army, led by Captains Fluellen, Macmorris, Jamy, and Gower, an Englishman, is typical of Renaissance dialect comedy in that no one seems able to articulate his thoughts, or communicate those thoughts to others. Fluellen attempts to initiate a conversation about his favorite martial subject, but between his own proclivity towards repetition and a series of angry or irrelevant interruptions, the discussion never gets off the ground:

> *Flu.*: Captain Macmorris, I beseech you now, will you voutsafe me, look you, a few disputations with you, as partly touching or concerning the disciplines of the war . . . in the way of argument, look you, and friendly communication; partly to satisfy my opinion, and partly for the satisfaction, look you, of my mind. . . .
>
> *Jamy.*: It sall be vary gud, gud feit, gud captens both, and I sall quit you with gud leve, as I may pick occasion; that sall I, mary.
>
> *Mac.*: It is no time to discourse, so Chrish save me. . . . The town is beseech'd, and the trumpet call us to the breach, and we talk, and be Chrish, do nothing . . .
>
> *Jamy.*: By the mess, ere theise eyes of mine take themselves to slomber, ay'll de gud service, or I'll lig i'th' grund for it. . . . Mary, I wad full fain heard some question 'tween you tway.
>
> *Flu.*: Captain Macmorris, I think, look you, under your correction, there is not many of your nation –
>
> *Mac.*: Of my nation? What ish my nation? Ish a villain, and a basterd, and a knave and a rascal. What ish my nation? Who talks of my nation?

Flu.: Look you, if you take the matter otherwise than is meant, Captain Macmorris, peradventure I shall think you do not use me with that affability as in discretion you ought . . .

Mac.: I do not know you so good a man as myself. So Chrish save me, I will cut off your head.

Gow.: Gentlemen both, you will mistake each other.
. . .

Flu.: Captain Macmorris, when there is more better opportunity to be required, look you, I will be so bold as to tell you I know the disciplines of war; and there is an end.

(3.2.94–141)[40]

For some, this scene is emblematic of the play's idealization of national unity, an England that had successfully incorporated the British Isles as a first step towards global sovereignty. In the dialogue of the four captains, according to Stephen Greenblatt, "Hal symbolically tames the last wild areas in the British Isles, areas that in the sixteenth century represented . . . the doomed outposts of a vanishing tribalism."[41] The rambling, repetitive quality of Shakespeare's dialect speakers, for Greenblatt, transforms speech that is potentially alien into something predictable and automatic, and therefore readily "mastered" by the English.[42] Jonathan Dollimore and Alan Sinfield, in a similar vein, argue that the jokes made at the expense of Fluellen and his dialect refer to the suppression of Welsh language and culture that attended the Union of 1536.[43] They suggest that Shakespeare's Welshman is given more attention than the other British captains because the annexation of Wales was the first real success story of English imperialism, and a model for subsequent ventures. Although Dollimore and Sinfield cite the play's "obsessive preoccupation with insurrection," they maintain that the Welsh, Irish, and Scottish captains represent "an ideal subservience of margin to centre."[44] Fluellen, in particular, is "totally committed to the king and his purposes." Henry's conquest of France, finally, stands in for sixteenth-century attempts to subdue Ireland, offering "a displaced, imaginary resolution of the states' most intractable problems."[45]

These readings of Henry's relationship to Fluellen concur in a judgment that the Welshman's dialect is ineffectual, disarmed of signification by the laughter it invites. While it is true that Shakespeare portrays dialect as a kind of linguistic reflex, this does not mean that his dialect speakers are trapped in a Jonsonian game of vapours. In *The Merry Wives of Windsor*, Shakespeare had hinted that "making fritters" of words is a way to displace other forms of violence. Putting a stop to the duel about to be fought between Caius and Evans, the Host charges, "Disarm them, and let them question. Let them keep their limbs whole and hack our English" (3.176–8). The same notion recurs in *Henry V*: "For Pistol, he hath a killing tongue and a quiet sword; by the means wherof 'a breaks words, and keeps whole weapons" (3.2.34–6). The joke, in both cases, seems to be that "breaking words" is utterly harmless, but Fluellen's example suggests otherwise. If the broken English assigned to foreign characters is a form of cultural disarmament, "killing tongues" occasionally strike at men as they do words.

In his well-known discussion with Gower concerning "Alexander the Pig," Fluellen's broken English disables an idealization of King Henry and his military practices. When Gower reports that the King has ordered his soldiers to cut the throats of their prisoners, in retaliation for burning down his tent, he exclaims, "O, 'tis a gallant king!" (4.7.10). Their dialogue continues:

> *Flu.*: Ay, he was porn at Monmouth, Captain Gower. What call you the town's name where Alexander the Pig was born?
> *Gow.*: Alexander the Great.
> *Flu.*: Why, I pray you, is not "pig" great? The pig, or the great, or the mighty, or the huge, or the magnanimous, are all one reckonings, save the phrase there is a little variations.

> (4.7.11–18)

So far, the joke is on Fluellen who, despite his theory of synonymy, cannot hear the huge discrepancies of meaning created by his Welsh accent. But then the target of Shakespeare's satire seems to shift:

> *Flu.*: I think it is in Macedon where Alexander is porn. I tell you, captain, if you look in the maps of the orld, I warrant you sall find, in the comparisions between Macedon and Monmouth, that the situations, look you, is both alike. . . . If you mark Alexander's life well, Harry of Monmouth's life is come after it indifferent well. . . . Alexander, God knows, and you know, in his rages, and his furies, and his wraths, and his cholers, and his moods, and his displeasures, and his indignations, and also being a little intoxicates in his prains, did, in his ales and his angers, look you, kill his best friend, Clytus.
> *Gow.*: Our King is not like him in that; he never kill'd any of his friends.
> *Flu.*: . . . I speak but in the figures and comparisions of it: as Alexander kill'd his friend Cytus; being in his ales and cups; so also Harry Monmouth, being in his right wits and his good judgments, turn'd away the fat knight with the great belly doublet.

> (4.7.22–48)

Fluellen's reference to the banishment of Falstaff is chilling, and the effect is hardly lessened by the fact that Harry, unlike the drunken Alexander, did away with his friend while he was in his "right wits." Suddenly, we are forced by Fluellen's "figures and comparisions" to place Harry's actions as King under moral scrutiny, and there is nothing funny whatsoever about what is revealed. After this Welsh history lesson, Gower's "gallant King" who orders the execution of French prisoners of war looks more and more like Fluellen's "Alexander the Pig": Both have lost something of their "greatness" in the translation.

As for why Fluellen, and not Jamy, for example, is given the most attention of the captains, Wales clearly occupies a special role in Harry's empire, and not because it adapted so readily to annexation. Fluellen makes a great deal of Harry's relationship to "Edward the Plack Prince of Wales," the king's Welsh derivation, his Welsh "plood":

> All the water in the Wye cannot wash your Majesty's plood out of your pody. . . . By Jeshu, I am your Majesty's countryman, I care not who know it. I will confess it to all the orld. I need not to be ashamed of your Majesty, praised by God, so long as your Majesty is an honest man.
>
> (4.7.106–7; 4.7.111–15)

When he is in disguise among his troops, Harry claims to be Harry le Roy, a Welshman, kin to Fluellen. The relationship between the King and his Welsh captain seems, at first, another comic juxtaposition; the idea that Fluellen could be "ashamed" of being the King's countryman, rather than the other way around, seems preposterous enough. Yet Fluellen repeatedly serves as Harry's historical conscience, reminding him of what he was, of a past that, despite his triumph in the French wars, continues to haunt him.[46] At the end of the play, Fluellen forces Pistol to eat the leek that he wears in commemoration of an ancient Welsh victory over their Saxon enemies. The leek may only be a prop for low comedy, but it stubbornly recalls native claims for Welsh sovereignty, and an ongoing struggle against English conquerors. King Harry sums up Fluellen accurately enough: "Though it appear a little out of fashion,/There is much care and valor in this Welshman" (4.1.83–4). Like Fluellen, the leek provides a lesson in ancient history that, however "out of fashion," has disturbing relevance to the larger history lesson related by the play as a whole. By way of Fluellen's dialectal "derivations," the King is made subject to Fluellen, rather than the other way around. His language is not "predictable and automatic," despite its formal limitations; though fully subject to English rule, Fluellen's broken English unexpectedly reforms the King who commands him. The English captain, Gower, says it best: "You thought, because he could not speak English in the native garb, he could not therefore handle an English cudgel. You find it otherwise, and henceforth let a Welsh correction teach you a good English condition" (5.2.75–9). In *Henry V*, Welsh "corrections" help redress the wrongs of the English King.

* * *

When the English lady pretends to receive the advances of Dekker's Welsh ambassador, one of the courtiers suggests a motive: "May bee shee longs/To study all the neighboringe languages" (4.3.13–14). While Welsh grammarians invited Englishmen to such pursuits, not even Shakespeare took them up on the offer; few English authors, with one notable exception, took the claims of Welsh seriously. In 1629, James Howell made Ben Jonson a gift of John Davies's *Welsh Grammar*, with verses composed for the occasion. By ruling Welsh with grammar, Howell writes, Davies accomplished

> thus to tame
> A wild and wealthy language, and to frame
> Grammatic toils to curb her so that she
> Now speaks by rules and sings by prosody:
> Such is the strength of Art rough things to shape,
> And of rude commons rich Enclosures make.[47]

According to Howell, Welsh was "rich" by nature, but still in need of the rule of art. Jonson furthered the English "domestication" of Welsh when he incorporated it into his court masque, *For the Honor of Wales* (1618).[48] The comic Welshmen who inhabit this masque occasionally engage in Welsh among themselves, but they address the royal audience in broken English. The result of Jonson's researches into the Welsh language, in fact, belongs to the small set of Renaissance works written almost entirely in dialect.

For the Honor of Wales was composed as a revision of an original introduction to the masque entitled *Pleasure Reconciled to Virtue*, first performed on Twelfth Night, 1618. The earlier version apparently met with great disapproval, including that of King James, who is reported as interrupting the performance to complain "What did you make me come here for? Devil take you all, dance."[49] Nathaniel Brent spoke for the rest of the court:

> The masque on 12th night is not comended of any. The poet is growen
> so dull that his devise is not worth the relating, much less the copying out.
> Divers thinke he should returne to his ould trade of bricke laying again.[50]

Pleasure Reconciled to Virtue is the only one of Jonson's masques that met with such disfavor, serious enough to call the poet's vocation into question.

Judging from *For the Honor of Wales*, which constitutes the record of his revisions, Jonson somehow determined that it was the original antimasques that were objectionable to his audience, and, perhaps, the particular pleasures they represented. In the original version, Comus, "the god of cheer, or the belly" (5) appears at the foot of a mountain, and wild music accompanies a chorus singing its praises for "the bouncing belly,/First father of sauce, and deviser of jelly,/Prime master of arts, and the giver of wit" (10–12). Though Comus is announced as a creative force, even "the prime master of arts," he is described in increasingly vulgar terms as the masque continues: "Some in derision call him the father of farts. But I say he was the first inventor of great ordnance, and taught us to discharge them on festival days" (54–7). The first antimasque, a dance of men in the shape of bottles and tuns, follows, and is then banished by Hercules. Hercules falls asleep after this labour, and a second antimasque, this time of dancing pygmies, takes the stage. When Hercules awakens these, too, are put to flight, and the masque concludes by establishing the proper relationship between pleasure and virtue: "Pleasure the servant, Virtue looking on" (192). It may be that the masque's portrayal of gluttony and drunkenness cut too close to the well-known excesses of James' court, but whatever the reason, Jonson chose to eliminate the dancing bottles and tuns, as well as the pygmies, in favor of singing and dancing Welshmen. It is a curious exchange, for it is not entirely evident what sort of "pleasure" the Welshmen, in lieu of wine and pygmies, represent, and what sort of "reconciliation" to virtue is required of them. At the second performance of the new masque, it was reported that it "was much better liked than twelfth night by reason of the newe Conceites and maskes, and pleasant merry speeches . . . by such as counterfeited Welse men."[51] Apparently, the "pleasant merry speeches" of sham Welshmen afforded some of the pleasure the King found wanting in the original.

Indeed, Jonson refocused his work on the "pleasures" of Wales: *For the Honor of Wales* is more than twice as long as the original masque. It begins in the middle of a heated argument among three Welshmen, Griffith, Jenkin, and Evan, "a Welsh Attorney" (3), who compete over who is best qualified to speak for the group:

> *Grif.:* I know what belongs to this place symwhat petter than you; and therefore give me leave to be pold to advise you. Is not a small matter to offer yourself into presence of a king, and all his court; be not too byssy and forward till you be called . . .
>
> *Jen.:* Cym, never talk any talks. If the king of Gread Prittain keep it assizes here, I will cym into court, loog you . . .
>
>   . . .
>
> *Ev.:* Do not discredit the nation and pyt wrong upon us all by your rassness.
>
>   . . .
>
> *Jen.:* . . . Why? Cannot yow and I talk too, cossin? The hall, God bless it, is big enough to hold both our talks.
>
> (4–10; 17–19; 83–4)

The Welshmen continue to abuse each other, until Evans is designated spokesman. Unfortunately, Evans forgets what it is they had to say to the King in the first place: "I know not a oord or a syllable of what I say" (113). The comedy of Welshmen barely able to speak before James was surely heightened by the defects of their English. But despite the low comedy of the opening scene, the Welshmen manage to make their point: They have the right to speak what they will, and how they will, before their King.

And what they have to say is this: James has incurred the anger of his Welsh subjects, on account of Jonson's earlier production:

> Is a great huge deal of anger upon yow from all Wales and the nation that your ursip would suffer our young master Sarles, your ursip's son and heir, and prince of Wales, the first time he ever play dance, to be pyt up in a mountain (Got knows where!) by a palterly poet.
>
> (37–42)

Evans, who is a poet as well as an attorney ("he has a sprig of laurel already towards his girlands" (51–2)), claims to have witnessed the performance on

141

Twelfth Night, and to have been appalled by what he saw: "I stand to it, there was neither poetries nor architectures nor designs in that belly-god" (182–3). The Welshmen explicitly take on the role of Jonson's critics, condemning the literary and artistic failure of *Pleasure Reconciled to Virtue*. The poet, it seems, uses the comical Welshmen to voice a lighthearted concession to the authorities who damned his earlier efforts.

But Evans does not only assume the role of the critic (or self-critic) but the role of the poet as well. From the start, the Welshmen hint of the "reformations" and "alterations" they have made to Jonson's original (82; 135), and finally reveal that the new masque will be written "for the honor of Wales" (139) with Welsh names and Welsh places to replace the material of the earlier version. The use of classical settings, they declare, was unnecessary in light of native settings that rival them:

> Is a very vile and absurd as a man would wiss, that I do say, to pyt the Prince of Wales in an outlandis mountain, when he is known his highness has a goodly mountain, and as tall a hills of his own . . . and of as good standing and as good descent as the proudest Adlas christened.
>
> (58–63)

Many of the "reformations" they recommend, in fact, are simply translations, as they explain of the mountain: "[It] is done without any manner of sharshes [charges] to your madesty, onely shanging his [the hill's] name"(140–1). Evans sums up their suit:

> The Welse nation, hearing that the Prince of Wales was to come into the hills again . . . have a desire of his highness, for the honor of Wales, [to] . . . have it all Welse, that is the short and the long of the requests. The prince of Wales we know is all over Welse.
>
> (137–9; 148–50)

The Welshmen, indeed, spend a great part of the antimasque rehearsing Welsh names, including those of some of the great English families, such as the Montgomerys and the Howards, who are of Welsh descent. The name of the King himself, "Charles James Stuart" is an anagram of "Claims Arthur's Seat" (348); this linguistic "reformation" proves that the King is Welsh as well. According to their derivations, the English nation, including the royal family, is "all over Welse."

In a lavish display of the bounties of the region, the Welshmen continue by inviting James to partake in a feast of native offerings. Although Jonson abandoned Comus and his followers in his revisions, food and drink remain central preoccupations of the masque. The "belly" is the subject of the masque's many songs:

> Let us tell ye
> Of some provisions for the belly,
> As kid, and goat, and great goat's mother,

And runt, and cow, and good cow's uther:
And once but taste o' the Welse mutton,
Your Englis seep's not worth a button;
And then for your fiss, sall shoose it your diss:
Look but about, and there is a trout.

(230–7)

The goats, like the bottles, even perform a dance before the king. Jonson, in effect, simply recast the bottles and tuns of the original as Welsh commodities, explicitly offered for James' consumption:

2nd Woman: Ow, that her would come down into Wales,
1st Woman: Her sould be very welcome to Welse Alice.
2nd Woman: I have a cow –
1st Woman: And I have a hen –
2nd Woman: Sall give it milk –
1st Woman: And eggs for all his men.
Chorus: Itself sall have venison and other seer,
    And may it be starved that steal him his deer.

(322–7)

Jenkins applauds the fall of Comus: "Is not better this now? . . . this is no monsters . . . is no tuns, nor no bottles: . . . was drunkenry in his eyes that make that devise in my mind" (295–6; 298–300). But if Jonson found a way to make this material more palatable to his audience, the recent memory of Comus suggests that the enjoyment of Wales – taking Welsh pleasures – offers another opportunity for royal consumption. Like Jonson's masque, produced for the pleasure of the King, Wales seems to exists only to satisfy James's appetite, whether for food or for entertainment. But Jonson's Welshmen, unlike the bottles and tuns, find a way to ensure their own survival, and a "reconciliation" with the English crown that does not depend on their complete subordination to the king, or their banishment from his presence.

Mindful, again, of the fate of his first efforts, Jonson concludes *For the Honor of Wales* with an apology for the present material. Griffith admits that the new masque

> very homely done it is, I am well assured, if not very rudely; but it is hoped your madesty will not interpret the honor, merits, love and affection of so noble a portion of your people by the poverty of these who have so imperfectly uttered it. . . . Though the nation be said to be unconquered, and most loving liberty, yet it was never mutinous.

(358–62; 372–3)

Griffith denies that the Welsh nation had been conquered by the English, a peculiar assertion, considering that the Union had occurred almost 100 years earlier. Presumably, Griffith is referring to certain resilient facets of Welsh

143

culture, or, on an even greater level of abstraction, the Welsh spirit. The Welshmen, the apology goes, may have spoken "imperfectly," but they love and honor the King; they are unconquered, but they do not intend any revolt. Like Jonson himself, the Welshmen appear to regret the utterances they have made in the past, to the extent that these have offended the King. The relationship between Jonson and the Welshmen who claim authorship over his masque culminates in this final passage, as Griffith concludes by reiterating the dependence of Wales on the English crown: "It is a nation bettered by prosperity so far, as to the present happiness it enjoys under your most sacred majesty, it wishes nothing to be added, but to see it perpetual in you and your issue" (379–82). Jonson, too, is dependent on the King and his issue; Jonson, too, admits to speaking "imperfectly" to them on occasion. But if Jonson's role is to provide pleasure for the King, he yet insists that his art remains "unconquered." By translating everything and everyone, including the King himself, into "Welsh," Jonson creates a line of literary and linguistic descent that "unites" the artist with his royal patron, and gives him a share of the conquest.

According to the conventions of the masque form, the Welsh and their dialect are implicitly reconciled, by subordination, to the "virtues" of their colonizers, yet it is crucial to note that these antimasquers are never formally banished from the piece. Comus may have been dismissed, but Jonson's Welsh survive, with their "pleasant merry speeches" attended, even applauded, by the King. For Jonson, the "imperfections" of the Welsh dialect may express his apologies to the crown, but not the subjection of that voice to the King or "his" English. On the contrary, Jonson presses the claims of Welsh over a king whose sovereignty depends, in the imaginative space of the masque, on a Welsh derivation, his own Welsh "plood."

* * *

> So that the speech being Irish, the heart must needs be Irish.
> Edmund Spenser, *A View of the Present State of Ireland* [52]

From the perspective of English writers, it seems, the Union with Wales had gone off without a hitch, although the unification of language was still slow in coming. The "broken English" of Welshmen in Renaissance English drama thus remains a sign of the failure as well as the success of the Anglicization of that people. The Irish were also identified, by English writers, as a bilingual nation, in the sense that both an indigenous Irish language (Irish Gaelic) and English were in use there. But, for Ireland, bilingualism was widely understood as a token of biculturalism, the coexistence of two races – Irish and English – whose integration was, as we shall see, never really encouraged by the English crown. Although English had been used in official records since the end of the medieval period, English as a spoken language was confined, in 1600, to Dublin and to two rural provinces, the baronies of Forth and Bargy in County Wexford, and to Fingall, a region north of Dublin. In these two areas, in fact, a dialect of the

"Old English," the descendants of the original, medieval English colonial stock, survived until about the end of the eighteenth century.[53] Many Renaissance English writers were preoccupied not so much with the language of the "wild Irish," but with the English of those countrymen who lived alongside a people considered barbaric. For these writers, the "broken English" of the Anglo-Irish demonstrated the threat of cultural and racial degeneration, the possibility that not only English customs and forms, but Englishmen themselves, might "become" Irish. Their preoccupation, in other words, was not so much with the "Anglicization" of the Irish as with the "Gaelicization" of the English.

Union with Ireland, after centuries of native resistance, was openly described by contemporary writers on Anglo-Irish relations in terms of conquest and subjugation, rather than integration and assimilation. Philip Sidney, in his *Discourse on Irish Affairs* (1577) denigrates the Irish as barbarians who by nature choose "rather all filthiness than any law," and who cling to the memory of freedom: "For until by time they find the sweetness of due subjection, it is impossible that any gentle means should put out the fresh remembrance of their lost liberty."[54] It is often noted that England's colonial aspirations began with Ireland. Sir Walter Ralegh, Sir Humphrey Gilbert, Ralph Lane – the leaders of the early English colonies in North America – all launched their imperial careers here.[55] There was a number of motives involved in the Tudors' decision to step up the pace and the vehemence of the long-standing project of colonizing Ireland. Among these were self-defense (the fear that Ireland might be used as a strategic base for enemies both domestic and foreign), and the desire to compete in the new European struggle for increased dominion and trade.[56] The official effort to suppress native Irish culture is generally dated to the fourteenth-century Statutes of Kilkenny, which, though they had never been repealed, were newly enforced in the early part of the sixteenth century. In 1534 Henry issued an act directed against Irish poets; in 1537, he promulgated "An act for the English order, habite, and language," which promised to "use various instruments, including education and religion, to propagate the English language" in Ireland.[57] The Tudors are generally credited with renewing the somewhat lapsed campaign directed at the extirpation of Irish culture, a project that came to some measure of fruition only with the Jacobean settlement policy, by which the English language was finally and securely "planted" along with an expanding English colony.[58]

But, as in Wales, the project of promoting a reformed religion led the crown to speak, once again, at cross-purposes on the question of Anglicization in Ireland. Queen Elizabeth, in fact, encouraged the use of Irish as means of disseminating the doctrines of the national church, even within the English Pale. Providing funds for a type and a press to print an Irish Bible, the Queen threatened to retract those funds as a means of stepping up the pace of translation. There is evidence, in fact, that Elizabeth herself made an effort to learn Irish, for a primer of the language was put together expressly for her. As historians have noted, the English policy towards the Irish language was remarkable for its ambivalence during the latter part of the sixteenth century. One notes, for example, that while Sir William Herbert in Munster was celebrating the translation of the Lord's Prayer and other religious materials into Irish in 1587, at about the same time the Lord Deputy in Dublin demanded that the statutes of Kilkenny, including its provisions on language, be put into effect "with all severity in due execution."[59]

It is essential to note that the "language policy" of Kilkenny was directed primarily at the Old English rather than at the native Irish. Written to maintain, rather than dissolve, the racial segregation of these peoples, the statutes of Kilkenny prohibited those of English descent, under the harshest penalties, to speak Irish, wear Irish dress, or intermarry with Irish – the latter defined as high treason.[60] These laws, in other words, were primarily concerned with forbidding English assimilation to Irish culture. Indeed, the problem of assimilation, the subversion of English civilization in Ireland, becomes a central theme of late sixteenth-century and early seventeenth-century treatises on the Irish conquest. Fynes Moryson, in his *Itinerary*, devotes a great deal of attention to the question of the "Irish-English"; especially, the consequences of linguistic assimilation or "Gaelicization":

> Contrary to the said laws, the Irish-English altogether used the Irish tongue, forgetting or never learning the English. And this communion or difference of language hath always been observed a special motive to unite or alienate the minds of all nations; so as the wise Romans as they enlarged their conquests, so they did spread their language with their laws, and the divine service all in the Latin tongue, and by rewards and preferments invited men to speak it, as also the Normans in England brought in the use of the French tongue in our Common Law and all words of art in hawking, hunting, and like pastimes. And in general, all nations have thought nothing more powerful to unite minds than the community of language.[61]

The use of Irish among the those of English ancestry (as well as the linguistic recusancy of the "mere Irish"), according to Moryson, was thus a deliberate effort to undermine the English conquest of the islands, to perpetuate their "alienation" from the English crown. Even the legal enforcement of Anglicization in Ireland, Moryson writes, had not contained the change in "affection" that the shift from English to Irish speech entailed:

> The law to spread the English tongue in Ireland was ever interrupted by rebellions, and much more by ill-affected subjects, so as at this time whereof I write, the mere Irish disdained to learn or speak the English tongue; yea, the English-Irish and the very citizens (excepting those of Dublin where the Lord Deputy resides), though they could speak English as well as we, yet commonly speak Irish among themselves and were hardly induced by our familiar conversation to speak English with us. . . . These outward signs, being the touchstones of the inward affection manifestly showed that the English-Irish held it a reproach among themselves to apply themselves any way to the English, or not to follow the Irish in all things.[62]

That the "English-Irish" deliberately chose to speak Irish, when they were fully conversant in English, accentuates their "inward" change.

Richard Stanyhurst also emphasizes the relationship between conquest and legally enforced Anglicization, and faults the Anglo-Irish for adopting an enemy tongue:

> Now whereas Irelande hath beene, by lawfull conquest, brought under the subjection of Englande, not onelye in king Henry the second his reigne, but also as well before as after . . . & the conquest hath béene so absolute and perfect, that all Leinster, Méeth, Ulster, the more parte of Connaght and Mounster, all the civities & burroughes in Irelande, have béene wholly Englished, and with Englishe conquerours inhabited, is it decent, thinke you, that theyr owne auncient native tongue shal be shrowded in oblivion, and suffer the enemies language, as it were a tettarre, or ring woorme, to herborow it self within the jawes of Englishe conquerours? no truely.[63]

The problem, according to Stanyhurst, was not the resistance of the Irish, who were being steadily and successfully "Englished," but the indecency of those English who had allowed an indigenous parasite – the Irish language – to infect the nation all over again. But it is Edmund Spenser, in his treatise, *A View of the Present State of Ireland* (1596), who most clearly articulates the notion that speaking Irish had adulterated the lifeblood of the English stock. In the fictional dialogue between Eudox ("honored"; "of good repute") and Iren ("Ireland") that constitutes his tract, Spenser considers the consequences of adopting the "bad and barbarous" ways of the Irish:

> *Iren*: And first I have to find fault with the abuse of language, that is, for the speaking of Irish amongst the English, which, as it is unnatural that any people should love another's language more than their own, so is it very inconvenient and the cause of many other evils.
>
> *Eudox*: It seemeth to me that the English should take more delight to speak that language than their own, whereas they should (methinks) rather take scorn to acquaint their tongues therto, for it hath been ever the use of the conqueror to despise the language of the conquered, and to force him by all means to learn his. So did the Romans always use, insomuch that there is almost no nation in the world but is sprinkled with their language. It were good therefore (methinks) to search out the original cause of this evil . . .
>
> *Iren*: I suppose that the chief cause of bringing in the Irish language amongst them was specially their fostering and marrying with the Irish, the which are two most dangerous infections, for first the child that sucketh the milk of the nurse must of necessity learn his first speech of her, the which being the first that inured to his tongue is ever after most pleasing to him, insomuch as though he afterwards be

taught English, yet the smack of the first will always abide with him, and not only of the speech, but also of the manners and conditions: for besides that young children be like apes, which will affect and imitate what they see done before them, specially by their nurses whom they love so well, they moreover draw into themselves, together with their suck, even the nature and disposition of their nurses, for the mind followeth much the temperature of the body; and also the words are the image of the minds, so as they, proceeding from the mind, the mind must be needs affected with the words; so that the speech being Irish, the heart must needs be Irish, for out of the abundance of the heart the tongue speaketh.[64]

Spenser thus invokes the traditional notion – urged by Dante in his claims for a "natural" Latin vernacular – that the infant acquires the "mother" tongue as it nurses at the mother's breast. But Spenser adds that when one nurses at the breast of a foreigner, one partakes both of a foreign language and a foreign constitution: "[Children] draw into themselves, together with their suck, even the nature and disposition of their nurses."[65] Iren goes on to reassert the necessity of enforcing the re-Anglicization, essentially, the renaturalization of the English-Irish by new, harsher laws. What is crucial about Spenser's formulation is the way that the "question of Irish" becomes not only a matter of foreign forms but foreign natures: Speaking Irish, Spenser suggests, is not a matter of linguistic difference alone, but a sign of a "natural" difference that is not fixed and determinate but dangerously subject to reform. Edmund Campion, in his *History of Ireland*, put it this way: "The very English of birth, conversant with the brutish sort of that people, become degenerate in short space and are quite altered into the worst rank of Irish rogues."[66] With Spenser, especially, the Renaissance ideal of linguistic community is exposed as a project of "translation" by which one culture, one "people," is transformed into another.

Stanyhurst describes the English spoken in Wexford and Fingall, expressing a common contemporary distaste for miscegenated languages, as a "mingle mangle, or gallamaufrey of both languages, that have in such medley or checker-wyse so crabbedly jumbled them both togyther, as commonly the inhabitants of the meaner sort speake neyther good English nor good Irishe."[67] An Englishman would barely recognize the language as his own, as he relates in an anecdote:

There was of late dayes one of the peeres of England sent to Weiseford as commissioner, to decide the controversies of that countrey, and hearing in affable wise the rude complaintes of the contrey clownes, he conceyved here and there, sometyme a worde, other whyles a sentence. The noble man beyng very glad that upon his first commyng to Ireland, he under-stood so many wordes. . . . He stoode in very great hope, to become shortly a well spoken man in the Irishe, supposing that the blunte people had pratled Irishe, all the while they jangled Englishe.[68]

148

Stanyhurst recognized that this dialect had retained numerous forms that had since become obsolete in England, and compared it to "the olde auncient Chaucer English." But the assignation of age did not redeem the dialect from the taint of contact and contamination by the Irish language. The Anglo-Irish that appears in Renaissance English literature sometimes incorporates features of this dialect,[69] along with Irish approximations of "common" English speech. The Anglo-Irish dialect of the English stage often includes the following features: *v* or *f* (often spelled *ph*) for English *wh*; *sh* for English *s*, *z*, and *ch*; *t* for *th* (and often, conversely, *th* for English *t* or *d*); and *p* for English *b*. Some of these phonetic features (*sh* for *ch*; *p* for *b*, for example) also appear in stage Welsh, showing that the English of these two groups was not always clearly distinguished. Here is a sample passage from *The Famous History of Captain Thomas Stukeley* (1605):

O Hamlon: Cresh blesh us, fo ish tat ish coughes.
Mackenor: Saint Patrick blesh us we be not betraid.
Oneale: . . . Tish some English churle in the toone that coughes, that is
    dree, some prood English souldior hees a dree cough, can drink no
    vater.[70]

Like the Welsh characters who appear in Renaissance English literature, the Anglo-Irish are often armed with a few Celtic phrases. But the "meere Irish" or the "wild Irish" are marginalized in Renaissance English literature nearly to the point of silence.[71]

It has often been observed that Macmorris, the Irish captain in Shakespeare's contingent of dialect speakers, seems to allude to the problem of the political and cultural identification of the Old English when he takes offence at a casual reference to his "nation." For convenience, I cite again the exchange between Fluellen and Macmorris (first quoted on pp. 136–7):

Flu.: Captain Macmorris, I think, look you, under your correction, there is
    not many of your nation –
Mac.: Of my nation? What ish my nation? Ish a villain, and a basterd, and
    a knave, and a rascal. What ish my nation? Who talks of my nation?
Flu.: Look you, if you take the matter otherwise than is meant, Captain
    Macmorris, peradventure I shall think you do not use me with that
    affability as in discretion you ought.

Macmorris's angry outburst has received various interpretations. His question "What ish my nation?" may be a rhetorical one; that is, he may be protesting that he is English and not Irish, despite Fluellen's implied identification. When he asks, "Who talks of my nation?" he may, again, be repudiating Ireland, but it is also possible that he is defending Ireland, by challenging Fluellen's right to "talk" of and for "his" people. It isn't clear, moreover, whether the "villain" he has in mind is Ireland, or Fluellen for invoking Ireland. Macmorris's dialect, along with Fluellen's, has been read as a sign of his marginalization; as a stage dialect, "predictable and automatic," Macmorris's speech has been said to dramatize English "control" over foreigners and foreign languages. But the fact that Macmorris's words allow a variety of readings – contradictory readings at that – shows that his dialect is not predictable at all, except in some strictly formal sense. He is clearly a loyal English subject, as his role in Henry's army confirms, but it is crucial to note that the Irishman's "broken English" is ambiguous in its allegiance, that by some readings, Macmorris places English under Irish "correction," rather than the other way around. We can be sure, at least, of one thing: Macmorris's questions articulate, by their "broken" forms, that he is not (from an English perspective) English; it records a difference that is never fully effaced.

In *The Irish Masque at Court* (1613),[72] a work written primarily in a literary dialect, Jonson portrays a band of Irish footmen who have come to celebrate a court wedding. These men identify themselves as Irish (not that they need to; the heavy stage Irish dialect they use makes that self-identification comically redundant). But from the start, they carefully distinguish themselves from the "wild Irish" in their willing subjection to the English crown. They represent the King's "good" subjects, and hail from the English colonies:

Dermock: We be Irishmen, an't pleash tee.
Donnell: Ty good shubshects of Ireland, an't pleash ty mayesty.
Dennice: Of Connough, Leimster, Ulster, Munster. I mine own shelf vash
    born in te English pale, an't pleash ty mayesty.

(47–50)

Like the Welshmen of Jonson's *For the Honor of Wales*, these "good subshects of Ireland" spend the first part of the masque arguing over who among them ought to speak before the King. But while the Welshman all claim the privilege, each of the Irish antimasquers finally insists that he is unworthy to speak, and tries to pass on the burden of speaking to another:

Patrick: Her'sh Dermock vill shpeak better ten eder oder on'em.
Dermock: No fait, shweet heart, tou liesht. Phatrick here ish te vesht man
    of hish tongue of all de four; pre tee now hear him.
Patrick: By Chreesh shave me, tou liesht. I have te vorsht tongue in te
    company at thy shervish. Vill shomebody shpeak?
Donnell: By my fayt, I vill not.
Dermock: By my goship's hand, I vill not.
Patrick: Speake, Dennish, ten.
Dennice: If I speake, te divel take me! I vill giue tee leave to cram my
    mout phit shamrocks ant butter, and vaytercreshes, in stead of pearsh
    and peepsh.

(33–44)

Later, their reluctance to speak will have been shown prudent, for the masque ultimately commands their silence. The Irishmen at last announce that they attend a company of Irish gentlemen who have come to entertain the court. These gentlemen, they insist, are among the King's "good [Irish] shubshects," who repudiate rebellion:

Dermock: Tou hasht very good shubshects in Ireland.
Dennice: A great good many o' great goot shubshects.
Donnell: Tat love ty mayesty heartily.
Dennice: Ant vil runne trough fire ant vater for tee, over te bog and te bank, be te graish o' Got and graish o' king.
Dermock: By Got, tey vill fight for tee, King Yamish . . .
    . . .
Donnell: Be not angry vit te honesht men for te few rebelsh and knavesh.
Patrick: Nor believe no tales, King Yamish.
Dermock: For by Got, tey love tee in Ireland.

(91–6; 105–8)

After the footmen dance to their "rude music" (122), the gentlemen perform a dance in Irish mantles, "which done [according to Jonson's stage directions] the footmen fell to speak again, till they were interrupted by a civil gentleman of the nation." This "civil gentleman" intervenes when Patrick expresses concern that the King might be weary:

He may be of your rudeness. Hold your tongues!
And let your coarser manners seek some place,
Fit for their wildness. This is none; begone!

(134–6)

It is instructive that these Irishmen, who clearly pose no threat at all to James, who rather assert, again and again, their subordination to the English King, are still characterized as "wild" – surely a reference to the "wild Irish" rebels they take pains to distinguish themselves from in the masque. The gentleman, moreover, demands more from the masquers than their silence. He introduces an Irish bard, a prophet who foretold of the king's power to "end our countrey's most unnatural broils," (141) and asks him for a "charm" that will confirm that prophecy:

This is the man thou promised should redeem,
If she would love his counsels as his laws,
Her head from servitude, her feet from fall,
Her fame from barbarism . . .
    . . .
Sing then some charm, made from his present looks,
That may assure thy former prophecies,
And firm the hopes of these obedient spirits.

(145–8; 150–2)

The bard's "charm" is indeed a magical one, for he announces that the King will "change" the Irish dancers, recreate them as fully obedient "creatures" of the crown:

151

> Bow both your heads at once and hearts;
> Obedience doth not well in parts.
> It is but standing in his eye
> You'll feel yourselves changed by and by;
> Few live that know how quick a spring
> Works in the presence of a king.
> 'Tis done by this: your slough let fall,
> And come forth newborn creatures all.
>
> (159–66)

With the bard's words, "the masquers let fall their mantles and discover their masquing apparel" (167–8); that is, they dramatize the bard's charge of letting their Irish "slough" fall to reveal themselves as "newborn" English courtiers. The bard makes it clear that this metamorphosis is about a change in nature, as he concludes the masque:

> So breaks the sun earth's rugged chains
> Wherein rude winter bound her veins;
> So grows both stream and source of price
> That lately fettered were with ice;
>
> . . .
>
> And all get vigor, youth, and sprite,
> That are but looked on by his light.
>
> (170–3; 176–7)

Jonson's masque offers a dramatic realization of a cultural fantasy that dominated the imaginations of so many early modern English writers: the metamorphosis of Irishmen into Englishmen, the recreation of one nation as another. True "obedience" demands the silencing of Irish speech (both the gentleman and the bard speak the King's English) – prologue to a full-scale translation from Irish to English.

Sir John Davies, writing in the early seventeenth century, brought the dream of a community of language to Ireland: "We may conceive an hope that the next generation will in tongue and heart and every way else become English, so as there will be no difference or distinction but the Irish sea betwixt us."[73] Jonson's *Irish Masque at Court* (1616) realizes that dream, but only within the realm of magic and fantasy rather than law and political action. The Anglicization of Ireland imagined by Jonson and other early modern English writers was nothing less than a fantasy of regeneration, not only of Irishmen but the English who had "degenerated" into their kind. The answer to Macmorris's question, "What ish my nation?" depended, it seems, on whether English colonialism could work wonders in Ireland.

* * *

My intention was always to effect a union by uniting Scotland to England, and not England to Scotland.

James I, *A Speach in the Starre-Chamber, the XX of June, Anno 1616*[74]

King James's qualification of what he meant by the "union" of his two kingdoms is instructive, not only in terms of understanding James' own efforts to sell the idea to his English parliaments, but for recognizing that "union," from an English perspective, was not intended as an invitation to political or cultural reciprocity. James, in fact, invoked Wales as testimony to the way such "unions" work to England's advantage, asking his first parliament: "Hath not the union of Wales to England added a greater strength thereto? Which though it was a great Principalitie, was nothing comparable in greatnesse and power to the ancient and famous Kingdome of Scotland."[75] James was largely successful in "uniting Scotland to England" as far as language was concerned, and championed Anglicization – a linguistic union that overwhelmingly privileged English over Scottish forms. The Anglicization of Scotland gained increasing momentum, in fact, only after a Scotsman ascended the throne of the "King's English." The remainder of this chapter will trace the linguistic border between England and Scotland, and the "naturalization" of Scots as English, on both sides of that border.

Although Gaelic was still in use in the Scottish Highlands, and in some parts of Galloway and Aberdeenshire, Scots in the middle of the sixteenth century was the national language of literature (and had been from the time of John Barbour's *Bruce* in 1375) and politics (the Acts of Scottish Parliaments were recorded in Scots from 1424). Linguistically, Scots closely resembled the dialect of English spoken just on the other side of the national border; both were descended from the Northumbrian dialect of Anglo-Saxon. For many Scotsmen, in fact, Scots and English were virtually the same language. Before 1500, the Scottish referred to their own vernacular as "Inglis" (English), and the term "Scots," first used by a Scottish writer in 1494, is used almost interchangeably with "Inglis" throughout the sixteenth century.[76] The author of *The Complaynt of Scotland* (*c.* 1549), responding to a barrage of English propaganda promoting union, argued defiantly that there was no natural affinity between the two nations. But despite his polemic, he made an exception for language:

> There is nocht tua nations undir the firmament that ar mair contrar and different fra uthirs nor is inglis men and scottis men quhoubeit that thai be . . . in ane ile, and nychtbours, and of ane langage.[77]

In England, Scots was not considered "Inglis" proper but rather the version of English spoken in the northern provinces. Andrew Boorde, describing the various languages spoken in England, wrote, "There is also the Northern tongue, the whyche is trew Scotysshe; and the Scottes tongue is the Northern tongue."[78] The earliest English grammars and dictionaries often recorded Scottish words, and the earliest researches into older forms of the language produced evidence that Scots, with northern English, had retained more features of Anglo-Saxon than southern English had. On the contemporary linguistic map as drawn by Renaissance English writers, Scots was a province of English, an English dialect that had attained the status of a foreign national language.

Like Welsh, the Celtic vernacular native to Scotland was repressed by Renaissance English legislation, but not until the early seventeenth century, after the accession of the Scottish James I. In 1609 James decreed that the highland clans send their eldest child to school in the lowlands to learn English. In 1616, he went further: An Act of the Privy Council required that "the vulgar Inglische toung be universallie plantit, and the Irishe language, whilk is one of the cheif and principall causis of the continewance of barbaritie and incivilitie amongis the inhabitants of the Ilis and Heylandis . . . be abolisheit and removit."[79] Under the "Irish" label, Scottish Gaelic and its speakers were designated as dangerous "foreigners" within their own nation, in an Act confirmed by the Scottish Parliament in 1631.[80]

The suppression of Scots, on the other hand, was never a matter of official policy. At least, neither the English nor the Scottish crown decreed Anglicization, the process by which the Scottish gradually assimilated their writing to southern forms. To a certain extent, the Anglicization of Scots was merely a by-product of cultural evolution, a process coterminous with the centralization of the vernacular in England. The Reformation of 1560 brought the English Geneva Bible and a largely English Psalter to the northern kingdom, but the Scottish, unlike the Welsh, did not revert to books of worship in their own tongue. A literary "reformation" of Scotland, however, long predated this; English poetry and prose circulated in Scotland from the fourteenth century or earlier, and Chaucer's influence on native poets is well known. Scottish *makars* of the fifteenth and sixteenth centuries not only imitated Chaucer's style, but tried out English spellings and English locutions as well. By 1560, Scots writing was already a mixed dialect, with pairs of spellings like *ony* and *any, gude* and *good, quha* and *who,* occuring side by side, sometimes in the same work.[81]

The Anglicization of Scots was thus promoted by many Scottish writers, who consciously sought to adapt their language to the more prestigious southern idiom. In 1513 Gavin Douglas wrote that Scots was "braid and plane" alongside "sudron."[82] Many sixteenth-century Scottish authors, such as George Buchanan, were bilingual, and alternately wrote in Scots and in "sudron"; others, like Sir William Alexander, gradually eliminated Scotticisms from their writings over the course of their careers. Alexander himself prepared the successive editions of his poetry published in 1604, 1606, and 1616; with each new edition, Alexander eliminated further traces of his Scottish ancestry, adapting his language to the "perfections" of English, as he explains in the preface to *Darius*: "For the more parte I use the Englishe phrase, as worthie to be preferred before our owne for the elegance and perfection thereof."[83] After 1603, authors such as Alexander quickly stepped up their efforts to make their language conform to that of the English court.

Seventeenth-century grammarians such as Alexander Gill generally sought to rule the English vernacular in conformity with the "general" language of London and the English court. But the union of the crowns inspired at least one attempt to renegotiate the terms of Anglicization while a Scotsman reigned over the

King's English. In his *Of the Orthographie and Congruitie of the Britan Tongue* (1619), the Scottish spelling reformer Alexander Hume tried to turn the tide of Anglicization by introducing Scots features into a new, integrated "Britan Tongue."[84] By insisting on the use of the word "Britan" to describe a "united" vernacular, Hume was appealing directly to James's designs for union. Like the Welsh grammarian William Salesbury, Hume used the term "Britan" to insinuate Scots into the new linguistic rule. He begins by invoking the King's personal interest in language, reminding James that he

> fel sundrie tymes on this subject reproving your courteoures, quha on a new conceat of sinnes sum tymes spilt (as they cal it) the King's language. Quilk thing it is reported that your Majestie not onlie refuted with impregnable reasones, but alsoe fel on Barret's opinion that you wald cause the universities mak an Inglish grammar to repres the insolencies of sik green heades.
>
> (p. 2)

Hume's reforms are thus intended to help enforce the "King's language" – or rather, Hume's own version of it – and to "repres" deviations from that standard. He explains that English and Scots are "dialectes of ane tonge" (p. 8) whose differences he seeks to settle: "My purpose is not to deal with impossibilities . . . but to conform (if reason will conform us) the south and north beath in latine and in English" (p. 9). He aims at an impartial estimate of the phonology of each dialect, and the way each represents sounds graphically. Sometimes "reason" finds in favor of southern English, sometimes Scots. The letter *a*, for example "the south soundes as beath thei and we sound it in *bare*, nudus; and we, as beath thei and we sound it in *bar*, obex. But without partialitie . . . we pronounce it better" (p. 8). Sometimes he finds both dialects lacking: "*u*, the south . . . pronounces *eu*, we *ou*, both, in my simple judgement, wrang" (p. 11). Hume championed certain Scottish spellings that Anglicization was phasing out:

> To reform an errour bred in the south, and now usurped be our ignorant printeres, I wil tel quhat befel my-self quhen I was in the south. . . . Ther rease, upon sum accident, *quhither quho, quhe, quhat*, etc. sould be symbolized with *q* or *w*. . . . At table my antagonist . . . began that I was becum an heretik . . . that I denyed *quho* to be spelled with a *w*, but with *qu*. . . . But *w* is a labial letter, *quho* a gutteral sound. And therfore *w* can not symboliz *quho*. . . . The proposition, said he, I understand; the assumption is Scottish, and the conclusion false.
>
> (p. 18)[85]

Whatever the merits of Hume's arguments, he was judged a "heretik" for suggesting that English adopt Scottish features. Needless to say, Hume's new "Britan" language was not adopted by speakers in any region of James's greater Britain. The Anglicization of Scottish writing proceeded, instead, at an increasingly rapid pace.

The accession of a Scot to the throne of England only accelerated the decline of Scots, and James personally presided over its fall. From his youth, James was proficient in both Scots and southern English; while he managed to avoid Scots diction in his letters to Queen Elizabeth, for example, he used it liberally in his earlier correspondence to his countrymen.[86] At the opening of the English Parliament in 1603, James made a case for the Union and for the naturalization of Scots born after his accession to the English throne, calling language as witness:

> Hath not God first united these two Kingdoms both in Language, Religion and similitude of maners? Yea, hath he not made us all in one island, compassed with one Sea, and of itselfe by nature so indivisible, as almost those that were borderers themselves on the late Borders, cannot distinguish, nor know, or discern, their own limits?[87]

James here reverses the argument of the Scottish nationalist who wrote the *Complaynt of Scotland*, suggesting that a "similitude" of language bespeaks a "similitude" of nature. James, in fact, repeatedly invoked "nature" as the grounds for uniting England and Scotland, arguing that the union of the kingdoms had already been effected in his body or person: "I desire a perfect Union of Lawes and persons, and such Naturalizing as may make one body of both Kingdomes under mee your King." To leave the nations divided was thus likened to regicide; to deny "that Union which is made in my blood," James argued, is "to cut me asunder the one halfe of me from the other."[88] But the Commons, who debated this for five years, persevered in their objections to two of James's terms of Union: First, the "naturalization" of the Scots, which would (in their view) make a foreign people possessors and inheritors of English property; second, the alteration of the "ancient and honourable name England" to Britain.[89]

These two objections, it is crucial to note, are not entirely unrelated. James, it seems, understood the name "Britain" as a sign of a "united" nature, as a representation of shared blood. Just as a father passes on his name, a single name, to his children, he declared, so he names his subjects "Britons" – "for we are Brethran."[90] This new name, moreover, would propagate a new accord: "The name will beget love, unity in diadem, in name and in government." James further decreed that the political border between the two nations be abolished linguistically, so that the marches or border regions between Scotland and England be renamed "the Middle Shires."[91] James's linguistic policy was thus an effort to create a "natural" relationship between England and Scotland, to reproduce two separate nations as a single body politic. James, in other words, hoped to realize the naturalization of the Scots by *producing* the linguistic grounds for union.

James was not alone in associating linguistic unity with "natural" ties of blood, or invoking a rhetoric of "family" to describe those who shared a common linguistic descent. William Camden celebrated the legacy of Germany in the Saxon blood and Saxon language of the English people, which had been "propagated" through conquest:

> This English tongue is extracted, as the nation, from the Germans the
> most glorious of all now extant in Europe for their morall, and martiall
> virtues, and preserving the libertie entire, as also for propagating their
> language by happy victories.[92]

Richard Verstegan, who worked to educate his countrymen about their glorious
Germanic roots, believed it a cultural imperative to translate French and other
foreign words to native English ones; Verstegan himself (né Rowlands) changed
his name as a means of announcing and affirming his German descent. For
Verstegan, names were not incidental to personhood, but embodied (racial)
identity. And Gill, when he entreated his countrymen to preserve the legacy
of Saxon, made the cause of language the cause of blood: "O you English, you
I appeal to, in whose veins flows that ancestral blood; retain, retain what
hitherto remaines of your native tongue."[93] For Gill, the English language
metonymically stood for the nation itself, and for a people bound together
by the same "ancestral blood," one that must never subject itself to the conquest
of foreign peoples or foreign tongues.

Although James claimed that the Scottish and the English were already united
by language, his own linguistic and literary practices reveal that he considered
their languages different enough; the progress of Anglicization in his own
writing is further evidence of how the King looked to language reform as a
means of "naturalizing" Scots as English. Although all of the printed editions
of the *Basilicon Doron*, for example, are in southern English, James's original
manuscript was written in Scots.[94] This manuscript marks a turning point in the
early modern history of this language, for it is one of the last major prose works
written in Scots before its rapid decline at the turn of the century.[95] James's
discussion of poetry in Book 3 originally read this way:

> The cheefe comendation of a poeme is that quhen the verse sall be shaiken
> sindrie in prose it sall be founde sa riche of quike inventions & poetike
> flouris, as it sall retaine the lustre of a poeme althoch in prose, & I walde
> also advyse you to writte in youre awin langage. . . . It best becumis a king
> to purifie & make famouse his awin langage quhairin he maye ga before
> all his subjectes as it settis him weill to doe in all laufull things.[96]

James's text was filled with Scottish spellings, including the use of *quh* and *i* for
the unstressed vowel in *flouris*, as well as Scottish phonemes (*a* for *o* in *sa* and
ga; *s* for *sh* in *sall*; *ch* for *gh* in *althoch*). All of the published editions, however,
eliminate these features. Here is the same passage from the edition of 1603:

> The chiefe commendation of a poeme is, that when the verse shall be
> shaken sundrie in prose, it shall be founde so riche in quick inventions, &
> poeticke floures . . . as it shall retaine the lustre of a poeme, although in
> prose. And I would also advise you to write in your owne language. . . . It
> best becommeth a king to purifie and make famous his owne tongue;
> wherein he may goe before all his subjectes; as it setteth him well to doe
> in all honest and lawfull things.[97]

James's original manuscript also contained forty-five Scottish locutions with over 150 occurrences, only a few of them surviving into print.[98] It is likely that James, like the poet William Alexander, supervised the Anglicization of his works, but it is important to note that it did not come naturally, even to the King of England. James, it seems, worked to naturalize not only the Scottish people, but the Scots language, and in both cases "naturalizing" meant uniting with England by assimilating to English rule.

James apparently planned to submit his poetical writings to a similar procedure, for there is evidence that he was preparing an edition of his poetry as a companion to his 1616 prose works.[99] A manuscript whose title page reads "All the kings short poesis that ar not printed," written between 1616 and 1618, reveals some of the ways in which James planned to reform some of his earlier poetry for publication. His translations from Du Bartas, originally written in the 1580s, included these lines:

> Nou even as quhen a prince or king dois over us so command
> as underneath the yoake of lau he garris his greatness stand
> he reulis without suspicion and the comounuelth enjoyes
> most happelie a quyet state uithout tirannike toyes
> but if that cruel tirrant lyke he never satiat be
> uith his goode subjectes saikless bloode & if his suorde do flee
> . . .
> the lyke falls out quehen as one of the elementis empyres
> over his three fellouis modestly & not thaire urake requyres
> & quhen as a proportion affeirant joynes ue see
> the subject humouris uith the cheif thoch thay unaequall be
> . . .
> but if that lyke unto that king quo barbarous did desyre
> that all the cittizenis of his most michtie great empyre
> baire but one craige that by that meanes (o crueltie) he micht
> by one great blou bereave the lyves of all the romanis quicht.

Twenty years later, the passage was revised for publication this way:

> Now even as when a Prince or King does over us so commande,
> As underneath the yoake of law he gars his greatness stande;
> He rules without suspicion, and the common wealth enjoyes
> Most happilie a quiet state, without tyrannique toyes:
> Bot if that cruell Tyranne like, he never satiate be,
> With his good subjects saickles bloode, and if his sworde doe flie
> . . .
> The like falls out when as one of the elements empires,
> Over his three fellowes modestlie, and not there wracke requires;
> And when as a proportion, affeirand joynes we see
> The subject humours with the cheefe, though they unequall be:

. . .

> Bot if that like unto that King who barb'rous did desire
> That all the cittizens of his most mightie great empire,
> Boore bot one craige that by that means (o crueltie) he might;
> By one greate blowe bereave the lives of all the Romans quitt.[100]

The editors of this manuscript – Prince Charles, with the help of the Groom of the Chamber, Thomas Carey – carefully Anglicized James's spelling, emending forms such as *quhen* to *when* (line 51), *micht* to *might* (line 67) and *elementis* to *elements* (line 59).[101] Yet they allowed a Scottish participle to remain in line 61 ("And when as a proportion *affeirand* joynes we see") along with a number of other Scottish words – *gars* (line 52), *saickless* (line 56), and *craige* (line 67). There is no clear explanation for why James allowed these Scotticisms to remain. But one fact remains: Scots features were far more likely to survive Anglicization in James's poetry than in his prose.[102]

There may be at least a partial explanation for this in the fact that James was also the author of a treatise on Scots poetics, written in Scots and included in his published *Essayes* of 1584. The work, entitled, "Ane Schort Treatise Conteining some Reulis and Cautelis to be Observit and Eschewit in Scottis Poesie," was the first work of its kind in the native vernacular, as James is careful to establish. The language of the treatise, in contrast to everything else printed in the same volume, is nearly all Scots – as if it had bypassed Anglicization altogether.[103] James explains to his readers that he wrote the work because

> that as for thame that hes written on it of late, there hes never ane of thame written in our language. For albeit sindrie hes written of it in English, quhilk is lykest to our language, zit we differ from thame in sindrie reulis of Poesie, as ze will find be experience.[104]

James, who elsewhere denied that there was any significant distinction between English and Scots, set Scots apart as "our" language when it came to questions of literature. James became an English politician, but it seems he remained a Scottish poet, even contributing a text on Scots poetics. This surprising gesture of Scottish nationalism, of resistance to Anglicization, was perhaps prophetic, for literature remained one oasis of linguistic survival for Scots. While most seventeenth-century Scottish authors composed their works in English, Scots lived on in the Early and Middle Scots poetry that continued to be printed, and in a few new comic and satiric pieces composed in popular Scots.[105] In its own way, as we will see, English literature, too, provided such a haven. Somehow, English and Scottish literature maintained a border that even the King of Great Britain could not abolish.

There are relatively few representations of Scots in English literature of the period, and this surely has much to do with James's success in suppressing the articulation of cultural differences after his accession to the throne. Representations of Scots in English literature before 1603 are not clearly distinguished from those of northern English;[106] in practice, we can only be sure that Scots is intended if the character in question happens to hail from Scotland. If we were not told in *Henry V* that Shakespeare's Captain Jamy were a Scotsman, for example, we could not specify his dialect on the basis of his pronunciation alone: "It sall be vary gud, gud feith, gud captens bath, and I sall quit you with gud leve, as I may pick occasion; that sall I, mary" (3.2.102–4). In a few cases, however, features that are peculiar to Scots do occur in literary portraits of the period. Some of these include the spelling *quh* for *wh*, as in *quha* (who); the ending of the present participle in -*and*; and the third person preterite ending -*it* for English -*ed*. Some authors also employed diction that was uniquely Scottish. The problem is that it is impossible to determine how consciously authors were exploiting these elements, that is, whether they, themselves, were able to draw the boundaries that separated Scots from northern English. Before 1603, Scots appears in at least a half a dozen plays, as well as popular jest books, and its presence often indicates an underlying hostility towards the "ill neighborhood"[107] of the northern kingdom. Nathaniel Woodes, in *The Conflict of Conscience* (1581), may intend Scots in his characterization of an evil Catholic priest named Caconos. Woodes uses dialect to suggest that Caconos's Catholicism is as alien and perverse as his forms of his speech; he tells his close ally Hypocrisy:

> In gude feth sir, this newis de gar me lope,
> Ay is as light as ay me wend, gif that yo wol me troth,
> Far new ayen within awer lond installed is the Pope,
> Whese Legat & authoritie tharawawt awr cuntry goth,
> And charge befare him far te com, us Preests end lemen bath,
> Far te spay awt gif that he mea, these new sprang Arataykes,
> Whilk de disturb awr hally Kirke, laik a sart of saysmataykes.[108]

Robert Greene's *The Scottish History of James the Fourth* (c. 1590) concerns the treachery of a Scottish king who marries the daughter of the King of England, only to plot her murder. The English declare war on the Scottish, who are finally defeated, and James IV is redeemed by the love of his English bride. Greene's play is unhistorical, but there is a great deal of evidence to suggest that the author intended to comment on Anglo-Scottish relations in his own day. First, Greene gave his source, which dealt with a conflict between Ireland and Scotland, national significance by replacing Ireland with England. Greene's play continually alludes to England's fears of Scottish plots against Elizabeth.[109] The play is structured within a frame tale, in which a misanthropic Scot, Bohan, emerges from a tomb to tell Oberon a story of corruption at the old Scottish court, "much like our court of Scotland this day." Oberon declares himself Bohan's friend, but is rebuffed:

> What wot I or reck I that? Whay, guid man, I reck no friend, nor ay reck
> no foe; al's ene to me. Git thee ganging, and trouble not may whayet, or
> ay's gar thee reckon me nene of thay friend, by the mary mass sall I.[110]

160

Greene concentrated his use of Scots in Bohan's vituperative introduction, occasionally reminding us of the dialect by injecting a word like *guid* into the speech of his other Scottish characters. Like Bohan's diatribe in Scots, Greene's play as a whole seems to damn the Scots and their intentions. According to his most recent editor, *The Scottish History of James the Fourth* may have been one of the works which caused an outcry in late sixteenth-century Scotland that "comedians of London . . . scorn the king and the people of this land in their play."[111]

Shakespeare's Captain Jamy is the last Scotsman to use his native dialect in English literature before 1603. Fluellen's "marvellous falorous gentlemen" displays only the most vigorous commitment to the King's cause:

> By the mess, ere theise eyes of mine take themselves to slomber, ay'll de gud service, or I'll lig i'th'grund for it; ay, or go to death; and I'll pay't as valorously as I may, that sall I suerly do.

> (3.2.114–17)

Yet *Henry V* begins with the King's lengthy aside on the "ill neighborhood" of Scotland (1.2.154), and the threat of a Scottish invasion, which may cast a bit of a shadow over Jamy, despite his profession of loyalty. In a few years, however, even characters as benign as Captain Jamy disappear from English literature. After James's accession to the English throne, authors were afraid of offending the Scottish King, and with good reason. In 1605, George Chapman, Ben Jonson, and John Marston were imprisoned for their collaborative work on *Eastward Hoe*, in which two gentlemen refer, with hints of a Scots dialect, to James's practice of indiscriminately patronizing his fellow Scotsmen. Seagull, a sea captain, makes a snide reference to the union of the Scottish and English, as he discourses on the colony of Virginia:

> You shal live freely there, without Sergeants, or Courtiers, or Lawyers, or Intelligencers, onely a few industrious Scots perhaps, who indeed are disperst over the face of the whole earth. But as for them, there are no greater friends to English-men and England, when they are out an't, in the world, then they are. And for my part, I would a hundred thousand of 'hem were there, for wee are all one Countreymen now, yee know; and we shoulde finde ten times more comfort of them there, than we do heere.[112]

From 1603 to 1625, the duration of James's reign, Scottish characters rarely appear at all in English literature; the notable exception, Shakespeare's *Macbeth*, has been fully Anglicized, although he retains the northern habit of talking to witches. The disappearance of Scots from English literature during James's rule suggests that the portrayal of the dialect itself was considered a form of slander.

James largely succeeded in eradicating Scots from English literature, along with the allegation that the two nations were not, as he claimed, of one language. But there was one channel of linguistic transmission over the border that James was unable to block. Throughout the sixteenth and seventeenth centuries, popular ballads, many originating in Scotland, circulated in England, and were occasionally set down in manuscripts or prepared in broadsheet form for the popular press. The best-known ballad of the period, popularly known as "Chevy Chase," comes down to us in several versions, and it is impossible to know whether Philip Sidney had to "confess his own barbarousness" for enjoying a Scottish or an English song. Although we do not know the details of their transmission, ballads were obviously subject to translation as they crossed the border, with traces occasionally remaining of the exchange. Sidney may have heard the story of the encounter between the Northumbrian Percy and the Scottish Douglas in the ballad "The Battle of Otterburn," which, in the extant version from 1550, contained northern or Scottish elements:

> Over Hoppertope hyll they cam in,
> And so down by Rodclyffe crage;
> Upon Greme Lynton they lyghted dowyn,
> Styrande [stirrring] many a stage [stag].
> And boldley brente Northumberlond,
> And haryed many a towyn;
> They dyd owr Ynglysshe men grete wrange,
> To batell that were not bowyn.[113]

It seems likely, in any case, that Scots entered the English imagination through the songs that circulated freely on both sides of the border.

In fact, the re-entry of Scots into Renaissance English literature may have occurred, indirectly, by way of the ballads. Ben Jonson's unfinished play, *The Sad Shepherd, or a Tale of Robin Hood* (*c.* 1635) sets traditional ballad material to the tune of pastoral drama. We have no decisive evidence concerning the dating of the fragment, but Jonson's prologue, which begins "He that hath feasted you these forty yeares," is no doubt the strongest proof we have that Jonson wrote it at the end of his career.[114] Jonson's sad shepherd is Aeglamour, mourning the death of his beloved Earine, whom he believes has drowned in the Trent. But Earine has in fact been abducted by the evil witch Maudlin, who has trapped the girl inside of a tree as a prize for her son Lorel. Maudlin further torments Aeglamour by dressing her daughter, Douce, in Earine's clothes, and sending her running, phantom-like, before him. Meanwhile Robin Hood is planning a feast for all his companions of Sherwood Forest, complete with venison prepared by Maid Marian. Determined to wreak havoc throughout the forest, Maudlin disguises herself as Marian and abducts the venison for her own pleasure. At the end of the fragment, which runs for almost two and a half acts, Robin Hood is beginning to suspect Maudlin of treachery. When he tries to capture her, she escapes, and Robin Hood is left holding the belt he had grabbed onto in the struggle.

There is much here that evokes Spenser – the pastoral loves of Aeglamour and his fellow shepherds recall Colin Clout and company, while Maudlin recalls the wiles of Duessa, and in the final scene, Florimell in flight. As many have noted, Jonson's debt to Spenser is also evident in the dialect that he created especially for the piece. We know that Jonson disapproved of the more elevated pastoral diction of Sidney and his continental predecessors, for he told Drummond that such authors "make every man speak as well as themselves, forgetting decorum." Jonson, however, was unlikely to turn to archaisms as a source of pastoral diction, for he denounced the Elizabethan poet who "in affecting the Ancients, writ no Language."[115] Instead, Jonson devised a diction based almost entirely on contemporary dialect, containing both northern and Scottish features. Here is Maudlin the witch mocking her son for his ineptness as a lover:

> Fowle Limmer! drittie Lowne!
> Gud faith, it duills mee that I am thy Mother!
> . . .
> Thou woo thy Love? thy Mistresse? with twa Hedgehoggs?
> A stinkand brock? A polcat? out thou houlet!
> . . .
> (false Gelden) gang thy gait
> And du thy turnes, betimes: or I'is gar take
> Thy new breikes fra' thee, and thy duiblet tu.
> The Tailleur, and the Sowter sall undu'
> All they ha' made; except thou manlier woo!
> (2.3.2–4; 2.3.6–8; 2.3.20–4)

But crucially, Jonson did not distribute this language evenly among his characters, as Spenser had in *The Shepheardes Calender*. The dialect of *The Sad Shepherd*, in fact, is not a generalized "pastoral diction" at all, but the language of a few chosen characters. Unaccountably, one of Robin Hood's huntsmen, Scathlock, uses an occasional dialectalism ("quh'a suld let me?" (1.6.56)), although his own brother, Scarlet, does not. With this exception, Jonson concentrated the dialect in the speech of Maudlin and her son. Like Shakespeare's Caliban, the unregenerate Lorel has some poetry in him, and his use of dialect at times can only be described as lyrical. Lorel woos his prisoner Earine with an inventory of his possessions:

> A Chestnut, whilk hath larded money a Swine,
> Whose skins I weare, to fend me fra the Cold.
> A Poplar greene, and with a kerved Seat,
> Under whose shade I solace in the heat;
> And thence can see gang out, and in, my neat.
> Twa trilland brookes, each (from his spring) doth meet,
> And make a river, to refresh my feet.
> (2.2.23–9)

Earine, who fails to hear any music in the swineherd's suit, mocks Lorel by aping his dialect:

> O, the feind, and thee!
> Gar take them hence: they fewmand all the claithes,
> And prick my Coates: hence with 'hem, limmer lowne.
> (2.2.42–4)[116]

163

The other characters associate the dialect with rusticity and coarseness; Robin Hood, for one, remarks "Nay, you must give them all their rudenesses;/They are not else themselves, without their language" (1.6.59–60). But Jonson, like Spenser before him, opened the borders of literary language to the rude music of the native dialects.

Jonson may have borrowed from Spenser the idea of interspersing his pastoral with dialect, but he surely found another source for his diction in the native ballad tradition. After all, Robin Hood was known chiefly through the ballads sung of his exploits, and, as I have suggested, there is reason to believe that the English would have associated balladry with provincial language. What is less certain is whether the dialect Jonson borrowed for Maudlin and her family is northern English or Scottish in character, and indeed, whether the distinction would have been meaningful to Jonson at all. From a purely linguistic standpoint, it is impossible to say. Some of the features Jonson used were specifically northern, others were uniquely Scottish, while the great majority might have been found on either side of the border. Generic criteria also yield mixed results: The pastoral tradition behind Jonson's play called for northern English, but ballads might be expected to have a Scottish flavor. The traditional Robin Hood ballads, on the other hand, were English productions, and though northern English was not indigenous to Sherwood Forest, Jonson may have intended the dialect to enhance his rural English setting. To confuse matters further, the dialect of *The Sad Shepherd* is not the language of ordinary provincials, but of supernatural beings, and the idea of a special language for witches, who were often associated with Scottish lore, might tip the scales back in favor of Scots. Then again, the dramatists Thomas Heywood and Richard Brome discovered a few witches living in the north country of Lancashire.[117]

While it is true that the origins of Jonson's dialect cannot be determined on linguistic grounds alone, there is other, literary testimony that bears on the case. Some of the Scotticisms that appear in the witch's dialect do not occur in any other English text of the period, with the exception of *The Valiant Scot* (1637), written by a Scottish author. These include the use of *quh* for *wh*, the preterite ending in *-it* (Maudlin's "I have departit it 'mong my poore Neighbours" (2.6.37)), and the present participle in *-and* ("When our Dame Hecat/Made it her going-night, over the Kirk-yard/With all the barkeand parish tykes set at her/While I sate whyrland of my brasen spindle" (2.3.42–5)). Further, Jonson had already created a northern English character in *Bartholomew Fair*, whose dialect does not include these features. We know that Jonson visited Scotland in 1618–19, and may have gained a fuller acquaintance with Scots at that time. It seems likely, then, that Jonson had some sense of the distinction between northern and Scottish forms, and deliberately chose Scots as a constitutive element of Maudlin's dialect.

This is not to imply, however, that Jonson intended his dialect to reproduce Scots in a literal sense, that he meant his audience to imagine that Maudlin and her kin had emigrated from Scotland to Sherwood Forest. Jonson does not localize their language, but neither does he merely recreate, as it has been suggested, the "synthetic English Doric" of Spenser.[118] To treat the dialect Jonson employed selectively in *The Sad Shepherd* as the playwright's idea of a pastoral language ignores its very specialized function in the play. Aeglamour and Earine speak only the King's English, as do Robin Hood and Maid Marian; dialect, for Jonson, is the language of witches, louts, and thieves. If Jonson grants the dialect some charms, he does so with Maudlin herself as well, whose malice is tempered with a kind of puckishness.

Jonson's *Sad Shepherd* offers an important lesson in the production of literary dialects in the early modern period. The "provincial" language of Maudlin and her family are not intended to evoke a particular region of England (or Scotland); like many dialects that appear in Renaissance literary works, the "Scots" of *The Sad Shepherd* pertains more to person than to any specific place. In Scots, Jonson found a dialect that had often carried the presumption of evil-doings, at least before James I had forced the assignation underground. But if it was still unacceptable to portray Scotsmen speaking in Scots, Jonson displaced the dialect from its native ground and found a new set of "aliens" to embody its voice. The result is a language that, whatever its original derivation, is ascribed to men and women of a radically different nature.

It would be many years before Scots was to enjoy a genuine revival, either in Scottish or in English literature, so successfully had James and the politics of Anglicization suppressed the articulation of linguistic and cultural difference. Evoking the varied linguistic traditions of contemporary dialect literature, literary pastoral, and popular song, the Scottish forms of Jonson's *Sad Shepherd* managed to survive the siege.

* * *

By way of conclusion, I would like to return to Shakespeare's *Henry V*, and the idea of an English empire united by nature and by words. The notion of the British empire as a single "body," naturalizing the disparate peoples it contains as one people, permeates Shakespeare's play. Henry's conquest of France is put forward, from the start, as a matter of inheritance and rightful descent; once the technical matter of the French Salic law ("In terram Salicam mulieres ne succedant" (1.2.38)) is removed as an obstacle in the opening scene of the play, Henry's "natural" claim to France is repeatedly invoked: "By law of nature and of nations, 'longs/To him and to his heirs, namely, the crown" (2.4.80–1). The war itself is figured, again and again, as one that sets English "breeding" against that of the French they mean to disinherit. Calling his army into the breach of war, Henry invokes the claims of English blood:

> Dishonor not your mothers; now attest
> That those whom you call'd fathers did beget you.
> . . .
> And you, good yeomen,

> Whose limbs were made in England, show us here
> The mettle of your pasture; let us swear
> That you are worth your breeding.
>
> (3.1.22–3; 3.1.25–8)

The French, in turn, mourn their losses as a loss of "breeding" as well as blood, and imagine the "Englishing" of France as the propagation of their enemies:

> Our madams mock at us, and plainly say
> Our mettle is bred out, and they will give
> Their bodies to the lust of English youth
> To new-store France with bastard warriors.
>
> (3.5.28–31)

The French Princess, Katherine, will indeed give her body to the lust of an English youth, as part of the settlement of the war, for the conclusion of the play offers the promise that Henry, the *Héritier de France* (5.2.340), will "from her blood raise up/Issue" (5.2.348–9). From the perspective of the French queen, Isabella, the marriage offers the hope of complete cultural union, accomplished by the new "ties" of blood, and she prays that one day "English may as French, French Englishmen/Receive each other" (5.2.367–8).

The "Englishing" of Katherine's body is figured in an early scene in which the princess translates her own body, part by part, into the language of her conqueror. Katherine asks Alice, an "old gentlewoman," to teach her the English words for hand, finger, arm, elbow, nails, neck, and chin. The Princess is a conscientious but not a gifted student, and her pronunciation is often comical (*de bilbow* for the elbow, *de nick* for the neck, *de sin* for the chin, etc.). Her broken English leads her to utter what she hears as French obscenities: "Le foot et le count! O Seigneur Dieu! ils sont lest mots de son mauvais, corruptible, gros, et impudique, et non pour les dames de honneur d'user" (3.4.52–4). By implication, the "translation" from French to English in this play is one in which "dames de honneur" – especially, the Princess herself – are corrupted by the change; but then, King Henry never concerned himself with the degradation of French women: "What is't to me, when you yourselves are cause,/If your pure maidens fall into the hand/Of hot and forcing violation?" (3.2.19–21). Language, in this scene, enacts a change in nature, a degrading alteration of the body of the foreigner, that Anglicization puts in force.

But it is crucial to note that that change is never fully accomplished in the play, that Katherine is never fully "Anglicized," as Harry wills. In the final scene of *Henry V*, the King attempts to win the love of the French Princess, despite a language barrier that might obviate their union. Harry is gracious about her deficiency in English: "If you will love me soundly with your French heart, I will be glad to hear you confess it brokenly with your English tongue" (5.2.104–6). His wit is lost upon her, however, for Katherine does not understand him: "I cannot tell wat is dat" (5.2.177). The King overcomes her incomprehension much as Pistol had in an earlier scene that prefigures this one. Pistol is trying to extort money from a French soldier, but his prisoner speaks only French: "*O prenez miséricorde! ayez pitié de moi!*" (4.4.11). But Pistol, ever resourceful, simply hears what he wants to hear, in this case, that the prisoner is offering him money ("Moy shall not serve, I will have forty moys" (4.4.12)). The King, like Pistol, ultimately gets what he wants from his French "captive," despite her lack of English. Yet when Harry implores Katherine, for the last time, "Break thy mind to me in broken English" (5.2.245–6), Katherine's final answer is only this: "Dat is as it shall please de *roi mon père*" (5.2.247). Katherine's deference to her father is appropriate enough under the circumstances, but the fact is that she, like the French soldier, never directly consents to Harry's will. The princess subjects herself to the will of a king, but she does not name that king as Henry; she neither translates the phrase *le roi* fully into English nor the sovereignty over her body to her new English lord. Though the implication is that Katherine will become part of the English body politic, promising to "new-store France" with English blood, she, too, seems to have learned something from the language lessons taught throughout the play, breaking her mind with broken English – but not quite as her conqueror demands.

Spenser was not anomalous in his decision to make "Iren" (Ireland) herself articulate a language policy that would silence the native language of her own people. The foreigners who use dialect or broken English in Renaissance writing are often made to speak for their surrender to English rule, both linguistic and political. Indeed, the dialects described in this book are all, in a sense, languages imposed by speakers of the King's English, fully subject to the prescriptions of their authors. It is no coincidence that the invention of stage dialects – linguistic caricatures, easily recognized and easily imitated, produced and reproduced for literary purposes – can be traced to this period. Yet, if Renaissance literary dialects, with their limited repertoires of form, tend to contain or suppress differences, they also mark and enunciate them: Neither Fluellen nor the French Princess, for example, are fully "Englished," fully united by conquest to England. After all, in recreating dialects for the stage, Renaissance authors were not primarily concerned with verisimilitude, but rather with making difference, itself, unmistakable. The broken English of Renaissance literature sometimes exposes a fault-line in contemporary efforts towards political or cultural commonality, by making the difference of language speak.

Making a "difference of English," I have suggested throughout this book, was an implicit design of many early modern writers, even when they were not attempting to represent varieties of current speech – or dialects in the conventional sense. Many, instead, cultivated "hard words" such as neologisms, or thieves' cant, or archaisms; these, too, are dialects of early modern English that were defined in relation to a "common" national language. It is well known that English took multiple forms in this period; what is remarkable is how many of those forms were deliberately produced by poets, playwrights, and other early modern language reformers, despite all their talk of a common language.

Renaissance writers, in a word, invented the difference of English – not only by giving form to its dialects, but by systematically endowing those forms with cultural value and meaning – for the first time in the history of the language. We should no doubt continue to credit Renaissance literary writers – Shakespeare, Spenser, and Jonson among them – with developing, refining, and advancing the vernacular, as they have been credited since their own time. But we should consider, too, that the "triumph of English" we celebrate in this period was predicated on a process of dividing and conquering the national language.

There were many competing answers put forward to the question of the language in Renaissance England, the question of which forms, specifically, were really and truly "English." In many ways, the debate over national linguistic standards had just begun. For the moment, demarcating the boundaries between dialects, discriminating the "difference of English," was enough to confer linguistic authority on writers who claimed to be in a position to judge.

NOTES

INTRODUCTION

1 As quoted in M. Aston, *The Fifteenth Century: The Prospect of Europe*, New York, Harcourt Brace, 1968, p. 41.

2 R.F. Jones, *The Triumph of the English Language: A Survey of Opinions Concerning the Vernacular from the Introduction of Printing to the Restoration*, Stanford, Calif., Stanford University Press, 1953.

3 Robert Cawdrey, *A Table Alphabeticall* (1604), Ann Arbor, Mich., University Microfilms, "To the Reader."

4 Richard W. Bailey's *Images of English: A Cultural History of the Language* also focuses on "ideas about language – and the images used to express them" (Ann Arbor, Mich., University of Michigan Press, 1991, pp. viii–ix). I am indebted to Bailey's emphasis on the importance of understanding the history of the "images" of English.

Regarding the "imaginary" nature of dialects, Pierre Bourdieu in *Language and Symbolic Power* has suggested that the very idea that a language can be divided into discrete "dialects" is an illusion born and perpetuated by the ideology of nationalism: "Only by transposing the representation of the national language is one led to think that regional dialects exist, themselves divided into subdialects – an idea flatly contradicted by the study of dialectics" (trans. Gino Raymond and Matthew Adamson, ed. John B. Thompson, Cambridge, Mass., Harvard University Press, 1991, p. 258n).

5 *Oxford English Dictionary*, s.v. "dialect." The word "dialect," referring to a variety of language, was first recorded in 1577.

6 Alexander Gill, *Logonomia Anglica* (1619), part 2, *Stockholm Studies in English* 27, trans. Robin C. Alston, eds Bror Danielsson and Arvid Gabrielson, Stockholm, Almquist & Wiksell, 1972, p. 102.

7 E.K. admits to the readers of Spenser's eclogues that "of many things which in him be strange, I know [the language] will seem the strangest" (*Epistle* to Gabriel Harvey, *The Works of Edmund Spenser*, eds Edwin Greenlaw *et al.*, vol. 7, part 1, Baltimore, Md., Johns Hopkins University Press, 1932–57).

8 N.F. Blake, *Shakespeare's Language: An Introduction*, London, Macmillan, 1983, p. 19.

9 David Bevington, General Introduction, *The Complete Works of Shakespeare*, ed. Bevington, New York, HarperCollins, 1992, p. lxxxiv.

10 Such phrases have been used frequently in characterizations of the linguistic *ethos* of the period. The "linguistic exuberance" and "linguistic enthusiasm" of Renaissance writers are invoked, respectively, by Joseph M. Williams, ("'O! When Degree is Shak'd': Sixteenth-Century Anticipations of Some Modern Attitudes

Toward Usage," in *English in Its Social Contexts: Essays in Historical Sociolinguistics*, eds Tim William Machan and Charles T. Scott, Oxford, Oxford University Press, 1992, p. 72) and by Bryan A. Garner ("Shakespeare's Latinate Neologisms," *Shakespeare Studies* 15, 1982, p. 154). Most recently, Gert Ronberg has described the "Renaissance delight in English as a literary language," as seen especially in the "lexical creativity" of its dramatists (*A Way With Words: The Language of English Renaissance Literature*, London, Edward Arnold, 1992, p. 22).

1 THE RENAISSANCE DISCOVERY OF DIALECT

1 Alexander Gill, *Logonomia Anglica* (1619), part 2, *Stockholm Studies in English* 27, trans. Robin C. Alston, eds Bror Danielsson and Arvid Gabrielson, Stockholm, Almquist & Wiksell, 1972, p. 84.
2 *Oxford English Dictionary*, s.v. "dialect." There is an earlier recorded example of the use of the word "dialect," as a variant of "dialectic", in 1551.
3 John Bullokar, *An English Expositor: Teaching the Interpretation of the Hardest Words Used in our Language* (1616), Ann Arbor, Mich., University Microfilms, F1.
4 *Epistle* to Gabriel Harvey, *The Works of Edmund Spenser*, eds Edwin Greenlaw *et al.*, vol. 7, part 1, Baltimore, Md., Johns Hopkins University Press, 1932–57.
5 Ben Jonson, *Poetaster* (1602), in *Ben Jonson*, vol. 4, eds C.H. Herford and Percy and Evelyn Simpson, Oxford, Clarendon Press, 1966, 5.3.549–61.
6 See Tony Crowley, *Standard English and the Politics of Language*, Urbana, Ill., University of Illinois Press, 1989, especially pp. 91–163 for a history of the varied uses of the phrase "standard language."
7 William Caxton, Prologue to the *Eneydos* (1490), in *The Prologues and Epilogues of William Caxton*, ed. W.J.B. Crotch, Millwood, N.Y., Kraus Reprints, 1978, p. 109; Thomas Wilson, *The Arte of Rhetorique* (1553), ed. Thomas J. Derrick, New York, Garland Publishing, 1982, pp. 325–9; Gill, *Logonomia Anglica*, p. 102; George Puttenham, *The Arte of English Poesie* (1589), eds Gladys Doidge Willcock and Alice Walker, Cambridge, Cambridge University Press, 1970, p. 144.
8 Joseph M. Williams, "'O! When Degree is Shak'd': Sixteenth-Century Antici- pations of Some Modern Attitudes Towards Usage," in *English in its Social Contexts: Essays in Historical Sociolinguistics*, eds Tim William Machan and Charles T. Scott, Oxford, Oxford University Press, 1992, p. 70.
9 Dante Alighieri, *De Vulgari Eloquentia* (*c.* 1303), trans. Warren Welliver, Ravenna, Longo Editore, 1981, I, 2; I, 5. All further citations refer to this edition and appear parenthetically in my text.
10 As Welliver points out in the notes to his translation, Dante had elsewhere, in his *Convivio*, called Latin "more beautiful, more effective, and more noble" than Italian (*De Vulgari*, p. 238).
11 See Angelo Mazzocco, "Dante's Notion of the *Vulgare Illustre*: A Reappraisal" for a summary of the long-standing debate among Italianists as to whether Dante's *vulgare illustre* represents "an abstraction, or a concrete linguistic entity" (*Papers in The History of Linguistics: Proceedings of the Third International Conference on the History of the Language Sciences*, eds Hans Aarsleff, Louis G. Kelly, and Hans- Joseph Niederehe, Amsterdam, John Benjamins, 1987, p. 129). Dante's *vulgare illustre*, it seems to me, must be "concrete" because Dante identifies its use among poets; it is "abstract," however, in that it does not represent any of the regional dialects, but rather an "artificial" dialect cultivated by poets.

12 For example, Niccoló Machiavelli's *Dialogue on Language* (*c.* 1515) pits Machiavelli against Dante, whose views on Italian are refuted (*The Literary Works of Machiavelli*, trans. and ed. J.R. Hale, Westport, Conn., Greenwood Press, 1979, pp. 175–90).

13 As quoted in G.A. Padley, *Grammatical Theory in Western Europe 1500–1700*, vol. 2, Cambridge, Cambridge University Press, 1988, p. 6.

14 The French established the Academie Richelieu after the Italian model, although its own *Dictionnaire* did not appear until 1694. See Aldo Scaglione, "The Rise of National Languages: East and West," in *The Emergence of National Languages*, ed. Aldo Scaglione, Ravenna, Longo Editore, 1984, pp. 36–7. For a collection of essays on the rise of standard languages throughout Europe, see the Academy of the Crusca's *The Fairest Flower: The Emergence of Linguistic Consciousness in Renaissance Europe*, Florence, University of California, International Conference of the Center for Medieval and Renaissance Studies, 1983.

15 Baldassare Castiglione, *The Book of the Courtier* (1528), trans. and ed. W.B. Drayton Henderson, London, J.M. Dent, 1928, pp. 11, 50, 13, and 51, respectively.

16 Castiglione, *The Courtier*, p. 52.

17 See Padley, *Grammatical Theory*, vol. 2, pp. 47–9, for a discussion of Castiglione's *lingua cortegiana*.

18 Gladys M. Turquet in Joachim Du Bellay, *The Defence and Illustration of the French Language* (1549), trans. and ed. Turquet, London, J.M. Dent, 1939, p. 5.

19 Du Bellay, *Defence*, p. 100. See Pierre Villey, *Les Sources Italiennes de la* Deffense et Illustration de la Langue Françoise *de Joachim Du Bellay*, New York, Burt Franklin, 1908, for a discussion of Du Bellay's Italian sources.

20 Du Bellay, *Defence*, pp. 21–2.

21 F. Brunot, *Histoire de la France*, as quoted in Padley, *Grammatical Theory*, vol. 2, p. 327.

22 Du Bellay, *Defence*, pp. 49, 56–7, and 45, respectively.

23 M.M. Bakhtin, *The Dialogic Imagination*, trans. Caryl Emerson and Michael Holquist, ed. Michael Holquist, Austin, Tex., University of Texas Press, 1981, p. 17. References to *Rabelais and His World* are from the translation of Helene Iswolsky (Bloomington, Ind., Indiana University Press, 1984). Further citations to these works appear parenthetically in my text.

24 Language historians commonly use the term "standardization" to refer to the rise of a dominant, though variable, dialect in vernacular writing. But "standardization," in this sense, does not refer to the codification of forms, but to the ascendance of one dialect over others. The term "centralization" is thus perhaps a more accurate way to characterize the rise of vernacular norms in the fourteenth through the seventeenth centuries in England.

25 Bakhtin writes, "Their [the dialects'] unique qualities began to be sensed in a new way, in the light of the evolving and centralizing norm of a national language" (*Dialogic Imagination*, p. 82).

26 See for example Albert C. Baugh and Thomas Cable, *A History of the English Language*, 3rd edn, Englewood Cliffs, N.J., Prentice-Hall, 1978, p. 193.

27 Sir Thomas Elyot, *The Book Named the Governor* (1531), ed. S.E. Lehmberg, London, J.M. Dent, 1962, p. 18.

28 As quoted in Williams, "'O! When Degree is Shak'd,'" p. 73.

29 As quoted in Eric Dobson, "Early Modern Standard English," *Transactions of the Philological Society*, 1955, pp. 40–1.

30 Notable beginnings include Dick Leith's *A Social History of English* (London, Routledge, 1983); Richard W. Bailey's *Images of English: A Cultural History of the Language*, (Ann Arbor, Mich., University of Michigan Press, 1991), and Tim William Machan and Charles T. Scott's *English in Its Social Contexts: Essays in Historical Sociolinguistics* (Oxford, Oxford University Press, 1992).

31 Pierre Bourdieu, *Language and Symbolic Power*, trans. Gino Raymond and Matthew Adamson, ed. John B. Thompson, Cambridge, Mass., Harvard University Press, 1991, pp. 48, 53, and 54, respectively.

32 Several sociolinguists have addressed the politics of the process by which certain forms of a language become authorized. See for example James Milroy and Lesley Milroy, *Authority in Language: Investigating Language Prescription and Standardization*, London, Routledge & Kegan Paul, 1985; Joshua A. Fishman, *Language and Nationalism: Two Integrative Essays*, Rowley, Mass., Newbury House, 1972; and John Earl Joseph, *Eloquence and Power: The Rise of Language Standards and Standard Languages*, New York, Basil Blackwell, 1987. Richard Helgerson has written a fascinating essay on the ideology of an age that sought to possess, in Edmund Spenser's words, "a kingdom of our own language" (see the introductory chapter of his *Forms of Nationhood: The Elizabethan Writing of England*, Chicago, Ill., University of Chicago Press, 1992, pp. 1–18).

33 S.S. Hussey, *The Literary Language of Shakespeare*, New York, Longman, 1982, p. 19.

34 From the statutes drawn up to define the purposes of the Academie Française (1635), as quoted in Baugh and Cable, *History of English*, p. 262.

35 As quoted in Robert L. Cooper, *Language Planning and Social Change*, Cambridge, Cambridge University Press, 1989, p. 11.

36 David Bevington in *The Complete Works of Shakespeare*, ed. Bevington, New York, HarperCollins, 1992, p. lxxxiv.

37 Gill, *Logonomia Anglica*, p. 191.

38 The first recorded comments on linguistic differences in England seem to be those of Giraldus Cambrensis who, in his *Description of Wales* (1190s), described the language of Devon as the purest form of English. Ranulf Higden, paraphrasing a passage from William of Malmesbury's *De Pontificabus* (*c.* 1125) critiqued the speech of his northern countrymen in his *Polychronicon* (*c.* 1330–50). John of Trevisa's 1387 translation reads:

> Al þe longage of þe Norþhumbres, and specialliche at York, is so scharp, slitting, and frotynge and unschape, þat we souþerne men may þat longage unneþe understonde. I trowe þat þat is bycause þat þey beeþ nyh to straunge men and naciouns þat speke strangliche, and also bycause þat the kynges of Engelond woneþ alwey fer from þat cuntrey.
>
> (quoted in W.A. Craigie, *The Critique of Pure English from Caxton to Smollett, Society for Pure English* 65, Oxford, Clarendon Press, 1946, p. 118).

Trevisa, by identifying southern English with the "kynges of Engelond", seems to presage the idea of the King's English.

Geoffrey Chaucer came even closer to the formulation when, in his *Treatise on the Astrolabe* (1392) he refers to "the King, that is lord of this langage" (*The Riverside Chaucer*, ed. Larry D. Benson, 3rd edn, Boston, Mass., Houghton Mifflin, 1987, pp. 56–7). Chaucer may have also been the first to introduce dialectal diversity into literature, to counterpose alternative dialects in a single text. Some Chaucerians identify *The Reeve's Tale* as the first in an ongoing tradition of dialect comedy in which northerners are depicted as provincial clowns for the amusement of a more sophisticated urban audience (see for example Derek Pearsall, *The Canterbury Tales*, London, George Allen & Unwin, 1985, p. 188). Yet the northern students are in fact superior to the miller in social and educational status, and the conclusion of the fabliau, in which the students get the last laugh, makes it unlikely that Chaucer's barbs are aimed entirely against them. While Chaucer demonstrates an awareness of dialect differences, there is no positive evidence that he considered some regional forms more "correct" or more prestigious than others.

The phrase "King's English" is usually attributed to the reign of Henry V, who is credited with re-establishing English (as opposed to Norman French) as the official language of the court. It takes on general currency, however, in the sixteenth century.

39 Caxton, Prologue to the *Eneydos*, p. 108.

40 Puttenham, *Arte of English Poesie*, p. 145. Willcock argues that Puttenham was exclusively interested in literary language, that "he is laying down no laws for ordinary communication." As proof, she cites Puttenham's concession that in daily talk gentlemen and even "learned clarkes" will "condescend" to their humbler neighbors and speak their dialect (p. xc). Yet it seems to me that Puttenham's word "condescension" is a clearly prescriptive one; i.e. that he is discriminating generally – and not only on behalf of poets – among "higher" and "lower" dialects.

41 Thomas Blount, *Glossographia* (1656), *Anglistica & Americana* 32, New York, Georg Olms Verlag, 1972, "To His Honored Friend."

42 Blount, *Glossographia*, Dedicatory poem.

43 Baugh and Cable, *History of English*, p. 232. A more recent estimate puts the number of new words introduced in the period at well over 25,000. See Bryan A. Garner, "Shakespeare's Latinate Neologisms," *Shakespeare Studies* 15, 1982, p. 151.

44 For a comprehensive account of this debate, see R.F. Jones, *The Triumph of the English Language: A Survey of Opinions Concerning the Vernacular from the Introduction of Printing to the Restoration*, Stanford, Calif., Stanford University Press, 1953, especially Chapter 4, "The Inadequate Language, Part II," pp. 94–141.

45 Caxton, Prologue to the *Eneydos*, pp. 108–9.

46 Puttenham, *Arte of English Poesie*, p. 145. The connection between dialect and "borrowed" words had a classical precedent. Quintilian had banned the use of dialect words in poetry, citing them, along with other "imported" words, as overly obscure (*The Institutione Oratoria*, trans. H.E. Butler, London, Loeb Classical Library, 1921, vol. 3, 8:13). Aristotle, before him, also seems to have implied that dialect was an example of "strange" poetic diction. See his *Poetics*, in *Works of Aristotle*, ed. Richard McKeon, 2nd edn, Chicago, Ill., University of Chicago Press, 1973, 1457b.

47 William Harrison, *The Description of England* (1577), ed. George Edelen, Ithaca, N.Y., Cornell University Press, 1968, p. 184.

48 Gill, *Logonomia Anglica*, p. 104.

49 See J.S. Cockburn, "Early Modern Assize Records as Historical Evidence," *Journal of Society of Archivists* 5, 1975, p. 223.

50 For a complete listing of cant glossaries and dictionaries of the seventeenth and eighteenth centuries, as well as English dictionaries that included cant terms, see De Witt T. Starnes and Gertrude E. Noyes, *The English Dictionary from Cawdrey to Johnson 1604–1755*, Chapel Hill, N.C., University of North Carolina Press, 1946. See Chapter 2, in the present volume, for a discussion of the literary appropriation of the canting language in the Renaissance.

51 Thomas Harman, *A Caveat or Warening, for Commen Cursetors* (1567), eds Edward Viles and F.J. Furnivall, Oxford, Oxford University Press, 1869, p. 82.

52 Harman, *Caveat*, p. 82.

53 Harman, *Caveat*, p. 85.

54 Samuel Daniel, *Defense of Ryme* (1603), in *Elizabethan Critical Essays*, ed. G. Gregory Smith, vol. 2, Oxford, Oxford University Press, 1904, p. 384.

55 Robert Cawdrey, *A Table Alphabeticall* (1604), Ann Arbor, Mich., University Microfilms, title page.

56 Cawdrey, *Table Alphabeticall*, "To the Reader." Cawdrey, in fact, took this passage directly from Wilson's *Arte of Rhetorique*, in a section devoted to convincing his readers that they must "never affect any straunge ynkehorne termes, but so speake as is commonly received" (p. 325).

57 Henry Cockeram, *The English Dictionarie* (1623), Ann Arbor, Mich., University Microfilms, "A Premonition from the Author to the Reader."
58 Cockeram, *English Dictionarie*, "A Premonition from the Author to the Reader."
59 Cockeram, *English Dictionarie*, A4.
60 John Bullokar, *An English Expositor*, "To the Courteous Reader."
61 There is little known about Robert Cawdrey and Henry Cockeram beyond the fact that they produced these works. John Bullokar was a physician.
62 Gill, *Logonomia Anglica*, p. 191.
63 For example Puttenham invented the words "multiformity," "predatory," "rotundity," "insect," "grandiloquence," "presupposal," "reminiscence," among others. See Willcock, in Puttenham, *Arte of English Poesie*, pp. xxxvii and xcii, for a discussion of Puttenham's coinings.
64 Puttenham, *Arte of English Poesie*, p. 145.
65 Richard Mulcaster, *The Elementarie* (1582), ed. E.T. Campagnac, Oxford, Clarendon Press, 1925, p. 77.
66 N.F. Blake, *Caxton and his World*, New York, Academic Press, 1973, p. 174.
67 Robert Robinson, *The Art of Pronunciation* (1617), Ann Arbor, Mich., University Microfilms, A5v.
68 An apology for the obscurities of the new spelling systems seems to have been *de rigueur*. William Bullokar, in his *Booke at Large, for the Amendment of Orthographie for English Speech* (1580), Ann Arbor, Mich., University Microfilms, accomplished this in verse:

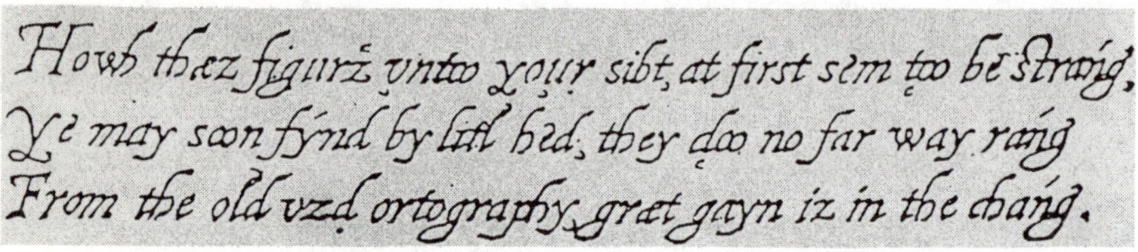
Howh thæz figurz vnto your siht, at first sēm too bē strang,
Ye may soon fynd by litl hēd, they doo no far way rang
From the old vzd ortography, great gayn iz in the chang.

Figure 1.5 William Bullokar's apology
Note: The text reads as follows:

Though these figures unto your sight, at first seem to be strange,
Ye may soon find by little heed they do no far way range
From the old used orthography, great gain is in the change.
("A Table Declaring the Contents of this Amendment of Ortography")

69 For an account of this controversy, see for example Bror Danielsson's introduction to Thomas Smith's *De Recta et Emendata Linguae Graecae Pronuntiatione* (1568), in *Sir Thomas Smith, Literary and Linguistic Works*, part 1, *Stockholm Studies in English* 50, Stockholm, Almquist & Wiksell, 1978, pp. 13–20.
70 Smith, *De Recta et Emendata Linguae Graecae*, part 2, p. 17.
71 Smith, *De Recta et Emendata Linguae Anglicae Scriptione* (1568) in *Sir Thomas Smith, Literary and Linguistic Works*, trans. and ed., Bror Danielsson, *Stockholm Studies in English* 56, Stockholm, Almquist & Wiksell, 1983, p. 41.
72 John Hart, *An Orthography, Conteyning the Due Order and Reason, Howe to Write or Paint Thimage of Mannes Voice, Most Like to the Life or Nature* (1569), Ann Arbor, Mich., University Microfilms, p. 4.
73 Edmund Coote, *The English Schoole-maister* (1596), *English Linguistics 1500–1800* 98, ed. R.C. Alston, Menston, The Scolar Press, 1968, title page.
74 Gill, *Logonomia Anglica*, p. 86.
75 Hart, *An Orthography*, p. 21.

76 John Hart, *A Methode or Comfortable Beginning* (1570), Ann Arbor, Mich., University Microfilms, B1r.

77 Gill, *Logonomia Anglica*, p. 87.

78 As quoted in E.J. Dobson, *English Pronunciation 1500–1700*, 2nd edn, vol. 1, Oxford, Clarendon Press, 1968, p. 34.

79 Hart, *An Orthography*, p. 12.

80 Mulcaster, *Elementarie*, p. 71.

81 Jonathan Goldberg, *Writing Matter: From the Hands of the English Renaissance*, Stanford, Calif., Stanford University Press, 1990, p. 195.

82 Mulcaster, *Elementarie*, p. 77.

83 Dobson, *English Pronunciation*, p. 195.

84 Dobson, "Early Modern Standard English," pp. 39–40.

85 Hart, *An Orthography*, p. 13.

86 Hart, *An Orthography*, p. 44.

87 Gill, *Logonomia Anglica*, p. 86.

88 Gill, *Logonomia Anglica*, p. 167. Spenser's stanza appears in *The Faerie Queene*, *Works of Edmund Spenser*, vol. 1, 2.12.71.

89 Hart, *An Orthography*, Preface.

90 Mulcaster, *Elementarie*, p. 112.

91 Bullokar, *Booke at Large*, "Bullokar to his Countrie" A1r.

92 Bullokar, *Booke at Large*, p. 48.

93 Timothy Bright, *Characterie: An Arte of Shorte, Swifte, and Secrete Writing by Character* (1588), Ann Arbor, Mich., University Microfilms, title page.

94 As quoted in Goldberg, *Writing Matter*, p. 205.

95 See Goldberg, *Writing Matter*, pp. 204–6, for a further discussion of the continuities between spelling reform and "swift writing" in the period.

96 Bright, *Characterie*, A3r.

97 Edmund Willis, *An Abreviation of Writing by Character* (1618), Ann Arbor, Mich., University Microfilms, title page.

98 Goldberg, *Writing Matter*, pp. 203–4.

99 None of the new spelling systems proposed during the sixteenth century gained currency; indeed, they barely attracted the interest of anyone in a position to effect such reforms. Goldberg has suggested that the court would never have endorsed the radical reforms of Hart and others because they "would have rewritten the language in ways that violated hierarchies of power maintained . . . by the vagaries of the English spelling system" (*Writing Matter*, p. 207).

100 Jane Donawerth, *Shakespeare and the Sixteenth-Century Study of Language*, Chicago, Ill., University of Illinois Press, 1984, p. 125.

101 Smith, *De Recta et Emendata Linguae Anglicae Scriptione*, p. 33.

102 N.F. Blake, *Shakespeare's Language: An Introduction*, London, Macmillan, 1983, p. 19.

103 Philip Sidney, to take another example, defends the vernacular in his *Defense of Poesie* (1595) (in *The Prose Works of Sir Philip Sidney*, ed. Albert Feuillerat, vol. 3, Cambridge, Cambridge University Press, 1968, pp. 43–4.

104 Puttenham, *Arte of English Poesie*, p. 249.

105 Puttenham, *Arte of English Poesie*, p. 249.

106 Gill, *Logonomia Anglica*, pp. 87 and 178–9, respectively. Gill borrowed the idea of "metaplasm" as the figure that distinguishes poetic from ordinary language from Quintilian. In his *Institutione Oratoria*, Quintilian writes that the grammarian's role is to

> point out what words are barbarous, what improperly used, and what are contrary to the laws of language. He will not do this by way of censuring the

poets for such peculiarities, for poets are usually the servants of their metres, and are allowed such license that faults are given other names when they occur in poetry: for we style them metaplasms, schematisms and schemata . . . and make a virtue of necessity.

(1:13–14)

Quintilian is an important classical source for the Renaissance idea that poets are licensed to break "the laws of language." See Jacqueline T. Miller, *Poetic License: Authority and Authorship in Medieval and Renaissance Contexts*, New York, Oxford University Press, 1986, pp. 24–9, for a review of classical theories of poetic license that informed Renaissance works.

107 Gill, *Logonomia Anglica*, p. 104. Gill makes an exception for the Northern dialect, which he held to be the "purest" version of English current. See Chapter 4 for a discussion of the place of northern English among Renaissance literary languages.

108 Gill, *Logonomia Anglica*, p. 104.

109 Derek Attridge has discussed the ways that Western writers from Aristotle on have tried to theorize the "peculiar language" of literature (*Peculiar Language: Literature as Difference from the Renaissance to James Joyce*, Ithaca, N.Y., Cornell University Press, 1988). I am indebted, throughout this study, to Attridge's formulation of the problem:

The conception of the special language of literature which we inherit from the Western aesthetic tradition seems to be based on two mutually inconsistent demands – that the language of literature be recognizably different from the language we encounter in other contexts, and that it be recognizably the same.

(p. 3)

See, especially, his Chapter 2, "Nature, Art, and the Supplement in Renaissance Literary Theory: Puttenham's Poetics of Decorum," pp. 17–45, for a discussion of how this paradox informs the debate on literary language in the Renaissance.

110 Thomas Heywood, *An Apology for Actors* (1612), ed. Richard H. Perkinson, New York, Scholars' Facsimiles and Reprints, 1941, F3r.

111 On the other hand, they were well aware that there were others at work on reforming the language. Moreover, many of the reformers spoke of the common goals of spelling reform, grammar-writing, and lexicography. Bullokar's orthography, for example, includes this verse:

A like consent in Dictionary (to Grammar joind hereto)
Will cause that English speech shall be, the perfectest I knowe.
(*Booke at Large*, Prologue)

Along with his treatise on spelling reform, Bullokar wrote a grammar in 1586 (the first of its kind in English) and a dictionary (no longer extant). In his *Orthography*, Hart noted that the progress of English grammar and lexicography depended on establishing a "sound" orthography (p. 5). Gill also incorporated a reformed orthography in his grammar. In this, they seemed to have envisioned national language reform on a broader scale.

112 Gill, *Logonomia Anglica*, p. 104.

113 *Oxford English Dictionary*, s.v. "license." Palsgrave (1530): " . . . which auctors do rather by a lycense poetycall." See Miller, *Poetic License*, especially pp. 9–33, for a list of additional references to "poetic license" in Renaissance works. Other Renaissance authors, without making use of the phrase "poetic license," invoked similar ideas of poetic "freedom." Ben Jonson, for example, stated: "I am not of that opinion to include a *Poet's* liberty within the narrowe limits of lawes, which either the *Grammarians*, or *Philosophers* prescribe" (*Discoveries*, in *Ben Jonson*, vol. 8, p. 641).

2 THE THIEVES OF LANGUAGE

1 The title of this chapter was stolen from Alicia Ostriker, "The Thieves of Language: Women Poets and Revisionist Mythmaking" (in *The New Feminist Criticism*, ed. Elaine Showalter, New York, Pantheon Books, 1985). Ostriker, in turn, took the title from Claudine Herrmann, *Les Voleuses de langue* (Paris, Des Femmes, 1976). Both authors call on women writers to "seize speech" and make it say what they mean, to create an *ecriture feminine* independent of patriarchal writing. My use of the phrase also hinges on the ways that authors take (or make) the language of others and appropriate it for their own purposes.

2 In William Camden, *Remaines Concerning Britain* (1614), Yorkshire, EP Publishing, 1974, pp. 47–8.

3 Camden, *Remaines*, p. 48.

4 Among the many Renaissance writers who, like Carew, refer to the "theft" of words, Puttenham speaks of "robbing" French poets "of his French termes" (*The Arte of English Poesie*, eds Gladys Doidge Willcock and Alice Walker, Cambridge, Cambridge University Press, 1970, p. 252), and Gill declares that "such pilfered progeny as [the neologisms] *pondering, perpending,* and *revoluting,* will always belong to Barbaralexis" (*Logonomia Anglica* (1619), part 2, *Stockholm Studies in English* 27, trans. Robin C. Alston, eds Bror Danielsson and Arvid Gabrielson, Stockholm, Almquist & Wiksell, 1972, p. 155).

5 Pierre Bourdieu, *Language and Symbolic Power*, trans. Gino Raymond and Matthew Adamson, ed. John B. Thompson, Cambridge, Mass., Harvard University Press, 1991, p. 66.

6 As quoted by Bourdieu, *Language and Symbolic Power*, p. 43.

7 Bourdieu, *Language and Symbolic Power*, pp. 57 and 64.

8 For example,Thomas Elyot debates whether English is "enryched and encreased" by the contemporary practice of neologism in *The Book Named the Governor* (1531) (ed. S.E. Lehmberg, London, J.M. Dent, 1962, I.I.5); and Thomas Wilson, in *The Arte of Rhetorique* (1553), notes that "wordes be received, as well Greke as Latine, to set furthe our meanyng in thenglishe tongue, either for lacke of store, or else because wee would enriche the language," (ed. Thomas J. Derrick, New York, Garland Publishing, 1982, p. 331). Modern histories of the language continue to employ the metaphor of "enrichment" in a way that has naturalized the trope, and thus obscured its historical significance. Albert C. Baugh and Thomas Cable, for example, speak of the "problem of enrichment" in the Renaissance in their *History of English of the English Language,* (3rd edn, Englewood Cliffs, N.J., Prentice-Hall, 1978, p. 213).

9 Francis Meres, *Palladis Tamia* (1598), ed. Arthur Freeman, New York, Garland Publishing, 1973, p. 280.

10 Stephen Greenblatt, *Shakespearean Negotiations: The Circulation of Social Energy in Renaissance England,* Berkeley, Calif., University of California Press, 1988, p. 45.

11 *Henry IV*, Part I, 2.4.18–19. All citations of Shakespeare's plays refer to *The Riverside Shakespeare*, ed. G. Blakemore Evans *et al.*, Boston, Mass., Houghton Mifflin, 1974; further citations are given parenthetically in my text.

12 Greenblatt, *Shakespearean Negotiations*, p. 44.

13 King Henry tells his son that Hotspur "hath more worthy interest to the state" – i.e., is more worthy to rule than he is (3.2.98).

14 The play's concern with discriminating between "true" and "counterfeit" kings pursues it to its end. In the battle at Shrewsbury, where the play concludes, Douglas confronts King Henry with the words, "What art thou/That counterfeit'st the person of a king?" (5.4.27–8).

15 Greenblatt, *Shakespearean Negotiations*, p. 42.

16   Max Beer, *Early British Economics*, New York, Augustus M. Kelley, 1967, p. 63.
17   John Hale, *A Discourse of the Common Weal of this Realm of England* (1581), ed. Elizabeth Lamond, Cambridge, Cambridge University Press, 1954, p. 69.
18   As quoted by Beer, *British Economics*, p. 64.
19   Hale, *Discourse of the Common Weal*, pp. 70–1.
20   For a comprehensive study of Renaissance economic thought, see Beer, *Early British Economics*; see also Joan Thirsk, *Economic Policy and Projects: The Development of a Consumer Society in Early Modern England*, Oxford, Clarendon Press, 1978; and C.G.A. Clay, *Economic Expansion and Social Change: England 1500–1700*, Cambridge, Cambridge University Press, 1984, 2 vols.
21   Hale, *Discourse of the Common Weal*, p. 32.
22   Beer, *British Economics*, p. 85.
23   James I, *The Basilicon Doron*, ed. James Craigie, vol. 1, Edinburgh and London, William Blackwood, 1944, pp. 89 and 91.
24   Beer, *British Economics*, p. 104.
25   As quoted in Beer, *British Economics*, p. 110.
26   Beer, *British Economics*, p. 104.
27   As quoted in Beer, *British Economics*, p. 85.
28   Hale, *Discourse of the Common Weal*, p. 78.
29   Camden, *Remaines*, p. 207.
30   As quoted in Beer, *British Economics*, p. 131.
31   Beer, *British Economics*, p. 59
32   See Sandra K. Fisher's *Econolingua: A Glossary of Coins and Economic Language in Renaissance Drama*, Newark, N.J., University of Delaware Press, 1985 for a comprehensive survey of economic rhetoric in the drama of the period. In her brief analysis of the early modern idea of words as coin, Fisher suggests that the metaphor "encapsulates the transition from intrinsic to exchange value," that "words . . . begin to be valuable not so much for what they represent (intrinsic worth) but for what profit or esteem their utterance can engender (exchange value)" (p. 21).
33   Puttenham, *Arte of English Poesie*, p. 145.
34   Puttenham, *Arte of English Poesie*, p. 144.
35   Willcock concurs that Puttenham "distinguishes this standard language partly on a regional and partly on a class basis." (*Arte of English Poesie*, p. lxxxix).
36   Puttenham, *Arte of English Poesie*, p. 144.
37   Attridge, *Peculiar Language*, p. 34.
38   Ben Jonson, *Discoveries* (1640), in *Ben Jonson*, eds C.H. Herford and Percy and Evelyn Simpson, vol. 8, Oxford, Clarendon Press, 1966, p. 622.
39   Alexander Gill, *Logonomia Anglica*, p. 87. Gill named these women after the dim-witted character Mopsa in Sidney's *Arcadia*.
40   Helge Kökeritz, "Alexander Gill on the Dialects of South and East England," *Studia Neophilologica* 11, 1939, p. 277.
41   W. Matthews, "The Vulgar Speech of London in the Fifteenth to Seventeenth Centuries," *Notes and Queries* 172, 1937, p. 3.
42   For studies of linguistic class markers in Shakespeare's works, for example, see G.L. Brook, *The Language of Shakespeare*, London, Andre Deutsch, 1976, pp. 181–5; Vivian Salmon, "Elizabethan Colloquial English in the Falstaff Plays," *Leeds Studies in English* 1, 1967, pp. 37–70, and Carol Replogle, "Shakespeare's Salutations: A Study in Stylistic Etiquette," in *A Reader in the Language of Shakespearean Drama*, eds Vivian Salmon and Edwina Burness, Amsterdam, John Benjamins, 1987, pp. 101–15.
43   By the term "neologism," I am referring to any word, regardless of its derivation, that was newly introduced into the language by writers during this period.

44 Bryan A. Garner, "Shakespeare's Latinate Neologisms," *Shakespeare Studies* 15, 1982, p. 151.

45 William Caxton, Prologue to the *Eneydos* (1490), in *The Prologues and Epilogues*, ed. W.J.B. Crotch, Millwood, N.Y., Kraus Reprints, 1978, p. 108.

46 P. Ashton (1556), as quoted by Manfred Gorlach, *Introduction to Early Modern English*, Cambridge, Cambridge University Press, 1991, p. 144.

47 Abraham Fraunce, *The Lawyers Logike, Exemplifying the Praecepts of Logike by the Practice of the Common Lawe* (1588), Ann Arbor, Mich., University Microfilms, "Epistle."

48 Wilson, *Arte of Rhetorique*, pp. 325–6.

49 Wilson, *Arte of Rhetorique*, pp. 327–8.

50 John Hart, *A Methode or Comfortable Beginning* (1570), Ann Arbor, Mich., University Microfilms, Preface.

51 Wilson, *Arte of Rhetorique*, pp. 330–1.

52 Ben Jonson, *Bartholomew Fair* (1631), in *Ben Jonson*, vol. 6, "The Induction on the Stage," lines 43–5.

53 Samuel Daniel, *Defense of Ryme* (1603), in *Elizabethan Critical Essays*, ed. G. Gregory Smith, vol. 2, Oxford, Oxford University Press, 1904, p. 384.

54 It is interesting to note that "audacious" was one such "foreign" word that had only recently been introduced into English. Puttenham, in fact, explicitly prohibited its use: "Many . . . words borrowed out of the Latin and French, were not so well to be allowed by us, as these words, *audacious*, for bold; *facunditie*, for eloquence: *egregious*, for great or notable," etc. (*Arte of English Poesie*, p. 147).

55 As quoted in W.A. Craigie, *The Critique of Pure English from Caxton to Smollett*, Society for Pure English, 65, Oxford, Clarendon Press, 1946, p. 143.

56 As quoted in Craigie, *Critique of Pure English*, pp. 141–2.

57 Garner has counted over 600 Latinate neologisms, not including old words used in new ways, or foreign loanwords, such as *passado* or *monarcho*. Only a third of these, however, have survived in our language. For these statistics, see Garner, "Shakespeare's Latinate Neologisms," pp. 158–70.

58 Garner, "Shakespeare's Latinate Neologisms," p. 151.

59 William Matthews, "Language in *Love's Labour's Lost*," *Essays and Studies*, 1964, p. 1.

60 Thomas Blount, *Glossographia* (1656), *Anglistica & Americana* 32, New York, Georg Olms Verlag, 1972, Dedicatory Poem.

61 Camden, *Remaines*, pp. 47–8.

62 As quoted in Gorlach, *Early Modern English*, p. 222.

63 As quoted in Craigie, *Critique of Pure English*, p. 145.

64 Garner refutes the common nineteenth-century view of Shakespeare as a "nativist" who eschewed foreign words; he also argues, persuasively, against Helge Kökeritz's "anti-Latinate" position on Shakespeare's language. See "Shakespeare's Latinate Neologisms," pp. 153–4.

65 Jonson, *Discoveries*, in *Ben Jonson*, vol. 8, p. 622.

66 The idea of linguistic "inflation" in *Love's Labor's Lost* has been explored by James Calderwood in his *Shakespearean Metadrama* (Minneapolis, Minn., University of Minnesota Press, 1971), pp. 68–70.

67 The French commission arrives in Navarre to settle a dispute over the possession of Aquitaine, which King Ferdinand holds as surety for a debt France owes him. The matter is never settled in the play. All quotations from *Love's Labor's Lost* are taken from *The Riverside Shakespeare*, ed. G. Blakemore Evans, Boston, Mass., Houghton Mifflin, 1974, and appear parenthetically in my text.

68 Calderwood, *Metadrama*, p. 68.

69 For example, "audacious" occurs in *A Winter's Tale* (2.3.42), and *1 Henry IV*

(4.3.45); "impudence" in *Measure for Measure* (5.1.363), *All's Well that Ends Well* (2.1.170), and *Pericles* (2.3.69); "excrement" in *Hamlet* (3.4.121), and *Merchant of Venice* (3.2.87); "eruption" in *1 Henry IV* (3.1.27), and *Julius Caesar* (1.3.78).

70 D.G. Scragg, *A History of English Spelling*, New York, Barnes & Noble, 1974, p. 61.

71 As quoted in Gorlach, *Early Modern English*, pp. 254–5.

72 Samuel Rowlands, *Martin Markall, Beadle of Bridewell* (1610), in *The Complete Works of Samuel Rowlands*, vol. 2, New York, Johnson Reprints, 1966, p. 58.

73 Thomas Harman, *A Caveat or Warening for Commen Cursetors* (1567), eds Edward Viles and F.J. Furnivall, Oxford, Oxford University Press, 1869, p. 27.

74 Thomas Dekker, *Lanterne and Candlelight: Or The Bellman's Second Night's Walke* (1608), in *Thomas Dekker*, ed. E.D. Pendry, London, Edward Arnold, 1967, p. 187.

75 Dekker, *Lanterne*, p. 191.

76 Rowlands, *Martin Markall*, p. 58.

77 Harman's description of thieves' cant as a "mingled" language (*Caveat*, p. 82) recalls contemporary descriptions of early modern English. Philip Sidney, for example, refers to the vernacular as "mingled" in his *Defense of Poesie* (1595), in *The Prose Works of Sir Philip Sidney*, ed. Albert Feuillerat, vol. 3, Cambridge, Cambridge University Press, 1968, p. 43.

78 William Harrison, *The Description of England* (1577), ed. George Edelen, Ithaca, N.Y., Cornell University Press, p. 184.

79 Harman, *Caveat*, p. 21.

80 Dekker, *Lanterne*, pp. 190–1.

81 Robert Greene, *A Notable Discovery of Coosnage* (1591), in *The Life and Complete Works in Prose and Verse of Robert Greene*, ed. Alexander B. Grosart, New York, Russell & Russell, 1964, vol. 10, p. 39.

82 Greene, *Notable Discovery* p. 33.

83 Dekker, *O per se O* (1612), in *Thomas Dekker*, p. 297.

84 Harman, *Caveat*, p. 82.

85 Greene, *A Disputation betweene a Hee Conny-Catcher and a Shee Conny-Catcher* (1592), in *Works of Robert Greene*, vol. 10, p. 204.

86 John Awdeley, *The Fraternitye of Vacabondes* (1565), eds E. Viles and F.J. Furnivall, Oxford, Oxford University Press, 1869, p. 5.

87 Harman, *Caveat*, pp. 44 and 58.

88 Robert Copland, *The Highway to the Spital-House* (1535/6), in *The Elizabethan Underworld*, ed. A.V. Judges, London, George Routledge & Sons, 1930, p. 10.

89 Greene, *The Defence of Conny-Catching*, (1592), in *Works of Robert Greene*, vol. 11, p. 50.

90 Greene, *Notable Discovery*, p. 6.

91 Greene, *Notable Discovery*, p. 12.

92 Greenblatt, *Shakespearean Negotiations*, p. 50.

93 Dekker, *Lanterne*, "To My Own Nation," p. 180.

94 Dekker, *Lanterne*, "To the Very Worthy Gentleman, Master Francis Muschamp," p. 176.

95 Dekker, *Lanterne*, p. 215.

96 Greene, *A Disputation*, p. 206.

97 Greene, *Defence of Conny-Catching*, pp. 51 and 75–6, respectively.

98 See, for example, Karl J. Holzknecht, ed., *Sixteenth-Century English Prose*, New York, Harper, 1954, p. 509.

99 Dekker, *Lanterne*, "To My Own Nation," p. 180.

100 Dekker, *Lanterne*, p. 195.

101 Rowlands, *Martin Markall*, p. 36.

102 Dekker, *Lanterne*, pp. 191 and 195, respectively.

103 Rowlands, *Martin Markall*, p. 5.

104 John L. McMullan, *The Canting Crew: London's Criminal Underworld 1550–1700*, New Brunswick, N.J., Rutgers University Press, 1984, p. 113.

105 Thomas Dekker and Thomas Middleton, *The Roaring Girl, or Moll Cutpurse* (1611), in *The Dramatic Works of Thomas Dekker*, ed. Fredson Bowers, vol. 3, Cambridge, Cambridge University Press, 1970, lines 25–6. All further citations refer to this edition and appear parenthetically in my text.

106 Francis Beaumont, John Fletcher and Philip Massinger, *Beggar's Bush* (c. 1637), in *Dramatic Works in the Beaumont and Fletcher Canon*, ed. Fredson Bowers, vol. 3, Cambridge, Cambridge University Press, 1970, 1.3.163–7. Further citations refer to this edition and appear parenthetically in my text.

107 Stephen Orgel in *Ben Jonson: The Complete Masques*, ed. Orgel, New Haven, Conn., Yale University Press, 1969, p. 30.

108 Dale Randall, *Jonson's Gypsies Unmasked*, Durham, N.C., Duke University Press, 1975, p. 49. For a description of Romany, see Bath C. Smart, *The Dialect of the English Gypsies*, London, Asher & Co., 1895.

109 Harrison, *Description of England*, p. 184.

110 Randall, *Gypsies Unmasked*, p. 51.

111 The Porter's prologue was delivered at the first performance of the masque only.

112 All citations of Jonson's *Gypsies Metamorphosed* refer to the Orgel edition and the line numbers are given parenthetically in my text.

113 Jonson, *Discoveries*, p. 662.

114 Randall, *Gypsies Unmasked*, p. 124.

115 Randall, *Gypsies Unmasked*, p. 162.

116 Jonathan Goldberg, *James I and the Politics of Literature*, Baltimore, Md., Johns Hopkins University Press, 1983, p. 130.

117 Randall, *Gypsies Unmasked*, p. 104.

118 Goldberg, *James I*, p. 130.

119 Stephen Orgel, *The Jonsonian Masque*, Cambridge, Mass., Harvard University Press, 1965, p. 99. As Orgel has explained, Jonson adapted the traditional "antic-masque," an acrobatic entertainment, to his own purposes as an "antimasque," 'a foil or false masque,' representing rebellion or misrule (in *Ben Jonson: The Complete Masques*, p. 5).

120 Randall, *Gypsies Unmasked*, p. 151.

121 In legitimizing the gypsies' language, Jonson seems to contradict his emphasis, elsewhere, on "custom" as the only arbiter of usage. Similarly, Jonson in his *English Grammar* censured certain usages that he used liberally in his literary works. For example, he prohibits the use of the genitive construction in phrases such as "the King his English" in his grammar, yet it appears in his plays, even in the title of one of them: *Sejanus His Fall*. Many critics have noted such contradictions, in his writings as in his life; a recent biographer has compared him to "a prudent business man who periodically feels an irresistible urge to go to the racetrack" (David Riggs, *Ben Jonson: A Life*, Cambridge, Mass., Harvard University Press, 1989, p. 2). But I do not think Jonson's self-identification with gypsies is about indulging irresistible urges to transgress. Jonson recreates the criminal underworld as a society "licensed" to transgress. Richard Burt has recently offered a compelling resolution to the paradox of an author who "strikingly falls on both sides of the division – legitimation and critique, authority and subversion, opposition and orthodoxy – over which the politics of his writings have been hitherto constructed." Jonson, he suggests, contributed to "an emergent discourse of literary criticism which regulated the exercise of a relatively autonomous poetic liberty" by seeking a paradoxically "free rei(g)n for his literary production and consumption." See his *Licensed by Authority: Ben Jonson and the Discourses of Censorship*, Ithaca, N.Y., Cornell University Press, 1993, pp. 12 and 19, respectively.

122 Thomas Randolph, *The Muses' Looking Glass* (1638), in *Poetical and Dramatic Works of Thomas Randolph*, ed. W. Carew Hazlitt, vol. 1, London, Reeves & Turner, 1875, 4.4.

123 Thomas Nashe, *Summer's Last Will and Testament* (1600), in *The Works of Thomas Nashe*, ed. Ronald B. McKerrow, vol. 3, Oxford, Basil Blackwell, 1958, 3.4.2–3.

3 REGIONS OF RENAISSANCE ENGLISH I: SOUTH OF THE BORDER

1 Ben Jonson, *Bartholomew Fair*, in *Ben Jonson*, ed. C. H. Herford and Percy and Evelyn Simpson, vol. 6, Oxford, Clarendon Press, 1966, 4.4.10–19.

2 M.M. Bakhtin, *The Dialogic Imagination*, trans. Caryl Emerson and Michael Holquist, ed. Michael Holquist, Austin, Tex., University of Texas Press, 1981, p. 82.

3 i.e., these are the first works in which a provincial dialect is consciously selected as the primary language of a text.

4 Bakhtin observes that the Renaissance interest in provincial language spurred a concurrent interest in exploring the provinces themselves, the "space" of intra-national differences:

> If the interorientation and the mutual clarification of the major languages rendered the awareness of time and its changes more acute, it also stimulated the awareness of historic space in the dialects, which strengthened and expressed the local, provincial peculiarities. This awareness of space, whether of a specific land or of the entire world, is characteristic of that period.
>
> (*Rabelais and his World*, trans. Helene Iswolsky, Bloomington, Ind., Indiana University Press, 1984, p. 469)

5 For a full-length study of the construction of an English national identity in Renaissance England, see Richard Helgerson, *Forms of Nationhood: The Elizabethan Writing of England*, Chicago, Ill., University of Chicago Press, 1992.

6 Alan Everitt, *The Local Community and the Great Rebellion*, London, The Historical Association, 1969, p. 8. For discussions of the place of the county in seventeenth-century English politics, see also Anthony Fletcher, "National and Local Awareness in the County Communities," in *Before the English Civil War: Essays on Stuart Politics and Government*, ed. Howard Tomlinson, London, Macmillan Press, 1983, pp. 151–74; and L.M. Hill, "County Government in Caroline England 1625–1640," in *The Origins of the English Civil War*, ed. Conrad Russell, London, Macmillan, 1973, pp. 66–90. For an opposing view, arguing against the "provincialism" of the provinces, see Clive Holmes, "The County Community in Stuart Historiography," *Journal of British Studies* 19.2, 1980, pp. 54–73.

7 Anthony Fletcher, *Tudor Rebellions*, Harlow, Longman, 1968, p. 101.

8 For example, William Lambarde, *Perambulation of Kent* (1570), William Harrison, *Description of England* (1577), William Camden, *Britannia* (1586), Sampson Erdeswicke, *Survey of Staffordshire* (*c.* 1595), William Burton, *Description of Leicestershire* (1622), Tristram Risdon, *Survey of Devon* (*c.* 1630), among many others. See F.J. Levy, *Tudor Historical Thought*, San Marino, Calif., Huntington Library, 1967, pp. 124–66, for a discussion of these and other Renaissance chorographies.

9 Helgerson, *Forms of Nationhood*, pp. 131–9.

10 John Leland, *The Itinerary* (1535/43), ed. Lucy Toulmin Smith, Carbondale, Ill., Southern Illinois Press, 1964.

11 Harrison, *Description of England*, p. 87.

12   Harrison, *Description of England*, p. 83.

13   Harrison, *Description of England*, pp. 85–6.

14   Harrison, *Description of England*, p. 85.

15   Michael Drayton, *Poly-Olbion* (1622), in *The Works of Michael Drayton*, ed. J. William Hebel, vol. 4, Oxford, Basil Blackwell, 1961, Song 22.1591–1601. All further citations refer to this edition and are given parenthetically in my text.

16   See for example Richard F. Hardin, *Michael Drayton and the Passing of Elizabethan England*, Lawrence, Kans., Kansas University Press, 1973, p. 64. Helgerson also notes that importance of "multiplicity" to Drayton's poem (*Forms of Nationhood*, p. 141).

17   For a further discussion of the implicit anti-centrism of Drayton's poem, see Helgerson, *Forms of Nationhood*, pp. 105–47.

18   John Stow, *Survey of London* (1598), ed. Henry Morley, London, George Routledge & Sons, 1890, p. 200. Further citations refer to this edition and are given parenthetically in my text.

19   Stephen S. Hilliard, *The Singularity of Thomas Nashe*, Lincoln, Nebr., University of Nebraska Press, 1986, p. 221.

20   Jonathan Crewe, *Unredeemed Rhetoric: Thomas Nashe and the Scandal of Authorship*, Baltimore, Md., Johns Hopkins University Press, 1982, p. 92.

21   Thomas Nashe, *Nashes Lenten Stuffe* (1599), in *Works of Thomas Nashe*, vol. 3. Further citations refer to this edition and appear parenthetically in my text.

22   Lorna Hutson, *Thomas Nashe in Context*, Oxford, Clarendon Press, 1989, p. 245.

23   Nashe's coinings in these passages, according to the *OED*, include *inamorately*, *transcursive* (cursory), *reportory* (a report or account), *condecorate*, *perponder*, *sempiternity*, *paralogized* (falsely reasoned), *pretertense*, *rantantingly*, and *dribblements*. Nashe is also the first writer to enfranchise the Spanish word *Alteza* and the Latin *Induperator*. He also makes use of numerous words of very recent coinage, including *patronized* (1589), *architectures* (1563), *prevalence* (1592), and *burdensome* (1578).

24   See for example Hilliard, *Singularity of Thomas Nashe*, p. 222.

25   Crewe, *Unredeemed Rhetoric*, p. 98.

26   Hutson calls attention to Nashe's pun (*Thomas Nashe in Context*, p. 248).

27   Hilliard, *Singularity of Thomas Nashe*, p. 232.

28   Hilliard, *Singularity of Thomas Nashe*, p. 224.

29   Crewe, *Unredeemed Rhetoric*, p. 92.

30   By Shakespeare's day, the phrase "clubs and clouted shoon," was proverbial for peasant revolt. Charles Hobday has collected many contemporary uses of this phrase, in numerous shires, north and south. See "Clouted Shoon and Leather Aprons: Shakespeare and the Egalitarian Tradition," *Renaissance and Modern Studies* 23, 1979, pp. 63–78. Although Hobday glosses the form *shoon* as an archaism, it had also survived in Renaissance dialects.

31   As quoted in Annabel Patterson, *Shakespeare and the Popular Voice*, Cambridge, Basil Blackwell, 1989, p. 32.

32   Alexander Gill, *Logonomia Anglica* (1619), part 2, *Stockholm Studies in English* 27, trans. Robin C. Alston., eds Bror Danielsson and Arvid Gabrielson, Stockholm, Almquist & Wiksell, 1972, p. 103. Note that Gill distinguishes southwestern from southeastern dialects – a distinction that is not as clear in literary representations of these dialects.

33   Thomas Randolph, *The Muses' Looking Glass* (1638), in *Poetical and Dramatic Works of Thomas Randolph*, ed. W. Carew Hazlitt, vol. 1, London, Reeves and Turner, 1875, 4.4.

34   W. Matthews, "The Vulgar Speech of London in the Fifteenth to Seventeenth Centuries," *Notes and Queries* 172, 1937, p. 3.

35 Andrew Boorde, *The Fyrst Boke of the Introduction of Knowledge* (1542), ed. F.J. Furnivall, London, Early English Text Society, 1871, p. 123; emphasis added.

36 William Shakespeare, *The Tragedy of King Lear*, in *The Riverside Shakespeare*, Boston, Mass., Houghton Mifflin, 1974, 4.6.235; 237–9. All citations to Shakespeare's plays refer to this edition and are given parenthetically in my text.

37 Thomas Wilson, *The Arte of Rhetorique* (1553), ed. Thomas J. Derrick, New York, Garland Publishing, 1982, pp. 329–30.

38 Carew, *Survey of Cornwall* (1602), in *Richard Carew of Antony*, ed. F.E. Halliday, London, Andrew Melrose, 1953, p. 139. All citations refer to this edition and are given parenthetically in my text.

39 In *The Excellency of the English Tongue*, Carew celebrates the "copiousness" of English on the grounds of the "diversity of our dialectes, for wee have court, and wee have countrye Englishe, wee have Northern, & Southerne, grosse and ordinary, which differ ech from other, not only in the terminacions, but alsoe in many wordes termes and phrases, and expresse the same thinges in divers sortes, yeat all right Englishe alike" (in William Camden, *Remaines Concerning Britain* (1614), Yorkshire, EP Publishing, 1974, p. 49). Carew is rare, among Renaissance English writers, in his judgment that all of these dialects are "right English alike." By invoking Spenser as a precedent, Carew seems to imply that he recognized Spenser's use of northern dialect words in his poetry. See Chapter 4 for a discussion of Spenser's use of dialect.

40 Both *ywrought* and *ybought* are participial forms characteristic of the southwestern dialect of English in the period.

41 John Ferne, *The Blazon of Gentrie* (1586), Ann Arbor, Mich., University Microfilms, 2.23. Further citations are given parenthetically in my text.

42 Andrew Boorde, *The First and Best Part of Scoggins Jests* (*c.* 1565), in *Old English Jest Books*, ed. W. Carew Hazlitt, London, Willis & Sotheran, 1866, pp. 63–4.

43 John Redford, *Wit and Science* (*c.* 1550), in *'Lost' Tudor Plays*, ed. John S. Farmer, New York, Barnes & Noble, 1966, pp. 152–3.

44 Redford, *Wit and Science*, p. 155.

45 Anon., *The Contention between Liberality and Prodigality* (1602), Oxford, Malone Society Reprints, 1913, 2.4.447–9. All further citations refer to this edition and appear parenthetically in my text.

46 A southern dialect speaker is once again used as a foil for a representative of prodigality in *The London Prodigal* (Anon.) (1605), an apocryphal Shakespearean play. Here, a Devonshire man and a young prodigal are rival suitors, not for money but for a woman. Once again, the prodigal is reformed, and the southerner's claims rebuffed.

47 Nicholas Udall, *Respublica* (1553), ed. Leonard A. Magnus, London, Kegan Paul, 1905, 3.3.648–52. Subsequent citations refer to this edition and appear parenthetically in my text.

48 Shakespeare uses dialect words occasionally throughout the plays, including words from his native Warwickshire, but there is no evidence that he was conscious of their dialectal status. British dialects (as opposed to English ones), including Welsh, Irish, and Scottish, are represented in a few works, including *Henry V*. See Chapter 5 for a discussion of these literary dialects.

49 A.C. Bradley, *Shakespearean Tragedy*, New York, St. Martin's Press, 1985, p. 210.

50 See for example Lawrence Danson, *Tragic Alphabet: Shakespeare's Drama of Language*, New Haven, Conn., Yale University Press, 1974; and Sheldon P. Zitner, "*King Lear* and Its Language," in *Some Facets of King Lear: Essays in Prismatic Criticism*, eds Rosalie L. Colie and F.T. Flahiff, Toronto, University of Toronto Press, 1974.

51 Zitner, "*King Lear* and Its Language," p. 5.

52 See, for example, Jane Donawerth, *Shakespeare and the Sixteenth-Century Study of Language*, Chicago, Ill., University of Illinois Press, 1984, p. 16.

53 Margreta de Grazia, "Shakespeare's View of Language: An Historical Perspective," *Shakespeare Quarterly* 29, 1978, pp. 374–88.

54 Donawerth, *Shakespeare and the Study of Language*, p. 134.

55 Zitner has suggested that although "plainness" is another verbal "garb" in *King Lear*, it is presented as a "relatively truthful one"; for Zitner, "dialect and folk speech [in *Lear*] are reductions to the primitive and the predecorous in a search for authenticity," ("*King Lear* and Its Language," p. 9). I agree with Norman Atwood, who argues that the "plain style" in *Lear* is just another rhetorical choice that bears no privileged relation to meaning or to truth (see "Cordelia and Kent: Their Fateful Choice of Style," *Language and Style* 9.1, 1976, pp. 42–54).

56 For a discussion of the ways in which *Lear* concerns the early seventeenth-century debate over the unification of England and Scotland, see Marie Axton, *The Queen's Two Bodies: Drama and the Elizabethan Succession*, London, Royal Historical Society, 1977, pp. 131–47.

57 Harry V. Jaffa, "The Limits of Politics: *King Lear*, Act 1, sc. 1," in *Shakespeare's Politics*, ed. Allan Bloom with Harry V. Jaffa, New York, Basic Books, 1964, pp. 121–2.

58 De Grazia, "Shakespeare's View of Language," p. 385.

59 De Grazia, "Shakespeare's View of Language," p. 374.

60 Jonathan Dollimore, *Radical Tragedy: Religion, Ideology and Power in the Drama of Shakespeare and his Contemporaries*, Chicago, Ill., University of Chicago Press, 1984, p. 196.

61 See Judy Kronenfeld, "'So distribution should undo excess, and each man have enough': Shakespeare's *King Lear* – Anabaptist Egalitarianism, Anglican Charity, Both, Neither?," *English Literary Renaissance* 59.4, 1992, pp. 755–84, for a critical reassessment of the "radicality" of these sentiments in *King Lear*.

62 N.F. Blake, *Shakespeare's Language: An Introduction*, London, Macmillan, 1983, p. 33.

63 As with so many passages in *Lear*, there is considerable controversy over which of the quarto and Folio editions best represents Shakespeare's intentions. For a detailed comparison of how Edgar's speech is represented in successive editions of *Lear* from the 1608 quarto forwards, see N.F. Blake, "Standardizing Shakespeare's Non-Standard Language," in *Standardizing English: Essays in the History of Language Change in Honor of John Hurt Fisher*, ed. Joseph B. Trahern, Jr., Knoxville, Tenn., University of Tennessee Press, 1989, pp. 57–8. As Blake demonstrates, modern texts tend to make the passage more "southern" than any of the extant originals, and to "standardize" the nonstandard character of the speech. While we may never know how systematically Shakespeare worked southern forms into Edgar's speech, even the 1608 quarto makes generous use of them. For the purposes of this chapter, it is enough to be certain that Shakespeare succeeded in indicating regional language.

64 See Patterson, *Shakespeare and the Popular Voice*, for a study of "popular" voices in Shakespeare's plays, and the representation of popular protest. Patterson argues that Shakespeare's "ventriloquism" ultimately speaks against the people whose voices he borrows (pp. 41–2).

65 For example, "Blow, winds, and crack your cheeks! rage! blow!/You cataracts and hurricanoes, spout/Till you have drench'd our steeples!" (3.2.1–3). See de Grazia, "Shakespeare's View of Language," p. 385.

66 Alfred Hart has noted that *Lear* contains the greatest number of "peculiar" words (words not found elsewhere) of all the plays except *Hamlet*. See his article

"Vocabularies of Shakespeare's Plays," *Review of English Studies* 19, 1943, p. 132.

67 Once again, Shakespeare's celebration of "free speech" should not be confused with a desire for linguistic anarchy, which is dramatized on the heath. As I discuss in Chapter 2, Shakespeare seems to advocate a license with words, not an unregulated liberty. While he allows that characters such as Cordelia and Edgar should be free to choose, it is not so clear that Shakespeare would grant the same freedom to ordinary "people."

68 Other examples include *Gammer Gurton's Needle* (Anon.) (1575) (ed. John S. Farmer, Tudor Facsimile Texts, New York, Ams Press, 1970) and Jonson's *For the Honor of Wales* (1618) and *The Irish Masque at Court* (1616) (both in *Ben Jonson: The Complete Masques*, ed. Stephen Orgel, New Haven, Conn., Yale University Press, 1969). See Chapter 5 for a discussion of Jonson's "British" dialects.

69 *Ben Jonson*, vol. 8, p. 267.

70 Ben Jonson, *A Tale of a Tub* (1633/40), in *Ben Jonson*, vol. 3, lines 1–4; 11–12. All further citations refer to this edition and line numbers appear parenthetically in my text.

71 According to the *OED*, s.v. "bilk," Jonson was the first writer to use the word to mean "a statement having nothing in it." Later writers use it as a variant of "balk."

72 Levy, *Tudor Historical Thought*, p. 159.

73 *Oxford English Dictionary*, s.v. "turf": From 1585, the word "turf" refers to "a sod cut from the turf of an estate, etc., as a token or symbol of possession."

74 L.A. Beaurline, *Jonson and Elizabethan Comedy*, San Marino, Calif., Huntington Library, 1978, p. 285.

4 REGIONS OF RENAISSANCE ENGLISH II: THE NORTH COUNTRY

1 Alexander Gill, *Logonomia Anglica* (1619), part 2, *Stockholm Studies in English* 27, trans. Robin C. Alston, eds Bror Danielsson and Arvid Gabrielson, Stockholm, Almquist & Wiksell, 1972, p. 104.

2 The term "archaism" was not current in the Renaissance; according to the *OED*, the word came into use in the middle of the eighteenth century. Renaissance writers commonly refer to "Chaucer's words" or simply to "old words" in referring to English words no longer current in "common" speech.

3 As quoted in Manfred Gorlach, *Introduction to Early Modern English*, Cambridge, Cambridge University Press, 1991, p. 292.

4 John Cheke, *Letter to Hoby* (1557), as quoted in Gorlach, *Early Modern English*, p. 222.

5 Gorlach, *Early Modern English*, p. 165. The growing interest in the language of the ancient Saxons gained momentum from the scholarly pursuits of contemporary Germanists, who were proposing that German, and not Hebrew as was formerly believed, was the Edenic language, perhaps even the language of God. English linguists, in turn, held that Saxon was the noblest ancestor of contemporary English, and, like German, had a special birthright. By the early part of the seventeenth century, Old English studies had received institutional support: The first lectureship in the new discipline was established at Cambridge in 1623, and twenty years later two poems were composed in Anglo-Saxon (See R.F. Jones, *The Triumph of the English Language: A Survey of Opinions Concerning the Vernacular from the Introduction of Printing to the Restoration*, Stanford, Calif., Stanford University Press, 1953, p. 233).

6 As quoted in W.A. Craigie, *The Critique of Pure English from Caxton to Smollet*, *Society for Pure English* 65, Oxford, Clarendon Press, p. 146.

7   Gill, *Logonomia Anglica*, p. 84, emphasis added.
8   William Camden, *Remaines Concerning Britain* (1614), Yorkshire, EP Publishing, 1974, p. 35.
9   Gill, *Logonomia Anglica*, p. 84.
10 John Hare, *St. Edward's Ghost* (1647), as quoted in R.F. Jones, *Triumph of English*, p. 249.
11 George Puttenham, *The Arte of English Poesie* (1589), eds Gladys Doidge Willcock and Alice Walker, Cambridge, Cambridge University Press, p. 144.
12 William Caxton, Prologue to the *Eneydos* (1490), in *The Prologues and Epilogues of William Caxton*, ed. W.J.B. Crotch, Millwood, N.Y., Kraus Reprints, 1978, p. 109.
13 As quoted in Gorlach, *Early Modern English*, p. 144.
14 George Gascoigne, *Certayne Notes of Instruction Concerning the Making of Verse*, in *The Posies* (1575), ed. John W. Cunliffe, Cambridge, Cambridge University Press, 1907, p. 469.
15 Ben Jonson, *Discoveries*, in *Ben Jonson*, vol. 8, Oxford, Clarendon Press, 1966, p. 622.
16 As quoted in R.F. Jones, *Triumph of English*, p. 256.
17 Quintilian, *The Institutione Oratoria*, trans. H.E. Butler, London, Loeb Classical Library, 1921, 8:24.
18 Gascoigne, *Certayne Notes*, p. 470. It is interesting to note that the word *turkeneth* appears to have been of Gascoigne's coinage, according to the *OED*, s.v. *turken*. Apparently, Gascoigne applied the same license to his own prose.
19 As quoted in Veré Rubel, *Poetic Diction in the English Renaissance: From Skelton Through Spenser*, New York, Modern Language Association, 1941, p. 106.
20 Nashe, of course, deliberately employed a heavily Latinate diction in his travesty of Harvey's writing, including the neologisms *horizonant* (his own coining) and *inveterate* (in use in this sense, since the 1560s).
        R.F. Jones has confirmed Nashe's statement, noting that in the sixteenth century, "augmenting the language by restoring obsolete terms was largely restricted to poetry" (*Triumph of English*, p. 242).
21 Rubel, *Poetic Diction*, p. 47.
22 Rubel, *Poetic Diction*, pp. 47 and 98, respectively.
23 Rubel, *Poetic Diction*, p. 47.
24 Gill, *Logonomia Anglica*, p. 155.
25 Gascoigne, *The Epistle* to the Reverend Divines, in *The Posies*, p. 5; Gascoigne, *Jocasta*, in *The Posies*, p. 326.
26 As quoted in R.F. Jones, *Triumph of English*, p. 128.
27 Edmund Spenser, *The Shepheardes Calendar* (1579), in *The Works of Edmund Spenser*, eds Edwin Greenlaw *et al.*, vol. 7, part 1, Baltimore, Md., Johns Hopkins University Press, 1932–1957, 11 vols. All citations that follow refer to this edition and line numbers of Spenser's verses are given parenthetically in my text.
28 William Warner, *Albion's England* (1612), in *The Works of the English Poets from Chaucer to Cowper*, ed. Alexander Chalmers, vol. 4, London, 1810, 5.24.
29 John Skelton, *Merie Tales, Newly Imprinted and Made by Master Skelton* (1525), ed. W. Carew Hazlitt, London, Willis & Sotheran, 1866, pp. 5–6.
30 As quoted in Craigie, *Critique of Pure English*, p. 146.
31 As quoted in Hans H. Meier, "Past Presences of Older Scots Abroad," in *The Nuttis Schell: Essays on the Scots Language*, ed. Caroline Macafee and Iseabail MacLeod, Aberdeen, The University Press, 1987, p. 117.
32 John Hart, *A Methode or Comfortable Beginning* (1570), Ann Arbor, Mich., University Microfilms, Preface.
33 Puttenham, *Arte of English Poesie*, p. 145.

34 Rubel, *Poetic Diction*, p. 144.

35 Patricia Ingham, "Spenser's Use of Dialect," *English Language Notes* 8.3, 1971, p. 167.

36 Nicholas Grimald, "Concerning Virgils Eneids," in *Tottel's Miscellany* (1557), ed. Edward Rollins, vol. 1, Cambridge, Mass., Harvard University Press, 1928, lines 1–5, 8, 13–14, emphasis added.

37 Nowell never completed his *Vocabularium*, and in 1567 turned over his manuscript to William Lambarde, who added many of the seventeen regionalisms from outside of Lancashire. The first completed Anglo-Saxon dictionary did not appear until 1659, when William Somner published his *Dictionarium Saxonico-Latino-Anglicum*.

38 Laurence Nowell, *Vocabularium* (1565), ed. Albert H. Marckwardt, Ann Arbor, Mich., University of Michigan Press, 1952, p. 22.

39 In fact, it is more likely that the southeastern dialect of English spoken in Kent had retained a greater number of Anglo-Saxon features (Larry D. Benson, personal correspondence).

40 On the sixteenth- and seventeenth-century interest in "pure" language, see the excerpts collected by Craigie, *Critique of Pure English*, pp. 115–60.

41 Quintilian, *Institutione Oratoria*, 8:13.

42 Gill, *Logonomia Anglica*, pp. 87, 104, 104, and 169, respectively.

43 Puttenham, *Arte of English Poesie*, p. 145.

44 Thomas Heywood and Richard Brome, *The Late Lancashire Witches* (1634), in *The Dramatic Works of Thomas Heywood*, vol. 4, New York, Russell & Russell, 1.1. All further citations refer to this edition and appear parenthetically in my text.

45 Thomas Deloney, *Thomas of Reading, or the Sixe Worthie Yeomen of the West* (1612), in *The Works of Thomas Deloney*, ed. Francis Oscar Mann, Oxford, Clarendon Press, 1912, pp. 214 and 226, respectively. All additional citations refer to this edition and appear parenthetically in my text.

46 Francis Beaumont and John Fletcher, *Cupid's Revenge* (1615), in *Dramatic Works in the Beaumont and Fletcher Canon*, ed. Fredson Bowers, vol. 2, Cambridge, Cambridge University Press, 1907, 4.1.104–6; 4.1.111–13. All further citations refer to this edition and are given parenthetically in my text.

47 Richard Brome, *The Northerne Lass* (1632), in *The Dramatic Works of Richard Brome*, vol. 3, New York, Ams Press, 1966, 2.2. All further citations refer to this edition and are given parenthetically in my text.

48 Brome, *The Northerne Lass*, "To Richard Holford."

49 *Oxford English Dictionary*, 2nd edn, s.v. "unkent." The *OED* notes the following use of the word in 1647: "Unkent, unkist, as the Northern Proverb hath it."

50 It is interesting to note that "gallimaufray" was a very recent loanword from French. According to the *OED*, the word first appeared in print in 1551.

51 Bruce Robert McElderry, Jr., "Archaism and Innovation in Spenser's Poetic Diction," *Publications of the Modern Language Association* 47.1, 1932, p. 148.

52 As quoted in R.M. Cummings, *Spenser: The Critical Heritage*, New York, Barnes & Noble, 1971, p. 288.

53 In his sonnet sequence, *Delia*, Daniel apparently distinguished himself from the author of *The Faerie Queene* and his archaic idiom:

> Let others sing of Knights and Palladines,
> In aged accents and untimely words.

(in *The Complete Works of Samuel Daniel in Verse and Prose*, ed. Alexander B. Grosart, vol. 1, New York, Russell & Russell, 1963, lines 1–2).

Jonson, *Discoveries*, in *Ben Jonson*, vol. 8, p. 618.

54 Ingham, "Spenser's Use of Dialect," p. 166.

55 The sources of Spenser's northernisms are continually debated by critics of his

diction. Some, like N.F. Blake, contend that Spenser's knowledge of dialect came entirely from medieval authors like Malory (*Non-standard Language in English Literature*, London, Andre Deutsch, 1981, p. 59). Malory, for example, uses the word *gar* once in all his works, and it is always possible that a very observant Spenser took note of it. But others have suggested that regional speech provided a primary source, since certain northernisms that are unrecorded or rare in medieval texts occur in contemporary dialects. See for example John Draper, "The Glosses to Spenser's *Shepheardes Calender*," *Journal of English and Germanic Philology* 18, 1919, pp. 556–74. It seems fairly certain that Spenser took his northernisms from written and "living" sources alike.

56 Draper, "Glosses to Spenser's *Shepheardes Calender*," pp. 560–6.
57 McElderry, "Archaism and Innovation," p. 150.
58 McElderry, for example, lists 163 archaic words that appear in the *Shepheardes Calender*, nearly half of which occur only in this poem ("Archaism and Innovation," p. 153).
59 Partridge also notes the contradictions in E.K.'s theory of archaisms (*The Language of Renaissance Poetry: Spenser, Shakespeare, Donne, Milton*, London, Andre Deutsch, 1971, p. 97).
60 Sir Philip Sidney, *Defense of Poesie* (1595), in *The Prose Works of Sir Philip Sidney*, ed. Albert Feuillerat, vol. 3, Cambridge, Cambridge University Press, 1968, p. 37.
61 Rubel, *Poetic Diction*, p. 145.
62 Ingham, "Spenser's Use of Dialect," p. 164.
63 McElderry, "Archaism and Innovation," p. 150. Although he slights the novelty of Spenser's language in general, even McElderry deems the diction of the *Shepheardes Calender* "experimental" in comparison with the language of Spenser's later poetry, including *The Faerie Queene* (p. 169). By the time he returned to pastoral at the end of his literary career, with *Colin Clouts Come Home Again* (1595) (in *The Works of Edmund Spenser*, eds Edwin Greenlaw *et al.*, vol. 7, part 1, Baltimore, Md., Johns Hopkins University Press, 1932/57), Spenser uses a diction that E.K. would hardly have had to gloss at all; the few "strange" words he employs are Latinate neologisms (Rubel, *Poetic Diction*, p. 257). Again, the disappearance of archaism as well as dialect from *Colin Clout* suggests that the poet made deliberate choices in creating the diction of *The Shepheardes Calender*.
64 Draper, "Glosses to Spenser's *Shepheardes Calender*," p. 556.
65 Alexander Pope, *A Discourse on Pastoral Poetry* (1717), in *Selected Prose of Alexander Pope*, ed. Paul Hammond, Cambridge, Cambridge University Press, 1978, p. 155.
66 Merritt Y. Hughes, "Spenser and the Greek Pastoral Triad," *Studies in Philology* 20, 1923, p. 190.
67 Sidney, *Defense of Poesie*, p. 37.
68 Hughes, "Spenser and Greek Pastoral," pp. 188–9.
69 Ingham, "Spenser's Use of Dialect," p. 165.
70 As quoted in Rubel, *Poetic Diction*, p. 113.
71 Louis Montrose has shown how Renaissance literary pastorals eliminate the "taint" of agrarian activities in order to forge a metaphorical identification between shepherds and gentlemen. See "Of Gentlemen and Shepherds: The Politics of Elizabethan Pastoral Form," *English Literary History* 22, 1982, p. 431.
72 Rubel, *Poetic Diction*, p. 152. Sidney's poem appears in *The Countesse of Pembroke's Arcadia* (1593), in *The Prose Works of Sir Philip Sidney*, ed. Albert Feuillerat, vol. 4, Cambridge, Cambridge University Press, 1968, lines 8–10.
73 Anne Lake Prescott, *French Poets and the English Renaissance: Studies in Fame and Transformation*, New Haven, Conn., Yale University Press, 1978, p. 263n.
74 Alfred W. Satterthwaite, *Spenser, Ronsard and DuBellay: A Renaissance Comparison*, Princeton, N.J., Princeton University Press, 1960, p. 20.

75 A contemporary of Mulcaster's reported that the teachers at the Merchant Taylors' School "being northern men born . . . had not taught the children to speak distinctly, or to pronounce their words as well as they ought." See W.L. Renwick, "Mulcaster and DuBellay," *Modern Language Review* 17.3, 1922, p. 283. There is some evidence, too, that Spenser's family hailed from Lancashire; it may be that Colin's north country, where the poet apparently spent an extended holiday before returning to London, refers to the home of some of Spenser's relations.

76 Richard Mulcaster, *The Elementarie* (1582), ed. E.T. Campagnac, Oxford, Clarendon Press, 1925, p. 90.

77 Mulcaster, *Elementarie*, p. 175.

78 Edmund Spenser, *The Faerie Queene*, in *Works of Edmund Spenser*, vol. 4, 4.2.32.

79 Chaucer himself, of course, did not confine himself to "pure" English forms. Although E.K. echoes Lydgate's judgment of Chaucer as the "Loadstarre of the language," Gill would name him, instead, the "star of ill-omen," who "rendered his poetry notorious by the use of Latin and French words" (*Logonomia Anglica*, p. 84).

80 For a discussion of Spenser's neologisms, borrowings, and other variant forms, see McElderry, "Archaism and Innovation," pp. 161–8. Rubel notes that Spenser might have have derived some of his French forms, including the suffix -*ance*, from Chaucer. As Rubel suggests, "the fact that [these words] also have a peculiarly Chaucerian flavor may have given them, to Spenser, the same atmosphere of remoteness as that of the archaisms. E.K.'s glosses show that they were equally unusual" (*Poetic Diction*, p. 146).

81 Puttenham, *Arte of English Poesie*, p. 145.

82 Viola B. Hulbert, "Diggon Davie," *Journal of English and Germanic Philology* 50, 1942, pp. 349–50.

83 Ingham, "Spenser's Use of Dialect," p. 166.

84 Montrose has shown how the pastoral poet's suit for love may represent other forms of desire ("Amorous motives displace or subsume forms of desire, frustration, and resentment other than the merely sexual"), including the desire for professional advancement ("Of Gentlemen and Shepherds," p. 440).

85 Several critics have suggested that the two gestures are parallel in meaning. See for example Richard Mallette, *Spenser, Milton, and Renaissance Pastoral*, Lewisburg, Penn., Bucknell University Press, 1981, p. 59; and Richard Helgerson, *Self-Crowned Laureates: Spenser, Jonson, Milton, and the Literary System*, Berkeley, Calif., University of California Press, 1983, p. 69.

86 See for example D.M. Rosenberg's *Oaten Reeds and Trumpets: Pastoral and Epic in Virgil, Spenser, and Milton*, Lewisburg, Penn., Bucknell University Press, 1981. While I do not argue that Spenser may have had Virgil's example in mind when he forged his career, I don't believe that Spenser intended his pastoral to be merely a prologue to his later works. Spenser presented his eclogues as the fulfillment, not the promise, of his literary talents.

87 Charles Gildon, *Complete Art of Poetry*, as quoted by Greenlaw in *Works of Edmund Spenser*, vol. 7, p. 575.

88 Some of Spenser's contemporaries, however, credited him with just that. Gabriel Harvey, for example, listed Spenser among other poets as an improver of the native tongue (as quoted in Rubel, *Poetic Diction*, p. 147).

89 George Peele, "Ecologue Gratulatorie" (1589), in *The Works of George Peele* (1589), ed. A.H. Bullen, vol. 2, Port Washington, N.Y., Kennicat Press, 1988, lines 269–77. Rubel suggests that Peele "not only echoes Spenser but in places quite outdoes him" (*Poetic Diction*, p. 159). Other seventeenth-century poets who drew on Spenser's language include William Browne, John Davies of Hereford, Michael Drayton, Edward Fairfax, Giles Fletcher the younger, Phineas Fletcher, and Henry More. See Partridge, *Language of Renaissance Poetry*, p. 99.

5 LANGUAGE, LAWS, AND BLOOD: THE KING'S ENGLISH AND HIS EMPIRE

1 Edmund Spenser, *A View of the Present State of Ireland* (1596), in *Elizabethan Ireland: A Selection of Writings by Elizabethan Writers on Ireland*, ed. James P. Myers, Jr., Hamden, Conn., Archon Books, 1983, p. 96.

2 Fynes Moryson, *An Itinerary* (1617–*c.* 1626), in Myers, *Elizabethan Ireland*, p. 207.

3 For a discussion of Nebrija and early modern linguistic colonialism, see G.A. Padley, *Grammatical Theory in Western Europe 1500–1700*, vol. 2, Cambridge, Cambridge University Press, 1988, pp. 157–65; see also Jose Piedra, "Literary Whiteness and the Afro-Hispanic Difference," *New Literary History* 18, 1987, pp. 303–11.

4 John Hare, *St. Edward's Ghost* (1647), as quoted in R.F. Jones, *The Triumph of the English Language: A Survey of Opinions Concerning the Vernacular from the Introduction of Printing to the Restoration*, Stanford, Calif., Stanford University Press, 1953, p. 222.

5 R.F. Jones has traced the turn, in the latter part of the sixteenth century, from concerns about the "inadequacy" of English to a celebration of the sufficiency and power of English. See, especially, Chapter 6, "The Eloquent Language," *Triumph of English*, pp. 168–213.

6 Alexander Gill, *Logonomia Anglica* (1619), part 2, *Stockholm Studies in English* 27, trans. Robin C. Alston, eds Bror Danielsson and Arvid Gabrielson, Stockholm, Almquist & Wiksell, 1972, p. 86.

7 Samuel Daniel, *Musophilus* (1599), in *Samuel Daniel: The Complete Works in Verse and Prose*, ed. Alexander B. Grosart, vol. 1, lines 957–62.

8 Stephen Greenblatt notes that Daniel "hasn't the slightest sense that the natives might be reluctant to abandon their own tongue"; for Daniel, the New World is a "cultural void" or a *tabula rasa* "ready to take the imprint of European civilization." ("Learning to Curse: Aspects of Linguistic Colonialism in the Sixteenth Century," in *Learning to Curse: Essays in Early Modern Culture*, New York and London, Routledge, 1990, p. 17).

9 In 1580, Spenser wrote to Gabriel Harvey asking, "Why a God's name may not we, as else the Greeks, have the kingdom of our own language?" Helgerson cites this and discusses some of its ramifications in the introduction to his book *Forms of Nationhood: The Elizabethan Writing of England*, Chicago, Ill., University of Chicago Press, 1992, pp. 1–18.

10 Renaissance authors were apparently most familiar with Welsh, followed by Irish. Scottish Gaelic does not appear in English literature of the period. For a comprehensive list of Renaissance plays that contain Welsh and Irish, see J.O. Bartley, *Teague, Shenkin and Sawney*, Cork, Cork University Press, 1954.

11 P.M. Zall, *A Hundred Merry Tales and Other Jestbooks of the Fifteenth and Sixteenth Centuries*, Lincoln, Nebr., University of Nebraska Press, 1963, p. 132.

12 As quoted in Bartley, *Teague, Shenkin, and Sawney*, p. 24. This character uses dialect sparingly in his song, addressing, for example, the "good shentlemen" (p. 25).

13 All citations to Shakespeare's plays refer to *The Riverside Shakespeare*, eds G. Blakemore Evans *et al.*, Boston, Mass., Houghton Mifflin, 1974, and references are given parenthetically in my text.

14 Zall, *A Hundred Merry Tales*, p. 94.

15 Andrew Boorde, *Merie Tales of the Mad Men of Gotam* (1565), ed. Stanley J. Kahrl, Evanston, Ill., Northwestern University Press, 1965, p. 16.

16 A more general, comparative study of Anglo-Welsh, Anglo-Irish, and Anglo-Scottish relations in the period will not be attempted here. For an overview of these issues, see for example Michael Hechter, *Internal Colonialism: The Celtic Fringe in*

British National Development, 1536–1966, Berkeley, Calif., University of California Press, 1975.

17 Shakespeare, *Henry V*, 2.4.80–1.

18 These lines are spoken by a Welsh "bardh" in the play by "R.A., Gent.," *The Valiant Welshman* (1615), Edinburgh and London, Ams Press, 1970, 1.1.56–7.

19 Bartley, *Teague, Shenkin, and Sawney*, p. 48.

20 Hechter, *Internal Colonialism*, p. 70.

21 As quoted in R. Brinley Jones, *The Old British Tongue: The Vernacular in Wales, 1540–1640*, Cardiff, Avalon Books, 1970, p. 33.

22 Jones, *The Old British Tongue*, p. 34.

23 George Owen, *Survey of Pembrokeshire* (1603), in *Cymmrodorian Records*, ed. Henry Owen, series 1, part 1, London, Charles J. Clark, 1982, p. 36.

24 Owen, *Survey of Pembrokeshire* (1603), pp. 34 and 40, respectively.

25 George Owen, *Cruell Lawes against Welshmen* (1603), in *Cymmrodorian Records*, series 1, part 3, p. 120.

26 William Salesbury, *A Dictionary in Englyshe and Welshe* (1547), Ann Arbor, Mich., University Microfilms, "To the moost victoriouse and Redoubtede Prince Henry."

27 William Salesbury, *A Briefe and a Playne Introduction, Teachyng How to Pronounce the Letters in the British Tong* (1550), Ann Arbor, Mich., University Microfilms, title page.

28 Salesbury, *A Briefe and a Playne Introduction*, p. 37.

29 Salesbury, *A Briefe and a Playne Introduction*, "Wyllyam Salesbury to the Reader."

30 As quoted in Glanmor Williams, *Recovery, Reorientation and Reformation Wales c. 1415–1642*, Oxford, Clarendon Press, 1987, p. 450.

31 As quoted in R. Brinley Jones, *The Old British Tongue*, p. 39.

32 R. Brinley Jones, *The Old British Tongue*, pp. 38 and 76.

33 As quoted in R. Brinley Jones, *The Old British Tongue*, p. 68.

34 As quoted in Glanmor Williams, *Recovery, Reorientation and Reformation*, pp. 464, 465, and 436, respectively.

35 Thomas Dekker, *The Welsh Embassador* (1624), in *The Dramatic Works of Thomas Dekker*, ed. Fredson Bowers, vol. 1, Cambridge, Cambridge University Press, 1970, 3.2.117–18. Further citations refer to this edition and appear parenthetically in my text.

36 This is probably the least accurate feature of literary representations of Anglo-Welsh. In Welsh, impersonal expressions made use of feminine pronouns (as in "she's raining") so it may be that Englishmen believed they were hearing the word "her" in a great deal of expressions where it didn't seem to belong. See Bartley, *Teague, Shenkin, and Sawney*, p. 73 for a discussion of the accuracy of literary portraits of the language.

37 Thomas Dekker, *Patient Grissill* (1603), in *Dramatic Works of Thomas Dekker*, vol. 1, 2.1.186–9; Ben Jonson, *For the Honor of Wales* (1618), in *Ben Jonson: The Complete Masques*, ed. Stephen Orgel, New Haven, Conn., Yale University Press, 1969, lines 36–41). All further citations from this masque refer to this edition and line numbers are given parenthetically in my text.

38 A character named Penda, disguised as the ambassador, illustrates his poetic prowess with one of his own compositions, which includes the lines "Wud you kanaw her mistris nose/Tis fine pridge ore which pewtie goes" (4.1.87–8).

39 *Henry V* was published in quarto before appearing in the First Folio, and it is important to note that Captain Macmorris and Captain Jamy do not appear in the quarto version of the play. There has been some debate as to whether this omission was a matter of political expedience. In any case, it is widely accepted that the Folio was based on Shakespeare's manuscript, and is therefore the closest we have to an authoritative text.

Fluellen appears in both versions, but for the most part, the Folio represents a more sustained effort to represent Anglo-Welsh. See N.F. Blake, "Standardizing Shakespeare's Non-Standard Language," in *Standardizing English: Essays in the History of Language in Honor of John Hurt Fisher*, ed. Joseph B. Trahern, Jr., Knoxville, Tenn., University of Tennessee Press, 1989, for a detailed comparision of the use of dialect in the two versions of the play.

40 Fluellen uses little in the way of dialect in this scene, which comes late in the play. Like most other dialect speakers in Renaissance English literature, Fluellen uses dialect inconsistently and unsystematically.

41 Stephen Greenblatt, *Shakespearean Negotiations: The Circulation of Social Energy in Renaissance England*, Berkeley, Calif., University of California Press, 1988, p. 56.

42 Greenblatt, *Shakespearean Negotiations*, p. 57.

43 Jonathan Dollimore and Alan Sinfield, "History and Ideology: The Instance of *Henry V*," in *Alternative Shakespeares*, ed. John Drakakis, London, Methuen, 1985, p. 224.

44 Dollimore and Sinfield, "History and Ideology," pp. 216–17.

45 Dollimore and Sinfield, "History and Ideology," pp. 216–17, 223, and 225, respectively.

46 Even on the verge of triumph over the French, King Henry recalls his father's usurpation of the crown, and his inherited guilt:

> Not to-day, O Lord,
> O, not to-day, think not upon the fault
> My father made in compassing the crown!
> I Richard's body have interred new
> And on it have bestowed more contrite tears,
> Than from it issued forth drops of blood.
> Five hundred poor I have in yearly pay,
> Who twice a day their wither'd hands hold up
> Toward heaven, to pardon blood; and I have built
> Two chauntries, where the sad and solemn priests
> Sing still for Richard's soul. More will I do;
> Though all that I can do is nothing worth,
> Since that my penitence comes after all,
> Imploring pardon.
>
> (4.1.292–305)

47 James Howell, *Epistolae Ho-Elianae: The Familiar Letters of James Howell*, vol. 2, Boston, Mass., Houghton Mifflin, 1907, p. 142.

48 In fact, Jonson had demonstrated an interest in Welsh linguistics at least ten years before Howell made his gift, for he used a Welsh grammar of the 1590s when he wrote *For the Honor of Wales*. See Bartley, *Teague, Shenkin, and Sawney*, p. 57.

49 As quoted in Stephen Orgel, *The Jonsonian Masque*, Cambridge, Mass., Harvard University Press, 1965, p. 70.

50 As quoted in Orgel, *Jonsonian Masque*, p. 71. All quotations from *Pleasure Reconciled to Virtue* and *For the Honor of Wales* are taken from *Ben Jonson: The Complete Masques*, ed. Stephen Orgel, New Haven, Conn., Yale University Press, 1969, and are given parenthetically in my text.

51 As quoted in Orgel, *Jonsonian Masque*, p. 72.

52 In Myers, *Elizabethan Ireland*, p. 97.

53 Alan Bliss, "The English Language in Early Modern Ireland," in *A New History of Ireland*, eds T.W. Moody, F.X. Martin and F.J. Byrne, vol. 3, Oxford, Clarendon Press, 1976, pp. 546–7. Moody, in the introduction to the volume, notes that the term "Old English" has been used variously by historians, sometimes to represent the descendants of the original English colonists (my usage), and other times in

reference to those Anglo-Irish who remained loyal to the English crown during the Civil Wars. The latter usage was current in the seventeenth century. See Moody *et al.*, p. xlii.

54 Sir Philip Sidney, *Discourse on Irish Affairs* (1577), in Myers, *Elizabethan Ireland*, p. 36.

55 G.A. Hayes-McCoy, "The Tudor Conquest," in *The Course of Irish History*, ed. T.W. Moody and F.X. Martin, Cork, Mercier Press, 1978, p. 174.

56 Hayes-McCoy, "Tudor Conquest," p. 175.

57 The ordinance of 1534 decreed that "no Yrishe mynstrels, rymours, shannaghes, new bardes, unchaghes, nor messangers, come to desire any goodes of any man dwellinge within the Inglyshrei, upon peyne of forfayture of all theyr goodes, and theyr bodyes to prison." See Brian O'Cuiv, "The Irish Language in the Early Modern Period", in *A New History of Ireland*, p. 520. On the 1537 ordinance, see O'Cuiv, "The Irish Language," pp. 509–10.

58 O'Cuiv, "The Irish Language," p. 529.

59 O'Cuiv, "The Irish Language," pp. 511–13.

60 Myers, *Elizabethan Ireland*, p. 4.

61 Moryson, *An Itinerary*, p. 207.

62 Moryson, *An Itinerary*, pp. 207–8.

63 As quoted in Bliss, "English Language in Early Modern Ireland," p. 546.

64 Spenser, *A View of the Present State of Ireland*, pp. 96–7.

65 Spenser, *A View of the Present State of Ireland*, p. 97.

66 Edmund Campion, *A History of Ireland* (1571), in Myers, *Elizabethan Ireland*, p. 25.

67 It is interesting to note that Stanyhurst describes "English Irish" in exactly the terms that E.K. had used to describe the state of the "common" vernacular in England – as a "gallamaufrey of . . . languages." The fact that English itself was a "mingle mangle" of native and foreign forms often made arguments against the incursion of additional foreign elements inconsistent.

68 As quoted in Bliss, "English Language in Early Modern Ireland," p. 547.

69 See Bliss, "English Language in Early Modern Ireland," for a philological analysis of these literary dialects, pp. 549–55.

70 Anon. *The Famous History of Captain Thomas Stukeley* (1605), Oxford, Malone Society Reprints, 1970, 7. 944–50.

71 Bartley, *Teague, Shenkin, and Sawney*, p. 27.

72 Ben Jonson, *The Irish Masque at Court* (1613), in *Complete Masques*. All further citations refer to this edition and are given parenthetically in my text.

73 Sir John Davies, *A Discovery of the True Causes Why Ireland Was Never Entirely Subdoed, Nor Brought Under Obedience of the Crown of England, Until the Beginning of His Majesty's Happy Reign* (1612), in Myers, *Elizabethan Ireland*, p. 174. For a related view of the treatment of Anglo-Irish in Renaissance literature and culture, see Michael Neill, "Broken English and Broken Irish: Nation, Language, and the Optic of Power in Shakespeare's Histories" (*Shakespeare Quarterly*, 45.1, 1994, pp. 1–32). Neill also discusses English fears of "degeneration" through contact with the Irish, and argues that Shakespeare's histories reflect a Tudor goal of cultural assimilation.

74 James I, *A Speech in the Starre-Chamber, the XX of June, Anno 1616* (1616), in *Political Writings*, ed. Johann P. Sommerville, Cambridge, Cambridge University Press, 1994, p. 209.

75 James I, *A Speech, As It Was Delivered in the Upper House of Parliament . . . the First Day of the First Parliament* (1603), in *Political Writings*, p. 135.

76 Mairi Robinson, *The Concise Scots Dictionary*, Aberdeen, Aberdeen University Press, 1985, Introduction, p. x.

77 Robert Wedderburn (alleged author), *The Complaynt of Scotlande* (1549), ed. James A.H. Murray, Early English Text Society, Extra Series No. 17, London, 1872, p. 106.

78 Andrew Boorde, *The Fyrst Boke of the Introduction of Knowledge* (1542), ed. F.J. Furnivall, Early English Text Society, London, 1871, p. 120. Boorde did find a way to distinguish between them, however, by suggesting that the Scottish, like the Welsh, were prone to swearing and profane oaths: "They [the Welsh] can not speke x wordes to-gyther of Welshe, but 'deavol,' that is to say, 'the devyl,' is at the end of one of the wordes, as 'the foule evyll,' whyche is the fallyng sycknes, is at the end of every skottysh mans tale" (p. 127).

79 Bailey, "The Conquests of English," pp. 15–16.

80 Nancy C. Dorian, *Language Death: The Life Cycle of a Scottish Gaelic Dialect*, Philadelphia, Penn., University of Pennsylvania Press, 1984, p. 20.

81 Robinson, *Scots Dictionary*, Introduction, p. x.

82 As quoted in Robinson, *Scots Dictionary*, p. x.

83 As quoted in Clausdirk Pollner and Helmut Rohlfing, "The Scottish Language from the Sixteenth to the Eighteenth Century: Elphinston's Works as a Mirror of Anglicisation," *Scottish Studies* 4, ed. Horst W. Drescher, Frankfurt am Main, Verlag Peter Lang, 1986, pp. 126–7.

84 Alexander Hume, *Of the Orthographie and Congruitie of the Britan Tongue* (1619), ed. H.B. Wheatley, London, Early English Text Society, 1865. All further references to Hume are taken from this edition and are given parenthetically in my text.

85 Hume was arguing that the initial phoneme in words like *what*, *where* and *when* is aspirated, and that aspiration is a gutteral rather than a labial sound (that is, it is articulated in the back of the throat, rather than by the lips).

86 See G. P. V. Akrigg, ed. *Letters of King James VI and I*, Berkeley, Calif., University of California Press, 1984. James's orthography, on the other hand, retained many Scotticisms, but after 1603, many of these began to disappear as well, even in informal letters. Hume would have been delighted to know that one of the Scottish features that persisted in James's writing was the use of *quh*, although by 1623, he reveals some confusion on this point, addressing a letter from "qwhitehall" (Akrigg, *Letters*, p. 32).

87 James I, *A Speach . . . Delivered . . . the First Day of the First Parliament*, p. 135.

88 James I, *A Speach . . . Delivered . . . the First Day of the First Parliament*, pp. 135–7.

89 Marie Axton, *The Queen's Two Bodies: Drama and the Elizabethan Succession*, London, Royal Historical Society, 1977, p. 134.

90 As quoted in Axton, *The Queen's Two Bodies*, p. 134.

91 Maurice Lee, Jr., *Government by Pen: Scotland under James VI and I*, Urbana, Ill., University of Illinois Press, 1980, p. 13.

92 William Camden, *Remaines Concerning Britain* (1614), Yorkshire, EP Publishing, 1974, p. 24.

93 Gill, *Logonomia Anglica*, p. 84.

94 James I, *The Basilicon Doron of King James VI*, ed. James Craigie, vol. 2, Edinburgh and London, William Blackwood, 1944, p. 6.

95 Craigie cites the *Basilicon Doron* as a work written "while that [i.e. Scots] was still a national literary dialect and before it had sunk to the level of a rustic dialect" (vol. 2, p. 117).

96 James I, *Basilicon Doron*, vol. 1, p. 186.

97 The other editions of the *Basilicon Doron* do not vary significantly with respect to James's Scotticisms, and the orthographic differences among them have little bearing on this argument. In the passage above, for example, the 1616 edition has *flowers* for *floures*, *quicke* for *quick*; otherwise they are identical.

98 James I, *Basilicon Doron*, vol. 2, pp. 113–15.

99 James I, *The Poems of James VI of Scotland*, ed. James Craigie, vol. 2, Edinburgh and London, William Blackwood, 1955, p. xxiii.

100 James I, *Poems of James VI*, vol. 2, lines 51–6, 59–62, 65–8.

101 Craigie argues that it is likely that James supervised these changes. See *Poems of James VI*, vol. 2, p. xli.
102 Craigie confirms that anglicization of vocabulary was not fully carried out in earlier published editions of James's poetry, the *Essayes* and *His Majesties Poetical Exercises*. See Craigie, *Poems of James VI*, vol. 1, p. 293.
103 James I, *Poems of James VI*, vol. 1, p. 306.
104 James I, *Poems of James VI*, vol. 1, p. 67.
105 Robinson, *Scots Dictionary*, p. xi. These works, in fact, served as the basis for the revival of Scots in eighteenth-century literature.
106 See Chapter 4, pp. 104–5, for an account of Renaissance representations of northern English. These forms are often used to represent Scots as well.
107 Shakespeare's Henry V reminds the English court of the "ill neighborhood" (1.2. 154) of Scotland, and the persistent threat the "auld enemy" had posed for centuries.
108 Nathaniel Woodes, *The Conflict of Conscience* (1581), Oxford, Malone Society Reprints, 1952, 3.4.905–11.
109 For a detailed discussion of the parallels between Greene's play and Anglo-Scottish relations between 1580 and 1590, see Catherine Lekhal, "The Historical Background of Robert Greene's *The Scottish History of James IV*," *Cahiers Elisabethains* 35, 1989, pp. 27–45.
110 Robert Greene, *The Scottish History of James the Fourth*, ed. Norman Sanders, London, Methuen, 1970, Induction, lines 3–6.
111 As quoted by Sanders in Greene, *Scottish History of James the Fourth*, pp. xxxiv–xxxv.
    One important exception to the idea that Scots was held in disdain by English authors of the sixteenth century is Surrey's use of Scotticisms in his translation of Books II and IV of the *Aeneid* (1554/7). Although Surrey never explicitly mentioned his Scottish source, he borrowed freely from Gavin Douglas's *Eneados* (1513). Gregory Kratzmann suggests that Surrey was trying to make his poetic language more flexible by augmenting it with Scots terms, but his examples indicate that, for the most part, Surrey misunderstand what these terms meant, and tried to force them to make English sense. See his *Anglo-Scottish Literary Relations, 1430–1550*, Cambridge, Cambridge University Press, 1980, pp. 169–94.
112 George Chapman, John Marston, and Ben Jonson, *Eastward Hoe* (1605), in *Ben Jonson*, eds C.H. Herford and Percy and Evelyn Simpson, vol. 4, Oxford, Clarendon Press, 1966, 3.3.40–8.
113 Helen Child Sargent and George Lyman Kyttredge, eds *English and Scottish Popular Ballads: Edited from the Collection of Francis James Child*, Boston, Mass., Houghton Mifflin, 1904, pp. 3–4.
114 Ben Jonson, *The Sad Shepherd, or a Tale of Robin Hood* (c. 1655), in *Ben Jonson*, vol. 7. Further citations refer to this edition and line numbers are given parenthetically in my text.
115 Jonson, *Conversations with Drummond* (1618/19), in *Ben Jonson*, vol. 1, p. 149; Jonson, *Discoveries* (1640), in *Ben Jonson*, vol. 8, p. 618.
116 Earine speaks standard English in her other appearances in the play. Further evidence that Earine is mocking Lorel's dialect is that while Jonson used the present participle in -*and* correctly throughout the play, Earine's "fewmand," presumably meaning "to make fume or smell," is egregiously ill-formed (Bartley, *Teague, Shenkin, and Sawney*, p. 92).
117 Thomas Middleton includes a character "from the northern parts" in his play *The Witch* (1610/16) who uses the words "bonny" and "varray." There is no reason to assume, however, that this walk-on is a Scotsman rather than a provincial from the north country of England.
118 Bartley, *Teague, Shenkin, and Sawney*, p. 84.

BIBLIOGRAPHY

Note: Each author's works are cited alphabetically by title. However, where several individual works are cited which appear in a collection, the collection is given first and the individual works follow in alphabetical order.

Academy of the Crusca, *The Fairest Flower: The Emergence of Linguistic Consciousness in Renaissance Europe*, Florence, University of California, International Conference of the Center for Medieval and Renaissance Studies, 1983.

Akrigg, G.P.V., ed., *Letters of King James VI and I*, Berkeley, Calif., University of California Press, 1984.

Anon., *The Contention between Liberality and Prodigality* (1602), Oxford, Malone Society Reprints, 1913.

——, *The Famous History of Captain Thomas Stukeley* (1605), Oxford, Malone Society Reprints, 1970.

——, *Gammer Gurton's Needle* (1575), ed. John S. Farmer, Tudor Facsimile Texts, New York, Ams Press, 1970.

——, *The London Prodigal* (1605), ed. John S. Farmer, Tudor Facsimile Texts, New York, Ams Press, 1970.

Aristotle, *Poetics*, in *Works of Aristotle*, ed. Richard McKeon, 2nd edn, Chicago, Ill., University of Chicago Press, 1973.

Aston, M., *The Fifteenth Century: The Prospect of Europe*, New York, Harcourt Brace, 1968.

Attridge, Derek, *Peculiar Language: Literature as Difference from the Renaissance to James Joyce*, Ithaca, N.Y., Cornell University Press, 1988.

Atwood, Norman, "Cordelia and Kent: Their Fateful Choice of Style," *Language and Style* 9.1, 1976, pp. 42–54.

Awdeley, John, *The Fraternitye of Vacabondes* (1565), eds E. Viles and F.J. Furnivall, Oxford, Oxford University Press, 1869.

Axton, Marie, *The Queen's Two Bodies: Drama and the Elizabethan Succession*, London, Royal Historical Society, 1977.

Bailey, Richard W., "The Conquests of English," in *The English Language Today*, ed. Sidney Greenbaum, Oxford, Pergamon, 1985, pp. 9–19.

——, *Images of English: A Cultural History of the Language*, Ann Arbor, Mich., University of Michigan Press, 1991.

Bakhtin, M.M., *The Dialogic Imagination*, trans. Caryl Emerson and Michael Holquist, ed. Michael Holquist, Austin, Tex., University of Texas Press, 1981.

——, *Rabelais and His World*, trans. Helene Iswolsky, Bloomington, Ind., Indiana University Press, 1984.

Bartley, J.O., *Teague, Shenkin, and Sawney*, Cork, Cork University Press, 1954.

Baugh, Albert C. and Thomas Cable, *A History of the English Language*, 3rd edn, Englewood Cliffs, N.J., Prentice-Hall, 1978.

Beaumont, Francis and John Fletcher, *Cupid's Revenge* (1615), in *Dramatic Works in the Beaumont and Fletcher Canon*, ed. Fredson Bowers, vol. 2, Cambridge, Cambridge University Press, 1970.

————, and Philip Massinger, *The Beggar's Bush* (*c.* 1647), in *Dramatic Works in the Beaumont and Fletcher Canon*, ed. Fredson Bowers, vol. 3, Cambridge, Cambridge University Press, 1970.

Beaurline, L.A., *Jonson and Elizabethan Comedy*, San Marino, Calif., Huntington Library, 1978.

Beer, Max, *Early British Economics*, New York, Augustus M. Kelley, 1967.

Blake, N.F., *Caxton and his World*, New York, Academic Press, 1973.

——, *Non-standard Language in English Literature*, London, Andre Deutsch, 1981.

——, *Shakespeare's Language: An Introduction*, London, Macmillan, 1983.

——, "Standardizing Shakespeare's Non-Standard Language," in *Standardizing English: Essays in the History of Language Change in Honor of John Hurt Fisher*, ed. Joseph B. Trahern, Jr., Knoxville, Tenn., University of Tennessee Press, 1989, pp. 57–81.

Bliss, Alan, "The English Language in Early Modern Ireland," in T.W. Moody, F.X. Martin, and F.J. Byrne, eds, *A New History of Ireland*, vol. 3, pp. 546–60.

Blount, Thomas, *Glossographia* (1656), *Anglistica & Americana* 32, New York, Georg Olms Verlag, 1972.

Boorde, Andrew, *The First and Best Part of Scoggins Jests* (*c.* 1565) in *Old English Jest Books*, ed. W. Carew Hazlitt, London, Willis & Sotheran, 1866.

——, *The Fyrst Boke of the Introduction of Knowledge* (1542), ed. F.J. Furnivall, London, Early English Text Society, 1871.

——, *Merie Tales of the Mad Men of Gotam* (1565), ed. Stanley J. Kahrl, Evanston, Ill., Northwestern University Press, 1965.

Bourdieu, Pierre, *Language and Symbolic Power*, trans. Gino Raymond and Matthew Adamson, ed. John B. Thompson, Cambridge, Mass., Harvard University Press, 1991.

Bradley, A.C., *Shakespearean Tragedy*, New York, St. Martin's Press, 1985.

Bright, Timothy, *Characterie: An Arte of Shorte, Swifte, and Secrete Writing by Character* (1588), Ann Arbor, Mich., University Microfilms.

Brome, Richard, *The Dramatic Works of Richard Brome*, New York, Ams Press, 1966, 3 vols.

——, *A Joviall Crew, or the Merry Beggars* (1641), in *The Dramatic Works of Richard Brome*, vol. 3.

——, *The Northerne Lass* (1632), in *The Dramatic Works of Richard Brome*, vol. 3.

Brook, G.L., *The Language of Shakespeare*, London, Andre Deutsch, 1976.

Bullokar, John, *An English Expositor: Teaching the Interpretation of the Hardest Words Used in our Language* (1616), Ann Arbor, Mich., University Microfilms.

Bullokar, William, *Booke at Large, for the Amendment of Orthographie for English Speech* (1580), Ann Arbor, Mich., University Microfilms.

Burt, Richard, *Licensed By Authority: Ben Jonson and the Discourses of Censorship*, Ithaca, N.Y., Cornell University Press, 1993.

Calderwood, James, *Shakespearean Metadrama*, Minneapolis, Minn., University of Minnesota Press, 1971.

Camden, William, *Remaines Concerning Britain* (1614), Yorkshire, EP Publishing, 1974.

Campion, Edmund, *A History of Ireland* (1571), in James P. Myers, Jr., ed., *Elizabethan Ireland: A Selection of Writings by Elizabethan Writers on Ireland*, pp. 22–35.

Carew, Richard, *The Excellency of the English Tongue*, in William Camden, *Remaines Concerning Britain*, pp. 42–51.

——, *Survey of Cornwall* (1602), in *Richard Carew of Antony*, ed. F.E. Halliday, London, Andrew Melrose, 1953.

Castiglione, Baldassare, *The Book of the Courtier* (1528), trans. and ed., W.B. Drayton Henderson, London, J.M. Dent, 1928.

Cawdrey, Robert, *A Table Alphabeticall* (1604), Ann Arbor, Mich., University Microfilms.

Caxton, William, Prologue to the *Eneydos* (1490), in *The Prologues and Epilogues of William Caxton*, ed. W.J.B. Crotch, Millwood, N.Y., Kraus Reprints, 1978, pp. 107–10.

Chapman, George, John Marston, and Ben Jonson, *Eastward Hoe* (1605), in Ben Jonson, *Ben Jonson*, vol. 4.

Chaucer, Geoffrey, *Treatise on the Astrolabe* (1392), in *The Riverside Chaucer*, ed. Larry D. Benson, 3rd edn, Boston, Mass., Houghton Mifflin, 1987.

Clay, C.G.A., *Economic Expansion and Social Change: England 1500–1700*, Cambridge, Cambridge University Press, 1984, 2 vols.

Cockburn, J.S., "Early Modern Assize Records as Historical Evidence," *Journal of Society of Archivists* 5, 1975, pp. 215–31.

Cockeram, Henry, *The English Dictionarie* (1623), Ann Arbor, Mich., University Microfilms.

Cooper, Robert L., *Language Planning and Social Change*, Cambridge, Cambridge University Press, 1989.

Coote, Edmund, *The English Schoole-maister* (1596), *English Linguistics 1500–1800*, 98, ed. R.C. Alston, London, The Scolar Press, 1968.

Copland, Robert, *The Highway to the Spital-House* (1535/6), in *The Elizabethan Underworld*, ed. A.V. Judges, London, George Routledge & Sons, 1930, pp. 1–25.

Craigie, W.A., *The Critique of Pure English from Caxton to Smollett*, Society for Pure English 65, Oxford, Clarendon Press, 1946.

Crewe, Jonathan, *Unredeemed Rhetoric: Thomas Nashe and the Scandal of Authorship*, Baltimore, Md., Johns Hopkins University Press, 1982.

Crowley, Tony, *Standard English and the Politics of Language*, Urbana, Ill., University of Illinois Press, 1989.

Cummings, R.M., *Spenser: The Critical Heritage*, New York, Barnes & Noble, 1971.

Daniel, Samuel, *The Complete Works of Samuel Daniel in Verse and Prose*, ed. Alexander B. Grosart, New York, Russell & Russell, 5 vols.

——, *Delia* (1592), in *The Complete Works of Samuel Daniel in Verse and Prose*, vol. 1.

——, *Musophilus* (1599), in *The Complete Works of Samuel Daniel in Verse and Prose*, vol. 1.

——, *Defense of Ryme* (1603), in *Elizabethan Critical Essays*, ed. G. Gregory Smith, vol. 2, Oxford, Oxford University Press, 1904, 2 vols., pp. 356–84.

Danson, Lawrence, *Tragic Alphabet: Shakespeare's Drama of Language*, New Haven, Conn., Yale University Press, 1974.

Dante Alighieri, *De Vulgari Eloquentia* (c. 1303), trans. Warren Welliver, Ravenna, Longo Editore, 1981.

Davies, Sir John, *A Discovery of the True Causes Why Ireland Was Never Entirely Subdoed, Nor Brought Under Obedience of the Crown of England, Until the Beginning of His Majesty's Happy Reign* (1612), in James P. Myers, Jr., ed., *Elizabethan Ireland: A Selection of Writings by Elizabethan Writers on Ireland*, pp. 146–84.

De Grazia, Margreta, "Shakespeare's View of Language: An Historical Perspective," *Shakespeare Quarterly* 29, 1978, pp. 374–88.

Dekker, Thomas, *The Dramatic Works of Thomas Dekker*, ed. Fredson Bowers, Cambridge, Cambridge University Press, 1970, 5 vols.

——, *Patient Grissill* (1603), in *The Dramatic Works of Thomas Dekker*, vol. 1.

——, *The Welsh Embassador* (1624), in *The Dramatic Works of Thomas Dekker*, vol. 1.

——, *Thomas Dekker*, ed. E.D. Pendry, London, Edward Arnold, 1967.

——, *Lanterne and Candlelight: or The Bellman's Second Night's Walke* (1608), in *Thomas Dekker*, pp. 187–282.

199

——, *O per se O* (1612), in *Thomas Dekker*, pp. 283–308.

—— and Thomas Middleton, *The Roaring Girle, or Moll Cutpurse* (1604/10), in *The Dramatic Works of Thomas Dekker*, vol. 3.

Deloney, Thomas, *Thomas of Reading, or the Sixe Worthie Yeomen of the West* (1612), in *The Works of Thomas Deloney*, ed. Francis Oscar Mann, Oxford, Clarendon Press, 1912, pp. 211–72.

Dobson, E.J., "Early Modern Standard English," *Transactions of the Philological Society*, 1955, pp. 25–54.

——, *English Pronunciation 1500–1700*, 2nd edn, vol. 1, Oxford, Clarendon Press, 1968, 2 vols.

Dollimore, Jonathan, *Radical Tragedy: Religion, Ideology and Power in the Drama of Shakespeare and his Contemporaries*, Chicago, Ill., University of Chicago Press, 1984.

—— and Alan Sinfield, "History and Ideology: The Instance of *Henry V*," in *Alternative Shakespeares*, ed. John Drakakis, London, Methuen, 1985, pp. 206–27.

Donawerth, Jane, *Shakespeare and the Sixteenth-Century Study of Language*, Chicago, Ill., University of Illinois Press, 1984.

Dorian, Nancy C., *Language Death: The Life Cycle of a Scottish Gaelic Dialect*, Philadelphia, Penn., University of Pennsylvania Press, 1984.

Draper, John, "The Glosses to Spenser's *Shepheardes Calender*," *Journal of English and Germanic Philology* 18, 1919, pp. 556–74.

Drayton, Michael, *Poly-Olbion* (1612/22), in *The Works of Michael Drayton*, ed. J. William Hebel, vol. 4, Oxford, Basil Blackwell, 1961, 5 vols.

Du Bellay, Joachim, *The Defence and Illustration of the French Language* (1549), trans. and ed. Gladys M. Turquet, London, J.M. Dent, 1939.

Elyot, Sir Thomas, *The Book Named the Governor* (1531), ed. S.E. Lehmberg, London, J.M. Dent, 1962.

Everitt, Alan, *The Local Community and the Great Rebellion*, London, The Historical Association, 1969.

Ferne, John, *The Blazon of Gentrie* (1586), Ann Arbor, Mich., University Microfilms.

Fisher, Sandra K., *Econolingua: A Glossary of Coins and Economic Language in Renaissance Drama*, Newark, N.J., University of Delaware Press, 1985.

Fishman, Joshua A., *Language and Nationalism: Two Integrative Essays*, Rowley, Mass., Newbury House, 1972.

Fletcher, Anthony, "National and Local Awareness in the County Communities," in *Before the English Civil War: Essays on Stuart Politics and Government*, ed. Howard Tomlinson, London, Macmillan Press, 1983, pp. 151–74.

——, *Tudor Rebellions*, London, Longman, 1968.

Fraunce, Abraham, *The Lawyer's Logike, Exemplifying the Praecepts of Logike by the Practice of the Common Lawe*, (1588), Ann Arbor, Mich., University Microfilms.

Garner, Bryan A., "Shakespeare's Latinate Neologisms," *Shakespeare Studies* 15, 1982, pp. 149–70.

Gascoigne, George, *The Posies* (1575), ed. John W. Cunliffe, Cambridge, Cambridge University Press, 1907.

——, *Certayne Notes of Instruction Concerning the Making of Verse*, in *The Posies*, pp. 465–73.

——, *The Epistle* to the Reverend Divines, in *The Posies*, pp.1–8.

——, *Jocasta*, in *The Posies*, pp. 244–326.

Gill, Alexander, *Logonomia Anglica* (1619), *Stockholm Studies in English* 26 and 27, trans. Robin C. Alston., eds Bror Danielsson and Arvid Gabrielson, Stockholm, Almquist & Wiksell, 1972, 2 parts.

Goldberg, Jonathan, *James I and the Politics of Literature*, Baltimore, Md., Johns Hopkins University Press, 1983.

——, *Writing Matter: From the Hands of the English Renaissance*, Stanford, Calif., Stanford University Press, 1990.

Gorlach, Manfred, *Introduction to Early Modern English*, Cambridge, Cambridge University Press, 1991.

Greenblatt, Stephen, "Learning to Curse: Aspects of Linguistic Colonialism in the Sixteenth Century," in *Learning to Curse: Essays in Early Modern Culture*, ed. Greenblatt, New York and London, Routledge, 1990, pp. 16–39.

——, *Shakespearean Negotiations: The Circulation of Social Energy in Renaissance England*, Berkeley, Calif., University of California Press, 1988.

Greene, Robert, *The Life and Complete Works in Prose and Verse of Robert Greene*, ed. Alexander B. Grosart, New York, Russell & Russell, 1964, 15 vols.

——, *The Defence of Conny-Catching* (1592), in *The Life and Complete Works of Robert Greene*, vol. 11, pp. 39–104.

——, *A Disputation between a Hee Conny-Catcher and a Shee Conny-Catcher* (1592), in *The Life and Complete Works of Robert Greene*, vol. 10, pp. 193–278.

——, *A Notable Discovery of Coosnage* (1591), in *The Life and Complete Works of Robert Greene*, vol. 10, pp. 1–61.

——, *The Scottish History of James the Fourth*, ed. Norman Sanders, London, Methuen, 1970.

Grimald, Nicholas, "Concerning Virgils Eneids," in *Tottel's Miscellany* (1557), ed. Edward Rollins, vol. 1, Cambridge, Mass., Harvard University Press, 1928, 2 vols.

Hale, John, *A Discourse of the Common Weal of this Realm of England* (1581), ed. Elizabeth Lamond, Cambridge, Cambridge University Press, 1954.

Hardin, Richard F., *Michael Drayton and the Passing of Elizabethan England*, Lawrence, Kans., Kansas University Press, 1973.

Harman, Thomas, *A Caveat or Warening, for Commen Cursetors* (1567), eds Edward Viles and F.J. Furnivall, Oxford, Oxford University Press, 1869.

Harrison, William, *The Description of England* (1577), ed. George Edelen, Ithaca, N.Y., Cornell University Press, 1968.

Hart, Alfred, "Vocabularies of Shakespeare's Plays," *Review of English Studies* 19, 1943, pp. 128–40.

Hart, John, *A Methode or Comfortable Beginning* (1570), Ann Arbor, Mich., University Microfilms.

——, *An Orthography, Conteyning the Due Order and Reason, Howe to Write or Paint Thimage of Mannes Voice, Most Like to the Life or Nature* (1569), Ann Arbor, Mich., University Microfilms.

Hayes-McCoy, G.A., "The Tudor Conquest," in *The Course of Irish History*, eds T.W. Moody and F.X. Martin, Cork, Mercier Press, 1978, pp. 174–88.

Hechter, Michael, *Internal Colonialism: The Celtic Fringe in British National Development, 1536–1966*, Berkeley, Calif., University of California Press, 1975.

Helgerson, Richard, *Forms of Nationhood: The Elizabethan Writing of England*, Chicago, Ill., University of Chicago Press, 1992.

——, *Self-Crowned Laureates: Spenser, Jonson, Milton, and the Literary System*, Berkeley, Calif., University of California Press, 1983.

Herrmann, Claudine, *Les Voleuses de langue*, Paris, Des Femmes, 1976.

Heywood, Thomas, *An Apology for Actors* (1612), ed. Richard H. Perkinson, New York, Scholars' Facsimiles and Reprints, 1941.

——, and Richard Brome, *The Late Lancashire Witches* (1634), in *The Dramatic Works of Thomas Heywood*, vol. 4, New York, Russell & Russell, 1964, 6 vols.

Hill, L.M., "County Government in Caroline England 1625–1640", in *The Origins of the English Civil War*, ed. Conrad Russell, London, Macmillan, 1973, pp. 66–90.

Hilliard, Stephen S., *The Singularity of Thomas Nashe*, Lincoln, Nebr., University of Nebraska Press, 1986.

Hobday, Charles, "Clouted Shoon and Leather Aprons: Shakespeare and the Egalitarian Tradition," *Renaissance and Modern Studies* 23, 1979, pp. 63–78.

Holmes, Clive, "The County Community in Stuart Historiography," *Journal of British Studies* 19.2, 1980, pp. 54–73.

Holzknecht, Karl J., ed., *Sixteenth-Century English Prose*, New York, Harper, 1954.

Howell, James, *Epistolae Ho-Elianae: The Familiar Letters of James Howell*, vol. 2, Boston, Mass., Houghton Mifflin, 1907, 4 vols.

Hughes, Merritt Y., "Spenser and the Greek Pastoral Triad," *Studies in Philology* 20, 1923, pp. 184–215.

Hulbert, Viola B., "Diggon Davie," *Journal of English and Germanic Philology* 50, 1942, pp. 349–67.

Hume, Alexander, *Of the Orthographie and Congruitie of the Britan Tongue* (1619), ed. H.B. Wheatley, London, Early English Text Society, 1865.

Hussey, S.S., *The Literary Language of Shakespeare*, New York, Longman, 1982.

Hutson, Lorna, *Thomas Nashe in Context*, Oxford, Clarendon Press, 1989.

Ingham, Patricia, "Spenser's Use of Dialect," *English Language Notes* 8.3, 1971, pp. 164–8.

Jaffa, Harry V., "The Limits of Politics: *King Lear*, Act 1, sc. 1," in *Shakespeare's Politics*, ed. Allan Bloom with Harry V. Jaffa, New York, Basic Books, 1964, pp. 113–45.

James I, *The Basilican Doron of King James VI*, ed. James Craigie, Edinburgh and London, William Blackwood, 1944, 2 vols.

——, *King James VI and I, Political Writings*, ed. Johann P. Sommerville, Cambridge, Cambridge University Press, 1994.

——, *A Speach, As It Was Delivered in the Upper House of Parliament . . . the First Day of the First Parliament* (1603), in *Political Writings*, pp. 132–46.

——, *A Speach in the Starre-Chamber, the XX of June Anno 1616* (1616), in *Political Writings*, pp. 204–29.

——, *The Poems of James VI of Scotland*, ed. James Craigie, Edinburgh and London, William Blackwood, 1955, 2 vols.

Jones, R. Brinley, *The Old British Tongue: The Vernacular in Wales, 1540–1640*, Cardiff, Avalon Books, 1970.

Jones, R.F., *The Triumph of the English Language: A Survey of Opinions Concerning the Vernacular from the Introduction of Printing to the Restoration*, Stanford, Calif., Stanford University Press, 1953.

Jonson, Ben, *Ben Jonson*, eds C.H. Herford and Percy and Evelyn Simpson, Oxford, Clarendon Press, 1966, 11 vols.

——, *Bartholomew Fair* (1631), in *Ben Jonson*, vol. 6.

——, *Conversations with Drummond* (1618/19), in *Ben Jonson*, vol.1.

——, *Discoveries* (1640), in *Ben Jonson*, vol. 8.

——, *Poetaster* (1602), in *Ben Jonson*, vol. 2.

——, *The Sad Shepherd, or a Tale of Robin Hood*, (*c.* 1635), in *Ben Jonson*, vol. 7.

——, *A Tale of a Tub* (1633/40), in *Ben Jonson*, vol. 3.

——, *Ben Jonson: The Complete Masques*, ed. Stephen Orgel, New Haven, Conn., Yale University Press, 1969.

——, *The Gypsies Metamorphosed* (1640), in *Ben Jonson: The Complete Masques*.

——, *For the Honor of Wales* (1618), in *Ben Jonson: The Complete Masques*.

——, *The Irish Masque at Court* (1616), in *Ben Jonson: The Complete Masques*.

Joseph, John Earl, *Eloquence and Power: The Rise of Language Standards and Standard Languages*, New York, Basil Blackwell, 1987.

Kökeritz, Helge, "Alexander Gill on the Dialects of South and East England," *Studia Neophilologica* 11, 1939, pp. 277–88.

Kratzmann, Gregory, *Anglo-Scottish Literary Relations, 1430–1550*, Cambridge, Cambridge University Press, 1980.

Kronenfeld, Judy, "'So distribution should undo excess, and each man have enough': Shakespeare's *King Lear* – Anabaptist Egalitarianism, Anglican Charity, Both, Neither?," *English Literary Renaissance* 59.4, 1992, pp. 755–84.

Lambarde, William, *Perambulation of Kent* (1570), ed. Richard Church, Bath, Adams & Dart, 1970.

Lee, Maurice, Jr., *Government by Pen: Scotland under James VI and I*, Urbana, Ill., University of Illinois Press, 1980.

Leith, Dick, *A Social History of English*, London, Routledge & Kegan Paul, 1983.

Lekhal, Catherine, "The Historical Background of Robert Greene's *The Scottish History of James IV*," *Cahiers Elisabethains* 35, 1989, pp. 27–45.

Leland, John, *The Itinerary* (1535/43), ed. Lucy Toulmin Smith, Carbondale, Ill., Southern Illinois Press, 1964.

Levy, F.J., *Tudor Historical Thought*, San Marino, Calif., Huntington Library, 1967.

McElderry, Bruce Robert, Jr., "Archaism and Innovation in Spenser's Poetic Diction," *Publications of the Modern Language Association* 47.1, 1932, pp. 144–70.

Machan, Tim William and Charles T. Scott, eds, *English in its Social Contexts: Essays in Historical Sociolinguistics*, Oxford, Oxford University Press, 1992.

Machiavelli, Niccoló, *Dialogue on Language* (*c.* 1515), in *The Literary Works of Machiavelli*, trans. and ed. J.R. Hale, Westport, Conn., Greenwood Press, 1979, pp. 175–90.

McMullan, John L., *The Canting Crew: London's Criminal Underworld 1550–1700*, New Brunswick, N.J., Rutgers University Press, 1984.

Mallette, Richard, *Spenser, Milton, and Renaissance Pastoral*, Lewisburg, Penn., Bucknell University Press, 1981.

Matthews, W., "The Vulgar Speech of London in the Fifteenth to Seventeenth Centuries," *Notes and Queries* 172, 1937, pp. 2–5.

Matthews, William, "Language in *Love's Labour's Lost*," *Essays and Studies*, 1964, pp. 1–11.

Mazzocco, Angelo, "Dante's Notion of the *Vulgare Illustre*: A Reappraisal," in *Papers in The History of Linguistics: Proceedings of the Third International Conference on the History of the Language Sciences*, eds Hans Aarsleff, Louis G. Kelly, and Hans-Joseph Niederehe, Amsterdam, John Benjamins, 1987, pp. 129–41.

Meier, Hans H., "Past Presences of Older Scots Abroad," in *The Nuttis Schell: Essays on the Scots Language*, eds Caroline Macafee and Iseabail MacLeod, Aberdeen, The University Press, 1987, pp. 116–23.

Meres, Francis, *Palladis Tamia* (1598), ed. Arthur Freeman, New York, Garland Publishing, 1973.

Middleton, Thomas, *The Witch* (1610/16), eds W.W. Greg and F.P. Wilson, Oxford, The Malone Society, 1948.

Miller, Jacqueline T., *Poetic License: Authority and Authorship in Medieval and Renaissance Contexts*, New York, Oxford University Press, 1986.

Milroy, James and Lesley Milroy, *Authority in Language: Investigating Language Prescription and Standardization*, London, Routledge & Kegan Paul, 1985.

Montrose, Louis, "Of Gentlemen and Shepherds: The Politics of Elizabethan Pastoral Form," *English Literary History* 22, 1982, pp. 415–53.

Moody, T.W., F.X. Martin, and F.J. Byrne, eds, *A New History of Ireland*, Oxford, Clarendon Press, 1976, 9 vols.

Moryson, Fynes, *An Itinerary* (1617– *c.* 1626), in James P. Myers, Jr., ed, *Elizabethan Ireland: A Selection of Writings by Elizabethan Writers on Ireland*, pp. 185–240.

Mulcaster, Richard, *The Elementarie* (1582), ed. E.T. Campagnac, Oxford, Clarendon Press, 1925.

Myers, James P., Jr., ed., *Elizabethan Ireland: A Selection of Writings by Elizabethan Writers on Ireland*, Hamden, Conn., Archon Books, 1983.

Nashe, Thomas, *The Works of Thomas Nashe*, ed. Ronald B. McKerrow, Oxford, Basil Blackwell, 1958, 5 vols.

——, *Nashes Lenten Stuffe* (1599), in *The Works of Thomas Nashe*, vol. 3, pp. 141–266.

——, *Summer's Last Will and Testament* (1600), in *The Works of Thomas Nashe*, vol. 3, pp. 227–95.

Neill, Michael, "Broken English and Broken Irish: Nation, Language, and the Optic of Power in Shakespeare's Histories," *Shakespeare Quarterly* 45.1, 1994, pp. 1–32.

Nowell, Laurence, *Vocabularium Saxiconum* (1565), ed. Albert H. Marckwardt, Ann Arbor, Mich., University of Michigan Press, 1952.

O'Cuiv, Brian, "The Irish Language in the Early Modern Period", in T.W. Moody, F.X. Martin, and F.J.Byrne, eds, *A New History of Ireland*, vol. 3, pp. 509–49.

Orgel, Stephen, *The Jonsonian Masque*, Cambridge, Mass., Harvard University Press, 1965.

Ostriker, Alicia, "The Thieves of Language: Women Poets and Revisionist Mythmaking," in *The New Feminist Criticism*, ed. Elaine Showalter, New York, Pantheon Books, 1985, pp. 314–38.

Owen, George, *Cruell Lawes against Welshmen, Cymmrodorian Records*, ed. Henry Owen, series 1, part 3, London, Charles J. Clark, 1982, pp. 120–60.

——, *Survey of Pembrokeshire* (1603), *Cymmordorian Records*, ed. Henry Owen, series 1, part 1, London, Charles J. Clark, 1982, pp. 1–285.

Padley, G.A., *Grammatical Theory in Western Europe 1500–1700*, Cambridge, Cambridge University Press, 1988, 2 vols.

Partridge, A.C., *The Language of Renaissance Poetry: Spenser, Shakespeare, Donne, Milton*, London, Andre Deutsch, 1971.

Patterson, Annabel, *Shakespeare and the Popular Voice*, Oxford, Basil Blackwell, 1989.

Pearsall, Derek, ed., *The Canterbury Tales*, London, George Allen & Unwin, 1985.

Peele, George, "Eclogue Gratulatorie" (1589), in *The Works of George Peele*, ed. A.H. Bullen, vol. 2, Port Washington, N.Y., Kennicat Press, 1988, 2 vols.

Piedra, José, "Literary Whiteness and the Afro-Hispanic Difference," *New Literary History* 18, 1987, pp. 303–11.

Pollner, Clausdirk and Helmut Rohlfing, "The Scottish Language from the Sixteenth to the Eighteenth Century: Elphinston's Works as a Mirror of Anglicisation," *Scottish Studies* 4, ed. Horst W. Drescher, Frankfurt am Main, Verlag Peter Lang, 1986, pp. 125–37.

Pope, Alexander, *A Discourse on Pastoral Poetry* (1717), in *Selected Prose of Alexander Pope*, ed. Paul Hammond, Cambridge, Cambridge University Press, 1978, pp. 152–6.

Prescott, Anne Lake, *French Poets and the English Renaissance: Studies in Fame and Transformation*, New Haven, Conn., Yale University Press, 1978.

Puttenham, George, *The Arte of English Poesie* (1589), eds Gladys Doidge Willcock and Alice Walker, Cambridge, Cambridge University Press, 1970.

Quintilian, *The Institutione Oratoria*, trans. H.E. Butler, London, Loeb Classical Library, 1921, 4 vols.

R.A., Gent., *The Valiant Welshman* (1615), Edinburgh and London, Ams Press, 1970.

Randall, Dale, *Jonson's Gypsies Unmasked*, Durham, N.C., Duke University Press, 1975.

Randolph, Thomas, *The Muses' Looking Glass* (1638), in *Poetical and Dramatic Works of Thomas Randolph*, ed. W. Carew Hazlitt, vol. 1, London, Reeves & Turner, 1875, 2 vols.

Ray, John, *A Collection of English Words not Generally Used* (1674), Ann Arbor, Mich., University Microfilms.

Redford, John, *Wit and Science* (*c.* 1550), in *'Lost' Tudor Plays*, ed. John S. Farmer, New York, Barnes & Noble, 1966.

Renwick, W.L., "Mulcaster and DuBellay," *Modern Language Review* 17.3, 1922, pp. 282–7.

Replogle, Carol, "Shakespeare's Salutations: A Study in Stylistic Etiquette," in *A Reader in the Language of Shakespearean Drama*, eds Vivian Salmon and Edwina Burness, Amsterdam, John Benjamins, 1987, pp. 101–15.

Riggs, David, *Ben Jonson: A Life*, Cambridge, Mass., Harvard University Press, 1989.

Robinson, Mairi, *The Concise Scots Dictionary*, Aberdeen, Aberdeen University Press, 1985.

Robinson, Robert, *The Art of Pronunciation* (1617), Ann Arbor, Mich., University Microfilms.

Ronberg, Gert, *A Way With Words: The Language of English Renaissance Literature*, London, Edward Arnold, 1992.

Ronsard, Pierre de, *Abbregé de l'art poetique françois* (1565), in *Oeuvres Complètes*, vol. 2, Paris, Bibliotheque de la Pléiade, 1950, 2 vols., pp. 995–1009.

Rosenberg, D.M., *Oaten Reeds and Trumpets: Pastoral and Epic in Virgil, Spenser, and Milton*, Lewisburg, Penn., Bucknell University Press, 1981

Rowlands, Samuel, *Martin Markall, Beadle of Bridewell* (1610), in *The Complete Works of Samuel Rowlands*, vol. 2, New York, Johnson Reprints, 1966, 3 vols.

Rubel, Veré, *Poetic Diction in the English Renaissance: From Skelton Through Spenser*, New York, Modern Language Association, 1941.

Salesbury, William, *A Briefe and a Playne Introduction, Teachyng How to Pronounce the Letters in the British Tong* (1550), Ann Arbor, Mich., University Microfilms.

——, *A Dictionary in Englyshe and Welshe* (1547), Ann Arbor, Mich., University Microfilms.

Salmon, Vivian, "Elizabethan Colloquial English in the Falstaff Plays," *Leeds Studies in English* 1, 1967, pp. 37–70.

Sargent, Helen Child and George Lyman Kyttredge, eds, *English and Scottish Popular Ballads: Edited from the Collection of Francis James Child*, Boston, Mass., Houghton Mifflin, 1904.

Satterthwaite, Alfred W., *Spenser, Ronsard and Du Bellay: A Renaissance Comparison*, Princeton, N.J., Princeton University Press, 1960.

Scaglione, Aldo, "The Rise of National Languages: East and West," in *The Emergence of National Languages*, ed. Aldo Scaglione, Ravenna, Longo Editore, 1984, pp. 9–49.

Scragg, D.G., *A History of English Spelling*, New York, Barnes & Noble, 1974.

Shakespeare, William, *The Complete Works of Shakespeare*, ed. David Bevington, New York, HarperCollins, 1992.

——, *The Riverside Shakespeare*, ed. G. Blakemore Evans, Boston, Mass., Houghton Mifflin, 1974.

Sidney, Sir Philip, *Discourse on Irish Affairs* (1577), in James P. Myers Jr., ed., *Elizabethan Ireland: A Selection of Writings by Elizabethan Writers on Ireland*, pp. 36–7.

——, *The Prose Works of Sir Philip Sidney*, ed. Albert Feuillerat, Cambridge, Cambridge University Press, 1968, 4 vols.

——, *The Countesse of Pembroke's Arcadia* (1593), in *The Prose Works of Sir Philip Sidney*, vol. 4.

——, *Defense of Poesie* (1595), in *The Prose Works of Sir Philip Sidney*, vol. 3, pp. 1–46.

Skelton, John, *Merie Tales, Newly Imprinted and Made by Master Skelton* (1525), ed. W. Carew Hazlitt, London, Willis & Sotheran, 1866.

Smart, Bath C., *The Dialect of the English Gypsies*, London, Asher & Co., 1895.

Smith, Sir Thomas, *De Recta et Emendata Linguae Anglicae Scriptione* (1568), in *Sir Thomas Smith: Literary and Linguistic Works*, trans. and ed. Bror Danielsson, *Stockholm Studies in English* 56, Stockholm, Almquist & Wiksell, 1983.

——, *De Recta et Emendata Linguae Graecae Pronuntiatione* (1568), in *Sir Thomas Smith, Literary and Linguistic Works*, trans. and ed. Bror Danielsson, *Stockholm Studies in English* 50, Stockholm, Almquist & Wiksell, 1978, 2 parts.

Spenser, Edmund, *The Works of Edmund Spenser*, eds Edwin Greenlaw *et al.*, Baltimore, Md., Johns Hopkins University Press, 1932–57, 11 vols.

——, *Colin Clouts Come Home Again* (1595), in *The Works of Edmund Spenser*, vol. 7, part 1.

——, *The Faerie Queen* (1590/6), in *The Works of Edmund Spenser*, vol. 4.

——, *The Shepheardes Calender* (1579), in *The Works of Edmund Spenser*, vol. 7.

——, *A View of the Present State of Ireland* (1596), in James P. Myers Jr., ed., *Elizabethan Ireland: A Selection of Writings by Elizabethan Writers on Ireland*, pp. 60–125.

Starnes, De Witt T. and Gertrude E. Noyes, *The English Dictionary from Cawdrey to Johnson 1604–1755*, Chapel Hill, N.C., University of North Carolina Press, 1946.

Stow, John, *Survey of London* (1598), ed. Henry Morley, London, George Routledge & Sons, 1890.

Thirsk, Joan, *Economic Policy and Projects: The Development of a Consumer Society in Early Modern England*, Oxford, Clarendon Press, 1978.

Udall, Nicholas, *Respublica* (1553), ed. Leonard A. Magnus, London, Kegan Paul, 1905.

Villey, Pierre, *Les Sources Italiennes de la* Deffense et Illustration de la Langue Françoise *de Joachim Du Bellay*, New York, Burt Franklin, 1908.

Warner, William, *Albion's England* (1612), in *The Works of the English Poets from Chaucer to Cowper*, ed. Alexander Chalmers, vol. 4, London, 1810, 21 vols.

Wedderburn, Robert, *The Complaynt of Scotlande* (1549), ed. James A. H. Murray, Early English Text Society, Extra Series No. 17, London, 1872.

Williams, Glanmor, *Recovery, Reorientation and Reformation Wales c. 1415–1642*, Oxford, Clarendon Press, 1987.

Williams, Joseph M., "'O! When Degree is Shak'd': Sixteenth-Century Anticipations of Some Modern Attitudes Toward Usage," in Tim William Machan and Charles T. Scott, eds, *English in Its Social Contexts: Essays in Historical Sociolinguistics*, pp. 69–101.

Willis, Edmund, *An Abreviation of Writing by Character* (1618), Ann Arbor, Mich., University Microfilms.

Wilson, Thomas, *The Arte of Rhetorique* (1553), ed. Thomas J. Derrick, New York, Garland Publishing, 1982.

Woodes, Nathaniel, *The Conflict of Conscience* (1581), Oxford, Malone Society Reprints, 1952.

Zall, P.M., ed., *A Hundred Merry Tales and Other Jestbooks of the Fifteenth and Sixteenth Centuries*, Lincoln, Nebr., University of Nebraska Press, 1963.

Zitner, Sheldon P., *"King Lear* and Its Language," in *Some Facets of King Lear: Essays in Prismatic Criticism*, eds Rosalie L. Colie and F.T. Flahiff, Toronto, University of Toronto Press, 1974, pp. 3–22.

INDEX